W9-BFL-808

The Bankruptcy Abuse Prevention and Consumer Protection Act of 2005

WITH ANALYSIS

By

ALAN N. RESNICK

and

HENRY J. SOMMER

Collier Editors-in-Chief

LexisNexis™

Matthew Bender®

ISBN 0–8205–6468–0

This publication is designed to provide accurate and authoritative information in regard to the subject matter covered. It is sold with the understanding that the publisher is not engaged in rendering legal, accounting, or other professional services. If legal advice or other expert assistance is required, the services of a competent professional should be sought.

LexisNexis, the knowledge burst logo, and Michie are trademarks of Reed Elsevier Properties Inc, used under license. Matthew Bender is a registered trademark of Matthew Bender Properties Inc.

Copyright © 2005 Matthew Bender & Company, Inc., a member of the LexisNexis Group. Originally published in 2005.

All Rights Reserved.
No copyright is claimed in the text of statutes, regulations, and excerpts from court opinions quoted within this work. Permission to copy material exceeding fair use, 17 U.S.C. §107, may be licensed for a fee of $1 per page per copy from the Copyright Clearance Center, 222 Rosewood Drive, Danvers, MA. 01923, telephone (978) 750-8400.

Editorial Offices
744 Broad Street, Newark, NJ 07102 (973) 820-2000
201 Mission St., San Francisco, CA 94105-1831 (415) 908-3200
www.lexis.com

Table of Contents

The Bankruptcy Abuse Prevention and Consumer Protection Act of 2005:
A Section-by-Section Analysis

ALAN N. RESNICK
HENRY J. SOMMER

COLLIER EDITORS-IN-CHIEF

S. 256, the "Bankruptcy Abuse Prevention and Consumer Protection Act of 2005" (the "2005 Act"), was passed by the United States Senate on March 10, 2005, and by the House of Representatives on April 14, 2005. The 2005 Act makes substantial changes to the Bankruptcy Code. A brief description of the significant substantive changes to the Code appears below.[1]

Means Test, Credit Counseling, and Related Provisions (Title I)

Conversion. Section 706(c) is amended to allow conversion of a chapter 7 case to a chapter 13 if the debtor consents to conversion. (S. 256, Sec. 101)

Dismissal for Abuse. Section 707(b) is amended to provide that a case may be dismissed for abuse, which may include bad faith or abuse demonstrated by the totality of the circumstances. Creditors and trustees are permitted to bring abuse motions for debtors above state median income as defined in the section. (S. 256, Sec. 102)

Means Test. Debtors above median income are subjected to a means test to determine if a presumption of abuse arises. Current monthly income, as defined in a new section 101(10A), is compared against expenses allowed under the Internal Revenue Service expense standards and other specified deductions and expenses, including payments due on secured and priority debts over 60 months after petition. A presumption of abuse arises if, after deduction of such expenses from income, the remaining amount over 60 months is at least the lesser of $10,000 or 25% of general unsecured claims, but not less than $6,000. The presumption may be rebutted if the debtor

---

[1] The headings for some of the titles and subtitles are those of the authors, and are more descriptive and accurate than the official titles regarding the content of those titles and subtitles.

shows that income and expenses should be adjusted to account for special circumstances for which there is no reasonable alternative and such adjustments bring the means test result below the minimum payment thresholds. Debtors must provide information in their schedules showing whether means test presumption arises. (S. 256, Sec. 102)

Attorney Sanctions. On motion under Federal Rule of Bankruptcy Procedure 9011, the court may order the attorney for a debtor to pay trustee's costs and attorney's fees in prosecuting a successful motion under section 707(b) if filing of the bankruptcy case violated Rule 9011. The court may also assess, under Rule 9011, a civil penalty against a debtor's attorney for violation of that rule. The court may award to a debtor, under Rule 9011, costs and attorney's fees incurred in contesting a motion under section 707(b) not filed by a trustee, United States trustee, or bankruptcy administrator if the motion is not granted and the party that filed the motion violated Rule 9011 or the attorney who filed the motion falsely certified that (i) the attorney had performed a reasonable investigation into circumstances giving rise to such motion, and (ii) the motion was well grounded in fact and was warranted by existing law or a good faith argument for extension, modification, or reversal of existing law or if the motion was made solely to coerce a debtor into giving up bankruptcy rights. However, no small business with a claim under $1,000 is subject to sanctions under this section for filing a motion under section 707(b). (S. 256, Sec. 102)

Attorney Certifications. The signature of an attorney for any party on a petition, pleading, or written motion is a certification that the attorney has performed a reasonable investigation into circumstances giving rise to such paper, the paper is well grounded in fact and is warranted by existing law or a good faith argument for extension, modification, or reversal of existing law, and does not constitute an abuse under section 707(b)(1). The signature of an attorney on a petition is a certification that the attorney has no knowledge after an inquiry that the information on the schedules is incorrect. (S. 256, Sec.102)

Dismissal for Certain Crimes. The court may, on motion of a victim of a crime of violence or drug trafficking crime, dismiss a chapter 7 case when it is in the best interest of the victim unless the case is necessary for the debtor to satisfy a domestic support obligation. (S. 256, Sec. 102)

Confirmation of Chapter 13 Plan. Good faith filing of the petition is added to the standards for confirmation of a chapter 13 plan. (S. 256, Sec. 102)

Confirmation of Chapter 13 Plan. For purposes of determining disposable income, the expenses of debtors above median income, as defined in the 2005 Act, are determined using the expense calculations in the means test of section 707(b). (S. 256, Sec. 102)

Modification of Chapter 13 Plan. The debtor is permitted to modify a chapter 13 plan to reduce payments in order to purchase reasonable and necessary health insurance. (S. 256, Sec. 102)

Modification and Study of Internal Revenue Service Expense Standards. It is the sense of Congress that the Internal Revenue Service can alter the living expense standards applicable in bankruptcy cases and the Executive Office of United States Trustees is directed to conduct a study of the use of those standards. (S. 256, Sec. 103)

Notice of Alternatives. The notice to be given by the clerk to bankruptcy debtors must contain a brief description of chapters 7, 11, 12, and 13, including the general purpose, costs, and benefits of proceeding under each chapter; the types of services available from credit counseling agencies; and statements that concealing assets or false oaths can lead to fines or imprisonment and that information supplied by bankruptcy debtors may be examined by the Attorney General. (S. 256, Sec. 104)

Financial Management Training Test Program. The Executive Office of United States Trustees is directed to develop a financial management curriculum, test that curriculum, evaluate the effectiveness of that and other consumer education programs, and report on that evaluation to Congress. (S. 256, Sec. 105)

Credit Counseling and Personal Financial Management Course. To be eligible for bankruptcy relief, an individual debtor must receive a briefing on credit counseling and budget analysis from a nonprofit budget and credit counseling agency approved by the United States trustee and meeting standards set forth in the 2005 Act. To receive a discharge in chapter 7 or chapter 13, an individual debtor must attend a personal financial management instructional course approved by the United States trustee. The briefing or course may be provided over the telephone or the Internet. These requirements may be waived or deferred in certain limited circumstances. (S. 256, Sec. 106)

Schedules of Chapter 13 Administrative Costs. The Executive Office of United States Trustees must issue schedules of reasonable and necessary chapter 13 administrative expenses for each judicial district for use in application of the means test. (S. 256, Sec. 107)

Assorted Consumer-Related Bankruptcy Provisions
(Title II)

ABUSIVE CREDITOR PRACTICES
(SUBTITLE A)

Refusal of Creditor to Accept Reasonable Prepetition Repayment Plan. The court is permitted to reduce an unsecured dischargeable consumer claim by up to 20% if the creditor refused to agree to a reasonable repayment plan, as defined by this section, with an approved credit counseling agency at a time more than 60 days prior to bankruptcy. Payments made through approved credit counseling agencies are protected from preference avoidance. (S. 256, Sec. 201)

Mortgage Payments. The willful failure to credit plan payments as provided in a plan is a violation of the discharge injunction if the debtor suffers material injury. Normal communications from a creditor about mortgage payments on the debtor's principal residence do not violate the discharge injunction. (S. 256, Sec. 202)

Reaffirmation. Lengthy disclosures specified by this section are required to be given to any debtor who reaffirms a debt. Forms for reaffirmation procedures are specified. A temporary presumption arises that a debtor cannot afford a reaffirmation agreement if the debtor's income minus the debtor's expenses leaves insufficient funds to make the payments, except if the creditor is a credit union. If such a presumption arises, the court may disapprove a reaffirmation agreement, even if the debtor is represented by an attorney. (S. 256, Sec. 203)

Section 363 Sales of Consumer Credit Obligations. Section 363 is clarified to ensure that a sale of consumer credit obligations under that section does not cut off consumer claims or defenses to the extent that they would not be cut off by a sale outside of bankruptcy. (S. 256, Sec. 204)

Reaffirmation Study. The Comptroller General of the United States is to conduct a study of reaffirmation practices and report to Congress with recommendations for legislation to address abusive or coercive practices. (S. 256, Sec. 205)

FAMILY LAW PROVISIONS
(SUBTITLE B)

Definition of Domestic Support Obligation. A definition of "domestic support obligation" is added to section 101. The definition is largely coextensive with debts that are currently nondischargeable under section 523(a)(5) as alimony, maintenance or support, but includes debts that accrue after the petition and includes support debts that from their inception are owed to a governmental unit. (S. 256, Sec. 211)

Priority of Domestic Support Obligations. Domestic support obligations are first in priority among unsecured debts. Among such obligations, those owed to spouse, former spouse or child of a debtor are given a higher priority than those that are assigned. Administrative expenses of a trustee are paid prior to domestic support obligations to the extent those expenses are incurred in administering assets to pay those obligations. (S. 256, Sec. 212)

Confirmation, Dismissal, and Discharge in Chapter 11, 12, and 13 Cases. The standards for confirmation of a plan in chapter 11, 12, and 13 cases are amended to include the debtor's payment of domestic support obligations that first become payable after the filing of the petition. A chapter 12 or chapter 13 plan that does not pay in full priority domestic support obligations that have been assigned may not be confirmed over the objection of a domestic support creditor unless the plan applies all of the debtor's projected disposable income to plan payments for five years. Grounds for dismissal of a chapter 12 or chapter 13 case are amended to include failure to pay domestic support obligations that first become payable after the filing of the petition. A full compliance chapter 12 or chapter 13 discharge for a debtor who is required by a judicial or administrative order or by statute to pay a domestic support obligation cannot be entered unless the debtor certifies that all payments due on such obligation have been paid, except to the extent the plan did not require payment of prepetition obligations. (S. 256, Sec. 213)

Automatic Stay. Additional exceptions to the automatic stay are created for commencement or continuation of proceedings concerning child custody, domestic violence, and divorce, to the extent the divorce proceeding does not involve division of property that is property of the estate; withholding of income to pay a domestic support obligation pursuant to a judicial or administrative order or a statute; interception of tax refunds for domestic support obligations; withholding of licenses from debtors who do not pay support obligations; reporting of credit reporting agencies of debtors who do not pay support; interception of tax refunds to collect support; and enforcement of medical support obligations. (S. 256, Sec. 214)

Dischargeability of Family-Related Obligations. All domestic support obligations are nondischargeable. All marital property settlement obligations not in the nature of support are nondischargeable under section 523(a)(15). The bankruptcy court no longer has exclusive jurisdiction over the dischargeability of such debts. (S. 256, Sec. 215)

Exemptions. All property exempted by the debtor is liable for domestic support obligations, even if such property would not have been liable for such obligations under applicable nonbankruptcy law. (S. 256, Sec. 216)

Preferences. A preference cannot be avoided to the extent the transfer was in payment of a domestic support obligation. (S. 256, Sec. 217)

Chapter 12 Disposable Income. Section 1225(b) is amended to exclude from disposable income amounts that become payable on a domestic support obligation after the date of the petition. (S. 256, Sec. 218)

Chapter 7 Trustee Notices to Domestic Support Obligees. The chapter 7, 11, 12, or 13 trustee must provide notice to any holder of a claim for a domestic support obligation of the availability of state child support enforcement agency services and an explanation of the rights of the holder to payment of the claim under chapter 7. The trustee must also provide notice to the state child support enforcement agency of the name, address, and telephone number of the holder of the domestic support obligation claim. In addition, at the time a discharge is granted, the trustee must provide notice to the claim holder and state child support enforcement agency of the granting of the discharge, the last known address of the debtor, the last known name and address of the debtor's employer, and the name of each creditor holding a claim not discharged under subsection 523(a)(2), (4), or (14A) or holding a claim that was reaffirmed. The holder of a domestic support obligation may request the debtor's address from such creditors whose debts have not been discharged or reaffirmed and the creditor may supply that information. (S. 256, Sec. 219)

Educational Loans. Educational loans, as defined by Internal Revenue Code section 221(d)(1), made by for-profit entities are made nondischargeable. (S. 256, Sec. 220)

OTHER CONSUMER-RELATED PROVISIONS
(SUBTITLE C)

Petition Preparers. New requirements are added to section 110 for bankruptcy petition preparers. If a petition preparer is not an individual, the required signatures and Social Security numbers under section 110 must be those of an officer, principal, responsible person, or partner. Petition preparers must give more detailed disclosures of their inability to practice law or give legal advice. The Supreme Court and Federal Judicial Conference are given authority to set maximum fees for petition preparers, and courts are directed to order turnover of excessive fees. Additional penalties are enacted for petition preparers who commit specific violations of the statute or court orders, including advising the debtor to conceal assets or use a false Social Security number or failing to inform the debtor that a bankruptcy petition is being filed. (S. 256, Sec. 221)

Sense of Congress on Financial Education. It is the sense of Congress that states should develop curricula on personal finance for elementary and secondary schools. (S. 256, Sec. 222)

Priority for Certain Drunk Driving and Boating Debts. Section 507(a) is amended to add a priority for debts for death or personal injury resulting from operating a motor vehicle or vessel if the operation was unlawful due to intoxication from alcohol, drugs, or another substance. (S. 256, Sec. 223)

Protection of Retirement Savings. Section 522 is amended to permit debtors to exempt all funds in any account exempt from taxation under sections 401, 403, 408, 408A, 414, 457, and 501(a) of the Internal Revenue Code. The only exception is an IRA account other than a SEP IRA under section 408(k) or a simplified employee pension under section 408(p), not created by a rollover from a non-IRA account, to the extent it exceeds $1,000,000, unless the court increases that amount in the interests of justice. An exception to the automatic stay is created for the withholding from a debtor's wages for such accounts pursuant to an agreement in which the debtor authorized such withholding to repay a loan from a plan under Internal Revenue Code section 408(b)(1) or subject to Internal Revenue Code section 72(p) or a thrift savings plan under 5 U.S.C. § 8433(g). Such loans are also excepted from discharge under a new section 523(a)(19), their terms may not be altered by a chapter 13 plan, and the funds used to pay them may not be considered disposable income under section 1325(b). (S. 256, Sec. 224)

Protection of Education Savings. Funds contributed more than 365 days before the petition to an education IRA, section 529 plan, or state tuition credit program are excluded from the bankruptcy estate if the beneficiary is a child, stepchild, grandchild, or stepgrandchild of the debtor. Exceptions to this rule include excess contributions to such plans and funds contributed between 365 and 720 days before the petition in excess of $5,000 per beneficiary.The debtor must file, under section 521, a listing of any interests the debtor has in such plans. (S. 256, Sec. 225)

Definitions for Debt Relief Agency Provisions. Definitions of "assisted person," "bankruptcy assistance," and "debt relief agency" are added to section 101. "Assisted person" means any individual with primarily consumer debts and nonexempt property worth less than $150,000. "Bankruptcy assistance" means any advice, goods, or services provided to an assisted person with respect to a title 11 case. "Debt relief agency" means, with certain specified exceptions, a bankruptcy petition preparer, or person that provides bankruptcy assistance to an assisted person for money or other valuable consideration. (S. 256, Sec. 226)

Restrictions on Debt Relief Agencies. Under a new section 526, a debt relief agency must provide all services promised to an assisted person, must refrain from advising assisted persons to make untrue or misleading statements, may not misrepresent services to be provided or benefits or risks of such services, and may not advise an assisted person or prospective assisted person to incur more debt in contemplation of a bankruptcy or to pay bankruptcy costs. Contracts that do not comply with these require-ments and those of new sections 527 and 528 are void and may not be enforced by any court or any person, other than the assisted person. A debt relief agency is liable for fees and charges paid if it intentionally fails to comply with sections 526–528 if a case is dismissed due to its negligent failure to file a required document or if it negligently or intentionally disregards material requirements of the Bankruptcy Code or Federal Rules of Bankruptcy Procedure. State law enforcement officials may enforce the requirements of section 526. The court may impose injunctive relief, civil penalties, and attorney's fees for intentional violations of section 526 or a pattern or practice of violations. Nothing in sections 526–528 is to be deemed a limitation on the ability of states to police the unauthorized practice of law. (S. 256, Sec. 227)

Disclosures by Debt Relief Agencies. Under a new section 527, a debt relief agency providing bankruptcy assistance to an assisted person must provide the written notice under section 342(b)(1) and other disclosures specified in section 527. To the extent applicable, a statement specified in section 527, or one substantially similar, must also be provided in a separate document. If a debt relief agency does not itself complete the petition, schedules, and statement of financial affairs, a debt relief agency must provide specified information to the assisted person about how to provide all information specified in section 521. (S. 256, Sec. 228)

Requirements for Debt Relief Agencies. Within five days of first provid-ing bankruptcy assistance services to an assisted person, a debt relief agency must execute a written contract with the person that explains the services the agency will provide and the fees for such service, provide the assisted person with a copy of the contract, disclose in any advertisement of bankruptcy assistance services that the services are with respect to bank-ruptcy relief, and include the following statement or a substantially similar statement in the advertisement: "We are a debt relief agency. We help people file for bankruptcy relief under the Bankruptcy Code." Any adver-tisement indicating that a debt relief agency provides assistance with respect to credit defaults, mortgage foreclosures, evictions, or debt problems must disclose that the assistance may involve bankruptcy relief and include the following statement or a substantially similar statement in the adver-tisement: "We are a debt relief agency. We help people file for bankruptcy relief under the Bankruptcy Code." These requirements apply regardless of whether the debt relief agency in fact represents consumer debtors in bankruptcy cases. (S. 256, Sec. 229)

GAO Study of Trustee Support Enforcement Tasks. The Comptroller General is directed to conduct a study of the feasibility and cost of requiring trustees to provide certain information to the Office of Child Support Enforcement promptly after the commencement of cases by individual debtors. (S. 256, Sec. 230)

Protection of Personally Identifiable Information. Section 363 is amended to provide that the transfer of personally identifiable information, as defined in the new provision, about individuals not affiliated with the debtor must be consistent with the debtor's disclosed policies for the disclosure of such information in effect on the date of the petition. The transfer may take place only after appointment of a consumer privacy ombudsman under new section 332 and after the court approves the transfer as not violating applicable nonbankruptcy law. (S. 256, Sec. 231)

Consumer Privacy Ombudsman. A new section 332 provides for the court to order the United States trustee to appoint a disinterested person to serve as the consumer privacy ombudsman if a hearing is required with respect to a debtor's transfer of personally identifiable information. The ombudsman shall appear and be heard at any hearing concerning the transfer and provide certain information to assist the court. The ombudsman is to be compensated from the estate. (S. 256, Sec. 232)

Disclosure of Names of Minor Children. Pursuant to a new section 112, the debtor may not be required to disclose the name of a minor child in public records, but may be required to disclose the name in a nonpublic record maintained by the court for examination by the United States trustee, the trustee, and any auditor in the case. (S. 256, Sec. 233)

Protection of Personal Information. Section 107 is amended to permit the court to enter an order protecting an individual from disclosure of information that would create an undue risk of identity theft or other unlawful injury to an individual or the individual's property. Information that may be protected from disclosure includes name, Social Security number, date of birth, driver's license or identification number, alien registration number, passport number, employer or taxpayer identification number, or any other information in a paper filed or to be filed with the court. However, the United States trustee, trustee, bankruptcy administrator, and any auditor shall have access to any paper filed or submitted in a case. Section 342(c) is amended to require only the last four digits of the debtor's Social Security number in notices, except that a notice to a creditor concerning an amendment of the schedules to add that creditor must have the full Social Security number. (S. 256, Sec. 234)

Consumer and Business Provisions
(Title III)

Prisoner Court Costs. Section 523(a)(17) is amended to make clear that it applies only to fees, costs, and expenses imposed on prisoners. (S. 256, Sec. 301)

Repeat Filings of Bankruptcy Cases. If a new case is filed within one year after an earlier dismissed case was pending, the automatic stay terminates 30 days after the new case is filed unless, after notice and a hearing, the court extends the stay because the new case is filed in good faith. A new case is presumptively not in good faith as to all creditors if the debtor had been a debtor in more than one prior case in the preceding year; or a prior case was dismissed during that period for failure to file documents without substantial excuse, failure to provide adequate protection, or failure to perform the terms of a confirmed plan; or there has been no substantial change of circumstances since the last dismissal that would make the new case likely to be successfully concluded. A new case is also presumptively in bad faith as to any creditor that filed a motion for relief from the automatic stay that was pending at the time of dismissal or had been resolved by terminating, conditioning, or limiting the stay. If a debtor files a case after two or more dismissed cases were pending in the previous year, no automatic stay under section 362 goes into effect. The court may order, after notice and a hearing, that the stay take effect upon a showing that the latest case is filed in good faith. The same presumptions of lack of good faith apply in this situation. (S. 256, Sec. 302)

In Rem Orders for Relief from Automatic Stay. A court may enter an *in rem* order with respect to the automatic stay of actions by a creditor secured by an interest in real property if the petition was part of a scheme to delay, hinder, and defraud creditors involving transfer of full or partial ownership interests or multiple bankruptcy filings affecting the property. Such an order, if recorded in compliance with state recording statutes, is binding on any case that would affect that property filed within two years after the order is entered. A debtor may obtain relief from such an order based upon changed circumstances or for good cause shown. An exception to the automatic stay is added to section 362(b) encompassing such orders. (S. 256, Sec. 303)

Exception to Automatic Stay. An additional exception is added for cases in which the debtor is ineligible for relief under section 109(g) or has filed the case in violation of a prior bankruptcy court order. (S. 256, Sec. 303)

Statement of Intention. Section 521 is amended to provide that an individual chapter 7 debtor shall not retain possession of personal property in which a creditor has a purchase-money security interest unless the debtor, within 45 days after the first meeting of creditors under section 341(a), either enters into a reaffirmation agreement on the creditor's claim or redeems the property under section 722. If the debtor fails to so act, the automatic stay with respect to such property is terminated, the property is no longer property of the estate, and the creditor can take whatever action with respect to the property is permitted by applicable nonbankruptcy law. However, the court, on motion of the trustee, may find that the property is of consequential value or benefit to the estate and order delivery of the property to the trustee. (S. 256, Sec. 304)

Statement of Intention. Section 362 is amended to provide that in an individual case the automatic stay is terminated as to personal property securing a claim or subject to an unexpired lease, and such property is no longer property of the estate if the debtor fails to file a timely statement of intention required under section 521(2) and indicate therein that the debtor will surrender the property, redeem it, enter into a reaffirmation agreement, or assume the personal property lease pursuant to new section 365(p). The stay is also terminated if the debtor does not timely take the action specified in the statement, unless the stated intention was to reaffirm on the original contract terms and the creditor refuses to agree to such reaffirmation. However, the court, on motion of the trustee, may find that the property is of consequential value or benefit to the estate and order delivery of the property to the trustee. (S. 256, Sec. 305)

Chapter 13 Treatment of Secured Debts. To be entitled to confirmation under section 1325(a)(5), a plan must provide that a secured creditor is to retain its lien until the earlier of full payment of its claim determined under nonbankruptcy law or discharge under section 1328 and that if the case is dismissed or converted the lien shall be retained to the extent recognized by nonbankruptcy law. For purposes of section 1325(a)(5), section 506 does not apply to a claim if the creditor has a purchase-money security interest and the debt was either incurred within the 910-day period before the petition for the purchase of a motor vehicle or incurred within the year before the petition for the purchase of any other thing of value. New definitions are added to section 101 for "debtor's principal residence," which includes a mobile home, and "incidental property," which includes property commonly conveyed with a principal residence. (S. 256, Sec. 306)

Exemption Domicile Requirements. The debtor's exemptions are determined based upon the law of the state where the debtor has been domiciled for the 730 days before the petition. If the debtor has not been domiciled in the same state for that period, exemptions are determined based upon the state where the debtor was domiciled for the 180 days before that period or for the longest portion of that 180 days. If the effect of this provision is to render the debtor ineligible for any state's exemption, the debtor may use the federal exemptions. (S. 256, Sec. 307)

Homestead Exemption Limitation. The debtor's homestead exemption is reduced to the extent it is attributable to nonexemptible property that the debtor disposed of within 10 years before the petition with the intent to hinder, delay, or defraud creditors. (S. 256, Sec. 308)

Conversion from Chapter 13 to Chapter 7. Section 348(f) is amended to provide that when a case is converted from chapter 13 to chapter 7 the claim of a creditor holding security as of the petition date continues to be secured by that security unless the claim, as determined under nonbankruptcy law, was paid in full during the case. Valuation of property and allowed secured claims in the chapter 13 case shall not be binding in the converted case. Any prebankruptcy default not cured by the date of conversion is given the effect it has under nonbankruptcy law. (S. 256, Sec. 309(a))

Personal Property Leases. If a lease of personal property is not timely assumed by the trustee, the property is no longer property of the estate and the automatic stay is terminated as to the property. An individual chapter 7 debtor may request in writing to assume a personal property lease. The lessor may give notice to the debtor that it is willing to have the lease assumed or that assumption is conditioned on cure of a default on the lease. If the debtor within 30 days thereafter notifies the lessor that the lease is assumed, the liability under the lease is assumed by the debtor and not the estate. The automatic stay and discharge injunction are not violated by the notice under this subsection or negotiation of a cure. In a chapter 13 case or individual chapter 11 case, a lease not assumed by a confirmed plan is deemed rejected, the leased property is no longer property of the estate, and the automatic stay is terminated as to such property. (S. 256, Sec. 309(b))

Adequate Protection. Periodic distributions to a secured creditor under section 1325(a)(5)(B) must be in equal monthly payments and sufficient to provide adequate protection. Beginning within 30 days after a chapter 13 petition, a debtor must make lease payments to a lessor of personal property and provide to the trustee evidence of such payments, which are credited against plan payments. Also, beginning within 30 days after a chapter 13 petition, a debtor must make adequate protection payments to a creditor with a purchase-money security interest in personal property and provide to the trustee evidence of such payments, which are credited against plan payments. If a chapter 13 plan is not confirmed, the trustee is to pay any court-ordered payments to creditors, as well as administrative expenses, prior to returning funds to the debtor. A chapter 13 debtor with a personal property lease or claim secured by a purchase-money security interest in personal property must provide to the lessor or secured creditor evidence of required insurance coverage within 60 days of a chapter 13 petition. (S. 256, Sec. 309(c))

Dischargeability Presumption. Section 523(a)(2)(C) is amended to create a presumption of fraud if the debtor incurs debt to a single creditor for purchases over $500 of luxury goods within 90 days before the order for relief or obtains cash advances on an open end credit account in excess of $750 within 70 days before the order for relief. (S. 256, Sec. 310)

Automatic Stay. New exceptions from the automatic stay of section 362(a)(3) are created for the continuation of proceedings to evict residential tenants if the lessor has obtained a judgment prior to the filing of the petition or if the lessor seeks possession based on endangerment of property or illegal use of controlled substances at the property. The latter exception comes into effect 10 days after the lessor files a certification with the court that such endangerment or use of substances occurred within 30 days before the certification, unless the debtor within 15 days of the certification objects to the certification, in which case the court shall determine whether grounds for the exception exist. The former exception does not apply until 30 days after the petition if the debtor has a right to cure the default and the debtor deposits with the court any rent that would become due during the 30 days after the filing of the petition. If the debtor files a further certification within 30 days after the petition that the debtor has cured the default, the exception does not apply, unless the court finds the certification is untrue. If a residential lessor has obtained a judgment for possession, the bankruptcy petition must so indicate and must state whether the debtor is attempting to cure the default. An exception to the stay is also created for any transfer not avoidable under section 544 or section 549. (S. 256, Sec. 311)

Time Between Bankruptcy Discharges. The time period in section 727(a)(8), governing a discharge after a prior chapter 7 or chapter 11 discharge, is changed from six to eight years. A chapter 7 discharge may not be entered if the debtor received a discharge in a case under chapter 7, 11, or 12 during the four years preceding the date of an order for relief under chapter 13 or in a prior chapter 13 case filed within two years before the date of the order for relief. (S. 256, Sec. 312)

Definition of Household Goods. Section 522(f) is amended to provide a definition of "household goods" for purposes of lien avoidance under section 522(f)(1)(B). The Executive Office of United States Trustees is to conduct a study of the use of this definition. (S. 256, Sec. 313)

Dischargeability of Debts Incurred to Pay Nondischargeable Taxes. A new section 523(a)(14A) is added, making debts incurred to pay nondischargeable taxes to governmental units other than the United States nondischargeable. (S. 256, Sec. 314(a))

Chapter 13 Discharge. Section 1328(a) is amended to make nondischargeable in chapter 13 cases debts of a kind described in subsections 523(a)(2) and (4). (S. 256, Sec. 314(b))

Notice. New notice provisions create a definition of "effective notice." If a creditor, within 90 days before a voluntary petition, supplies the debtor with an account number and the address at which the creditor requests to receive correspondence, a notice required by title 11 to be sent by the debtor to the creditor must be sent to that address and include the account number. If a creditor cannot communicate with the debtor within the 90-day period, and if the creditor provided such address and account number in its last two communications with the debtor, any notice required by title 11 to be sent by the debtor to the creditor must be sent to that address and include the account number. A creditor in an individual chapter 7 or chapter 13 case may file with the court and serve on the debtor a notice of address to be used for notices to the creditor in that case. An entity may also file with the court notice of an address to be used by all bankruptcy courts or by particular bankruptcy courts for all chapter 7 and chapter 13 cases in which that entity is a creditor. Notice other than in accordance with these provisions is not "effective" until it is brought to the attention of the creditor. If a creditor designates a person or department to receive notices and establishes reasonable procedures to deliver notices to that person or department, a notice is not deemed brought to the attention of the creditor until that person or department receives it. A monetary penalty may not be imposed on a creditor for a violation of a stay under section 362 or failure to comply with section 542 or 543 unless the creditor's conduct occurs after the creditor receives notice effective under this section of the order for relief. (S. 256, Sec. 315(a))

Additional Document Requirements. Section 521 is amended to require additional documents to be provided by the debtor. If section 342(b) applies, the debtor must file a certification that the debtor received the notice under section 342(b). The debtor must also file an itemized statement of monthly net income, copies of payment advices or other evidence of payment received within the 60 days before the petition from the debtor's employer(s), and a statement of any reasonably anticipated increases in income or expenses in the 12 months after the petition is filed. At least seven days before the first date set for the section 341(a) meeting, the debtor must provide to the trustee a copy of the federal tax return required under applicable law or a transcript thereof for the most recent tax year before the year the case was filed and for which a return was filed. The debtor must also supply a copy at the same time to any creditor that timely requests one. If the debtor fails to provide such copies the court must dismiss the case unless the failure is for reasons beyond the debtor's control. A chapter 7, 12, or 13 individual debtor must, at the request of the court, United States trustee, or a party in interest, file with the court federal tax returns or tax transcripts for each year ending while the case is pending and, if federal tax returns for any of the three years ending before the commencement of the case are filed during the case, the returns or tax transcripts for such years. Amendments to such returns must also be filed with the court. However, the filing and provision of such returns are subject to privacy protections to be developed by the Administrative Office of the United States Courts. Chapter 13 debtors must file annual statements of income and expenditures. If requested by the trustee or United States trustee, the debtor must provide information that establishes the identity of the debtor. (S. 256, Sec. 315(b))

Dismissal for Failure to File Documents. If an individual chapter 7 or 13 debtor fails to file all of the documents required by section 521(a)(1), the case is to be "automatically" dismissed. A party in interest may request such dismissal and the court must dismiss the case within five days of such request unless the court has granted the debtor an additional period of up to 45 days to file the information. The court may also decline to dismiss the case upon motion of the trustee if the debtor attempted in food faith to file the evidence of payment from the debtor's employer and that the best interests of creditors would be served by administration of the case. (S. 256, Sec. 316)

Scheduling of Chapter 13 Confirmation Hearing. Section 1324 is amended to provide that the confirmation hearing may be held no earlier that 20 days after the meeting of creditors and no later than 45 days after the meeting unless the court finds that it is in the best interests of creditors and the estate to hold it earlier and no party objects. (S. 256, Sec. 317)

Length of Chapter 13 Plan. Debtors with a current monthly income over the applicable state median income as defined in the 2005 Act may be required to file a five-year plan if their plans do not propose payment of 100% of unsecured claims. (S. 256, Sec. 318)

Sense of Congress Regarding Rule 9011. It is the sense of Congress that Federal Rule of Bankruptcy Procedure 9011 be amended to provide that all documents, including schedules, submitted to the court or to a trustee by pro se debtors and represented debtors be submitted only after reasonable inquiry to verify that the information in the documents is well grounded in fact and warranted by existing law or a good faith argument for the extension or reversal of existing law. (S. 256, Sec. 319)

Relief from Automatic Stay. In an individual chapter 7, 11, or 13 case, the automatic stay of section 362 shall terminate 60 days after a request for relief from the stay unless a final decision on the request is rendered by the court within the 60 days or the period is extended either by agreement or by the court for a specific period of time found necessary for good cause. (S. 256, Sec. 320)

Chapter 11 Cases Filed by Individuals. Chapter 11 is amended to include several features of chapter 13 for cases involving individual debtors. Property of the estate in a chapter 11 case for an individual debtor will include property acquired during the case, as well as earnings from postpetition services performed by the debtor. A chapter 11 plan for an individual debtor must provide for payment to creditors under the plan of all or a portion of postpetition earnings from personal services or other future income. Chapter 11 is also amended to add, as a requirement for confirmation when the debtor is an individual, the same disposable income standard used in section 1325(b)(2) of the Code. Chapter 11 is amended to delay granting a discharge to an individual debtor until completion of payments under the plan, but the court may grant a discharge if the debtor defaults on plan payments, the value actually distributed under the plan to unsecured creditors is not less than the amount they would have received in a chapter 7 liquidation, and modification of the plan is not practicable. In addition, if the debtor is an individual, the plan may be modified after confirmation on request of the debtor, the trustee, the United States trustee, or an unsecured creditor, either to increase or to reduce the amount or time periods regarding payments. (S. 256, Sec. 321)

Limitations on Homestead Exemption. A debtor may not exempt "any amount of interest" acquired by the debtor in the 1,215 days before the petition that exceeds $125,000 in a homestead or burial plot. The limitation does not apply to the principal residence of a family farmer or to an interest transferred from a previous principal residence in the same state. The debtor may not exempt any amount of interest exceeding $125,000 in such property if the debtor has been convicted of a felony that demonstrates the bankruptcy case to be an abuse or if the debtor owes a debt arising from various securities statutes or from criminal, intentional, willful, or reckless misconduct that caused serious physical injury or death to another in the preceding five years. (S. 256, Sec. 322)

Employee Benefits. Amounts that are withheld or received as contributions by an employer from employees for payment to employee benefit plans subject to title I of ERISA or section 414(d) of the Internal Revenue Code, or sections 403(b) or 457 of the Internal Revenue Code, or for health insurance are not property of the estate. Amounts that are withheld or received as contributions from employees by an employer for payment to employee benefit plans subject to title I of ERISA or section 414(d) of the Internal Revenue Code, or sections 403(b) or 457 of the Internal Revenue Code are not disposable income under section 1325(b)(2). (S. 256, Sec. 323)

Exclusive Jurisdiction in Matters Involving Bankruptcy Professionals. The district court in which the bankruptcy case is commenced or pending is given exclusive jurisdiction over matters involving the construction of section 327 and rules relating to disclosure requirements in connection with the employment of attorneys, accountants, and other professionals in bankruptcy cases. (S.256, Sec. 324)

Filing Fee Changes. The filing fees set by 28 U.S.C. § 1930(a) are changed to $200 for chapter 7, $150 for chapter 13, and $1,000 for chapter 11. Changes are made in allocation of amounts from fees to the United States Trustee System Fund and the Judiciary, effective immediately, but with a two-year sunset date. (S. 256, Sec. 325)

Fee Sharing with Attorney Referral Programs. Section 504 is amended so that it does not apply to sharing, or agreeing to share, compensation with a bona fide public service attorney referral program operating in accordance with nonfederal law regulating attorney referral services and applicable professional responsibility rules. (S. 256, Sec. 326)

Valuation of Collateral. Section 506(a) is amended to provide that in an individual chapter 7 or 13 case, personal property shall be valued for purposes of determining an allowed claim based on replacement value as of the petition date without deduction for costs of sale or marketing. Replacement value of property acquired for personal, family, or household purposes is defined to mean the amount a retail merchant would charge for property of that kind considering the age and condition at the time value is determined. (S. 256, Sec. 327)

Defaults Based on Nonmonetary Obligations. Section 365(b) is amended to clarify that the obligation to cure defaults as a condition to assuming a real property lease does not include a default arising from failure to perform a nonmonetary obligation (other than a penalty rate or penalty provision) if it is impossible to cure the default by performing nonmonetary acts at or after the time of assumption. However, if the default arises from the failure to operate in accordance with a nonresidential real property lease, the default must be cured by performance at and after the time of assumption in accordance with the lease and by paying any pecuniary damages. Nonmonetary defaults in other types of executory contracts, other than any penalty rate or penalty provision, must be cured as a requirement for assumption. Similar kinds of provisions on the obligation to cure nonmonetary defaults are added to section 1124(2) with respect to the impairment of a class of claims. (S. 256, Sec. 328)

Back Pay Awards of Wages and Benefits. Section 503(b) is amended to clarify that wages and benefits awarded in a judicial or NLRB proceeding as back pay attributable to the postpetition period as a result of a violation of federal or state law, regardless of the time of the unlawful conduct or whether services have been rendered, are administrative expenses if payment of such wages and benefits will not substantially increase the probability of layoff or termination of current employees, or of nonpayment of domestic support obligations, during the bankruptcy case. (S. 256, Sec. 329)

Delay of Discharge in Certain Cases. Sections 727, 1141, 1228, and 1328 are amended to provide that discharge is to be delayed if the court finds that there is reasonable cause to believe that the debtor may be subject to the new section 522(q) restrictions on the homestead exemption based on certain types of misconduct and there is a pending proceeding in which the debtor may be found guilty or liable with respect to a type of act specified in that subsection. (S. 256, Sec. 330)

Limitations on Retention Bonuses and Severance Pay. Section 503 is amended to prohibit the payment or allowance of an obligation for the benefit of an insider for the purpose of inducing the insider to remain with the debtor's business unless the insider has a bona fide offer for employment from another business for the same or greater compensation, the services provided by the insider are essential to the survival of the business, and the amount of the transfer or obligation does not exceed 10 times the amount of the mean transfer or obligation of a similar kind given to nonmanagerial employees within the calendar year, or, if there were no similar transfers or obligations to nonmanagerial employees, the amount is not greater than 25% of the amount of any similar transfer or obligation for the benefit of such insider for any purpose during the previous calendar year. In addition, a severance payment may not be paid or allowed to an insider unless payment is part of a program that is generally applicable to all full-time employees and the amount of the payment does not exceed 10 times the amount of the mean severance pay given to nonmanagerial employees during the calendar year. Other types of transfers or obligations outside the ordinary course of business and not justified by the circumstances, including transfers for the benefit of officers, managers, or consultants hired postpetition, are also prohibited. (S. 256, Sec. 331)

Fraudulent Involuntary Bankruptcy Petitions. Section 303 is amended to provide that if an involuntary petition against an individual is dismissed and contains any materially false, fictitious, or fraudulent statement, the court may seal the records of, and all references to, the petition. The court may enter an order prohibiting consumer reporting agencies from reporting an involuntary petition against an individual that has been dismissed. Upon expiration of certain criminal statutes of limitation, the court may for good cause expunge the records of any involuntary petition. Section 157 of title 18, relating to bankruptcy fraud, is amended to specifically include a fraudulent involuntary petition. (S. 256, Sec. 332)

General and Small Business Bankruptcy Provisions
(Title IV)

GENERAL BUSINESS BANKRUPTCY PROVISIONS
(SUBTITLE A)

Acts by Securities Self Regulatory Organization. Section 362 is amended to provide that an investigation or action by a securities self regulatory organization, such as a national securities exchange, to enforce its regulatory powers, including an act to delist, delete, or refuse to permit quotation of a stock, or the enforcement of an order, other than for monetary sanctions, obtained in an action to enforce the organization's regulatory powers, is not subject to the automatic stay. Section 101 is amended to add a definition of "securities self regulatory organization." (S. 256, Sec. 401)

Order Dispensing with Section 341 Meetings in Prepackaged Cases. The court may order the United States trustee not to convene a meeting of creditors or equity security holders if the debtor has filed a plan for which the debtor solicited acceptances prepetition. (S. 256, Sec. 402)

Grace Period for Perfecting Security Interests to Avoid Preference Risk. Section 547(e) is amended to provide that, for preference purposes, a transfer is made when it takes effect between the transferor and the transferee if it is perfected within 30 days thereafter. Otherwise, the transfer is made on the date of perfection. The grace period under current laws is 10 days. (S. 256, Sec. 403)

Reduced Time to Assume or Reject Nonresidential Real Property Leases. A nonresidential real property lease under which the debtor is the lessee is deemed rejected, and the property must be immediately surrendered, if the trustee does not assume the lease by the earlier of 120 days after the order for relief or entry of an order confirming a plan. The court may extend the 120-day period for an additional 90 days on motion of the debtor or lessor for cause, but any further extension may not be granted without written consent of the lessor. (S. 256, Sec. 404)

Change in Membership of Committees in Chapter 11 Cases. The court may order the United States trustee to change the membership of a committee appointed under section 1102 if the change is necessary to ensure adequate representation of creditors or equity security holders. The court may order that the committee be increased to include a creditor that is a "small business concern" (as defined in the Small Business Act) if such creditor holds claims the aggregate amount of which is disproportionately large when compared to the creditor's annual gross income. (S. 256, Sec. 405)

Duty of Committees to Provide Access to Information. A creditors' committee must provide access to information for nonmember creditors who hold claims of the kind represented by the committee, and must solicit and receive comments from such creditors. (S. 256, Sec. 405)

Goods Returned on Consent of the Seller. Section 546 is amended to provide that when the court, on a motion made within 120 days after the order for relief, finds it is in the best interest of the estate for goods delivered to the debtor before bankruptcy to be returned to the seller, with the seller's consent, the goods remain subject to prior rights of secured creditors. (S. 256, Sec. 406)

Protection of Warehouseman's Lien. Section 546 is amended to protect from a trustee's attack any warehouseman's lien for storage, transportation, or other costs incidental to the storage and handling of goods, consistent with state statutes applicable to such liens, such as section 7-209 of the Uniform Commercial Code. (S. 256, Sec. 406)

Limitation of Compensation Awarded to a Trustee. Section 330(a) is amended to provide that, in determining the amount of reasonable compensation to be awarded to a trustee, the court must treat the compensation as a commission based on the limitations set forth in section 326. (S. 256, Sec. 407)

Postpetition Solicitation of Votes Based on Prepetition Disclosure. To permit postpetition continuation of solicitation of votes on a chapter 11 plan based on prepetition disclosure, section 1125 is amended to provide that an acceptance or rejection of a plan may be solicited during the case from the holder of a claim or interest if the holder was solicited before the commencement of the case in a manner that complied with applicable nonbankruptcy law. (S. 256, Sec. 408)

Preferential Payments in the Ordinary Course. The protection from preference attack for payments made in the ordinary course of business under section 547(c)(2) is amended to require only that the debt was incurred by the debtor in the ordinary course of business or financial affairs of the debtor and *either* the payment was made in the ordinary course of business or financial affairs of the debtor and the transferee *or* the payment was made according to ordinary business terms. (S. 256, Sec. 409)

Small Preferences in Business Cases. If the debtor's debts are not primarily consumer debts, a preference is not recoverable if the aggregate value of all property that constitutes or is affected by the transfer is less than $5,000. (S. 256, Sec. 409)

Venue in Small Proceedings by the Trustee. Section 1409(b) of 28 U.S.C. is amended to provide that the only proper federal venue in which a trustee may commence litigation to recover a money judgment or property in a proceeding arising or related to a bankruptcy case is the district where the defendant resides, if the proceeding is based on a consumer debt of less than $15,000 or is against a noninsider based on a nonconsumer debt of less than $10,000. (S. 256, Sec. 410)

Limitation on Extension of Exclusivity. Section 1129(d) is amended to provide that the exclusive period in which only the debtor may file a chapter 11 plan may not be extended beyond the date that is 18 months after the order for relief and that the exclusive period in which the required acceptances must be obtained may not be extended beyond the date that is 20 months after the order for relief. (S. 256, Sec. 411)

Condominium, Cooperative, and Homeowner Association Fees. Section 523(a)(16) is amended to provide that fees arising with respect to a debtor's interest in a residential condominium, cooperative, or homeowner's association for as long as the debtor has a legal, possessory, or equitable interest in such property are nondischargeable. (S. 256, Sec. 412)

Creditor Representation at Meeting of Creditors. Section 341 is amended to permit a creditor holding a consumer debt, or a representative of the creditor, to appear and participate at the meeting of creditors in a chapter 7 or chapter 13 case, either alone or with an attorney for the creditor, notwithstanding any local rule or nonbankruptcy law that requires representation by an attorney. (S. 256, Sec. 413)

Relaxing of Disinterestedness Standard for Investment Bankers. The definition of "disinterested person" is amended so that a person will not be ineligible for employment as a professional under section 327 solely because the person was an investment banker for a security of the debtor, or was an attorney, director, officer, or employee of such investment banker. (S. 256, Sec. 414)

Factors for Determining Reasonable Compensation. Section 330 is amended to add as a new factor to be used in determining reasonable compensation for a professional person employed under section 327 or 1103 of the Code whether the person is board certified or otherwise has demonstrated skill and experience in the bankruptcy field. (S. 256, Sec. 415)

Appointment of Elected Trustee in Chapter 11 Cases. Section 1104 is amended to provide that if an eligible, disinterested trustee is elected at the meeting of creditors in a chapter 11 case, the United States trustee shall file a report certifying the election and the elected trustee shall be considered appointed for purposes of that section. Any dispute regarding the election shall be resolved by the court. (S. 256, Sec. 416)

Utility Service. A new subsection 366(e) is enacted to deal specifically with adequate assurance of payment to utilities in chapter 11 cases. A utility is permitted to terminate service to a chapter 11 debtor if it does not receive adequate assurance within 30 days of the petition. The term "adequate assurance" for purposes of section 366(e) is defined to mean a cash deposit, letter of credit, certificate of deposit, surety bond, prepayment, or other form of security to which the utility agrees. It does not include the availability of an administrative expense priority. The court may modify the amount of adequate assurance under section 366(e) but cannot take into account the absence of security before the petition, the timely payment of prepetition bills, or the availability of an administrative expense priority. A utility may recover or set off against a prepetition deposit by a chapter 11 debtor without notice or order of court. (S. 256, Sec. 417)

Waiver of Filing Fees. Section 1930 of title 28 is amended to provide that the filing fee for a chapter 7 debtor may be waived by the court, under procedures prescribed by the Judicial Conference of the United States, for an individual unable to pay the fee in installments and whose income is below 150% of the poverty level. (S. 256, Sec. 418)

Disclosure of Information Regarding Chapter 11 Debtor's Substantial or Controlling Interests in Subsidiaries. The Judicial Conference of the United States is required to propose amended Federal Rules of Bankruptcy Procedure and official forms directing debtors in chapter 11 to disclose information on the value, operations, and profitability of any closely held corporation, partnership, or any other entity in which the debtor holds a substantial or controlling interest. The purpose of the disclosure is to assist parties in interest taking steps to ensure that the debtor's substantial interest in another entity is used for the payment of claims against the debtor. (S. 256, Sec. 419)

GENERAL AND SMALL BUSINESS BANKRUPTCY PROVISIONS (SUBTITLE B)

Flexible Rules for Disclosure Statements. Section 1125(a) is amended to provide that in all chapter 11 cases, both large and small, the court shall consider the complexity of the case, the benefit of additional information to parties in interest, and the cost of providing additional information whenever the court is determining whether a disclosure statement provides adequate information. (S. 256, Sec. 431)

Flexible Standards for Disclosure Statements and Plans in Small Business Cases. Section 1125 is amended to provide that, in a small business case, the court may determine that the plan itself provides adequate information and that a separate disclosure statement is not necessary. The court also may approve a disclosure statement submitted on a standard form approved by the court or adopted by the Judicial Conference as an official form. (S. 256, Sec. 431)

Conditional Approval of Disclosure Statement in Small Business Case. Section 1125 is amended to give the court the authority to conditionally approve a disclosure statement in a small business case, subject to final approval after notice and a hearing. The conditionally approved disclosure statement must be mailed not later than 25 days before the confirmation hearing, and the hearing on final approval of the disclosure statement may be combined with the confirmation hearing. (S. 256, Sec. 431)

New Definitions for "Small Business Case" and "Small Business Debtor." A case is a "small business case" if it is filed under chapter 11 and the debtor is a "small business debtor." In general, a debtor is a "small business debtor" if (1) the debtor is engaged in commercial or business activities, including an affiliate of the debtor that is also in bankruptcy, but excluding any debtor whose primary activity is the business of owning or operating real estate; (2) the debtor has noncontingent, liquidated, secured, and unsecured debts that, in the aggregate, do not exceed $2 million on the date of the petition or order for relief, excluding debts owed to affiliates or insiders of the debtor; and (3) the United States trustee has not appointed a committee of unsecured creditors under section 1102 or the court has determined that the creditors' committee is not sufficiently active and representative to provide effective oversight of the debtor. If a creditors' committee has been appointed and is active in the case, the debtor is not a "small business debtor," regardless of the aggregate amount of debts. (S. 256, Sec. 432)

Standard Form Disclosure Statement and Plan for Small Business Cases. The Judicial Conference of the United States is required to prescribe official forms for a disclosure statement and plan for small business cases. The forms are intended to achieve a practical balance between reasonable needs of the courts and the parties for reasonably complete information, as well as economy and simplicity for debtors. (S. 256, Sec. 433).

Uniform Reporting Requirements for Small Business Debtors. New section 308 is added to the Code to require small business debtors to file periodic and other reports containing the following information: (1) the debtor's profitability; (2) reasonable approximation of projected cash receipts and disbursements over a reasonable period; (3) comparisons of actual cash receipts and disbursements with projections in prior reports; (4) whether the debtor is in compliance with postpetition requirements imposed by the Code or the Rules, and whether the debtor has been timely filing tax returns and other governmental filings and paying taxes and other administrative expenses when due; (5) if the debtor is not in compliance with such postpetition requirements or is not filing tax returns and other governmental filings or paying taxes and other administrative expenses when due, information of what the failures are and on how they will be remedied; and (6) information on such other matters as is in the best interest of the debtors and creditors, and in the public interest in fair and efficient chapter 11 procedures. These requirements become effective 60 days after the promulgation of Federal Rules of Bankruptcy Procedure to establish forms to be used to comply with the new section 308 of the Code. (S. 256, Sec. 434)

Promulgation of Rules and Official Forms on Uniform Reporting in Small Business Cases. The Judicial Conference is required to promulgate Federal Rules of Bankruptcy Procedure and Official Forms directing small business debtors to file periodic financial and other reports containing information about the debtor's profitability and cash receipts and disbursements, and whether the debtor is timely filing tax returns and paying taxes and other administrative expenses when due. (S. 256, Sec. 435)

Duties of Debtor in Possession or Trustee in Small Business Case. A new section 1116 is added to the Code to list duties of a small business debtor in possession or trustee, including the duty to (1) append to its petition the most recent balance sheet, statement of operations, cash-flow statement, and federal income tax return (or a statement that such documents have not been prepared or no such tax return has been filed); (2) attend, through its senior management and counsel, meetings scheduled by the court or the United States trustee, including initial debtor interviews; (3) timely file schedules and statements of financial affairs, with extensions that cannot exceed 30 days after the order for relief unless there are compelling circumstances justifying further time; (4) file postpetition reports as required under the Federal Rules of Bankruptcy Procedure or local rules; (5) maintain customary insurance; (6) timely file tax returns and other required governmental filings, and timely pay taxes entitled to administrative expense priority; and (7) allow the United States trustee or his or her designee to inspect the debtor's business premises, books, and records. (S. 256, Sec. 436)

Time for Filing Plan and Disclosure Statement in Small Business Cases. In a small business case, only the debtor may file a plan within 180 days after the order for relief. In addition, a plan and disclosure statement must be filed within 300 days after the order for relief, regardless of who files them. These time periods may be extended for cause only if the debtor demonstrates that it is more likely than not that the court will confirm a plan within a reasonable period of time, a new deadline is imposed when the time is extended, and the order extending the time is signed before the existing deadline has expired. (S. 256, Sec. 437).

Plan Confirmation Deadline in Small Business Cases. If a plan is timely filed in a small business case, the court must confirm the plan within 45 days after it is filed. The court may extend this time but only if it determines that it is more likely than not that the court will confirm a plan within a reasonable time, a new deadline is imposed at the time the extension is granted, and the order extending the deadline is signed before the existing deadline has expired. (S. 256, Sec. 438)

Duties of the United States Trustee in Small Business Cases. Section 586 of title 28 is amended to impose duties on the United States trustee in small business cases. These duties include the obligation to conduct an initial debtor interview early in the case at which the United States trustee must begin to investigate the debtor's viability, inquire about the debtor's business plan, explain the debtor's obligations to file monthly operating reports and inform the debtor of other obligations, and attempt to develop an agreed scheduling order. The United States trustee, if it is determined to be appropriate and advisable, must visit the debtor's business premises, ascertain the state of the debtor's books and records, and verify that the debtor has filed tax returns. The United States trustee also must review and monitor the debtor's activities to determine whether the debtor will be unable to confirm a plan, and must move to dismiss or convert the case to another chapter if the United States trustee finds material grounds for such relief. (S. 256, Sec. 439)

Scheduling Conferences. Section 105(d) is amended to provide that the court shall hold such status conferences as are necessary to further the expeditious and economical resolution of the case. This provision is not limited to small business cases. (S. 256, Sec. 440).

Serial Small Business Filers. Section 362 is amended to provide that the automatic stay does not apply if the debtor is a debtor in another small business case that is pending when the petition is filed, was a debtor in a small business case that was dismissed for any reason within the previous two years, or was a debtor in a small business case in which a plan was confirmed within the past two years. In addition, if the debtor is an entity that had acquired substantially all the assets or business of a small business debtor that fits the above description, the automatic stay will not apply in a bankruptcy case of such entity unless the entity establishes that it made the acquisition in good faith and not for the purposes of evading these new serial filer provisions. These amendments to section 362 for serial filers do not apply in a noncollusive involuntary case or, in a voluntary case, if the debtor establishes that filing the petition resulted from circumstances beyond the control of the debtor not foreseeable at the time the case then pending was commenced, and it is likely that the court will confirm a feasible reorganization (not liquidating) plan within a reasonable time. (S. 256, Sec. 441)

Expanded Grounds for Dismissal or Conversion of Chapter 11 Cases. Section 1112 is amended to require the court to dismiss or convert a chapter 11 case for cause unless there are unusual circumstances identified by the court that establish that such relief is not in the best interests of creditors and the estate, there is a reasonable likelihood that a plan will be confirmed in a timely manner, there is reasonable justification for the debtor's conduct giving rise to the ground for dismissal or conversion, and the ground for dismissal or conversion will be cured within a reasonable time. The section also provides that "cause" to dismiss or convert includes any of 16 acts or omissions, including the unauthorized use of cash collateral that is substantially harmful to one or more creditors, failure to maintain appropriate insurance, and failure to pay postpetition taxes. These provisions on dismissal and conversion apply in all chapter 11 cases, not only small business cases. (S. 256, Sec. 442)

Time to Rule on Motion to Dismiss or Convert Chapter 11 Case. The court is required to commence a hearing on a motion to dismiss or convert a chapter 11 case within 30 days after the motion is filed. The court also is required to decide the motion within 15 days after commencement of the hearing, unless the movant consents to a continuance for a specified period or compelling circumstances prevent the court from meeting these time limits. (S. 256, Sec. 442)

Appointment of Trustee or Examiner in Chapter 11 Case. Section 1104(a) is amended so that if grounds exist to convert or dismiss the case under section 1112, but the court determines that the appointment of a trustee or examiner is in the best interests of creditors and the estate, the court must order the appointment of a trustee or examiner. (S. 256, Sec. 442)

Study of Small Business Cases. Within two years after enactment of the 2005 Act, the Administrator of the Small Business Administration, in consultation with the various officials, shall conduct a study to determine (1) the factors that cause small businesses to become debtors in bankruptcy and that cause certain small businesses to succeed in chapter 11, and (2) how bankruptcy laws may be made more effective and efficient in assisting small businesses to remain viable. (S. 256, Sec. 443)

Automatic Stay Against Mortgagee of Single Asset Real Estate. Section 362(d)(3), which permits continuation of the automatic stay against a creditor with a claim secured by a mortgage on single-asset real estate, but only if certain interest payments are made, is modified in several ways, including the express application of the nondefault contract rate of interest for purposes of determining the amount of interest payments that must be made to continue the stay. (S. 256, Sec. 444)

Limit on Administrative Expense When Nonresidential Lease Is Assumed Followed by Rejection. Section 503(b) is amended to provide that when a nonresidential lease is rejected after being assumed, a sum equal to all monetary obligations due (excluding those arising from or relating to a failure to operate or a penalty provision) for a period of two years after the date of rejection or actual turnover of the premises (without reduction or setoff for any reason except for sums actually received or to be received from a third party) is an administrative expense. The claim for the remaining sums due for the balance of the lease term is a prepetition claim subject to the landlord's cap in section 502(b)(6). (S. 256, Sec. 445)

Debtor as Plan Administrator of an Employee Benefit Plan. Unless a trustee has been appointed in the case, the debtor is obligated under section 521 to continue to perform the obligations of an administrator of an ERISA employee benefit plan if, when the case was commenced, the debtor served as such an administrator. If a trustee is serving in the case, the trustee has such duties under sections 704(a) and 1106. (S. 256, Sec. 446)

Committees of Retired Employees. Section 1114 is amended to clarify that the court orders the appointment of a committee of retired persons but that the United States trustee does the appointing. (S. 256, Sec. 447)

Municipal Bankruptcy Provisions
(Title V)

Technical Amendment. A technical amendment is made regarding the court ordering relief under chapter 9. (S. 256, Sec. 501)

Application of Financial Contract Sections to Chapter 9 Cases. Section 901 is amended to make applicable in chapter 9 cases those provisions that govern contractual rights to liquidate, terminate, or accelerate securities contracts, commodities contracts, forward contracts, repurchase agreements, swap agreements, and master netting agreements, as well as the provision on the timing of damage measurements regarding these types of contracts. (S. 256, Sec. 502)

Bankruptcy Data
(Title VI)

Reporting of Statistics by the Courts. The Administrative Office of United States Courts is required to compile statistics collected by clerks of court in chapter 7, 11, and 13 cases, make the statistics available to the public, and on or before July 1, 2008 and annually thereafter provide an analysis of the statistics to Congress. The statistics must include, in the aggregate and itemized by chapter and district, the following: total assets and liabilities of debtors, also itemized by the categories in the schedules; current monthly income, average income and average expenses of debtors;

the aggregate amount of debt discharged, determined based on total debts reported and the amounts "in categories which are predominantly nondischargeable"; average time between filing and closing of cases; the number of reaffirmation agreements filed, the number of cases in which reaffirmation agreements were filed, the number of such cases in which the debtor was represented by an attorney, and the number of such cases in which a reaffirmation agreement was approved by the court; for chapter 13 cases only, the number of cases in which an order was entered valuing collateral and the number of such cases in which the order valued collateral at less than the amount of the claim, the number of cases dismissed, the number of cases dismissed for failure to make plan payments, the number of cases refiled after dismissal, and the number of cases in which a plan was completed, itemized by the number of plan modifications before plan completion, and the number of cases in which the debtor had filed another case during the six-year period before the petition; the number of cases in which fines or punitive damages were assessed against creditors for misconduct; and the number of cases in which sanctions or damages were awarded against debtors' attorneys under Federal Rule of Bankruptcy Procedure 9011. (S. 256, Sec. 601)

Trustee and Debtor in Possession Reporting. The Attorney General is required to develop forms for reports by trustees and debtors in possession that will facilitate the compilation of data and public access to such data. The data to be collected is such data that would be helpful in evaluating the bankruptcy system, with due regard for concerns of data collection costs and privacy issues. Final reports must include, in addition to other information required by law: time the case was pending; assets abandoned; assets exempted; estate receipts and disbursements; costs of administration; claims asserted; claims allowed; claims discharged without payment; and, for chapter 12 and chapter 13 cases, dates of confirmation, each modification of the plan, and defaults by the debtor under the plan. Forms for periodic reports in chapter 11 cases are required to contain additional types of information, including numbers of employees, receipts, disbursements, profitability, professional fees, and details of plans. (S. 256, Sec. 602)

Audits. The Attorney General and the Federal Judicial Conference are to develop procedures for use in audits of information submitted by individual chapter 7 and chapter 13 debtors, to be performed by independent certified public accountants and independent licensed public accountants using generally accepted auditing standards or alternative auditing standards developed by the Attorney General and the Federal Judicial Conference. The procedures must provide for audits of no less than one in 250 randomly chosen cases, and require audits of cases with greater than average variations above the statistical norm for income or expenses. Individual audit reports are to be filed with the court, and notice is to be given to creditors and the United States Attorney of material misstatements of income, expenditures, or assets that were discovered. Section 727(d) is amended to provide that a discharge may be revoked for failure to satisfactorily explain a material misstatement found in an audit or to make documents or property available in an audit. (S. 256, Sec. 603)

Sense of Congress Regarding Bankruptcy Data. It is the sense of Congress that all public electronic bankruptcy data should be released in usable bulk electronic form, subject to privacy safeguards, using uniform data definitions and aggregating data for each case in a specific record. (S. 256, Sec. 604)

Bankruptcy Tax Provisions
(Title VII)

Subordination of Certain Tax Liens and Determination of Ad Valorem Taxes. Section 724 is amended to give greater rights to holders of ad valorem tax liens on real or personal property by limiting the subordination of such liens in chapter 7 cases. In addition, section 724 is amended to provide that all tax liens subordinated under section 724 are not subordinated to administrative expenses, other than postpetition wages, salaries, and commissions, incurred while the case was in chapter 11. Section 505(a) is amended to provide that the bankruptcy court may not determine the amount or legality of an ad valorem tax if the period for contesting or redetermining the tax has expired under applicable nonbankruptcy law. (S. 256, Sec. 701)

Fuel Tax Claims. Section 501 is amended so that a claim arising from the debtor's liability for an assessed fuel use tax may be filed by the base jurisdiction designated under an International Fuel Tax Agreement and shall be allowed as a single claim. (S. 256, Sec. 702)

Notice of Request for a Determination of Taxes. Section 505(b) is amended to require the clerk to maintain a list on which a federal, state, or local governmental unit responsible for the collection of taxes within the district may designate an address for service of requests for determination of tax liability, as well as describe where further information concerning additional requirements for filing such requests may be found. If a taxing authority does not list this information with the clerk, the request for determination of tax liability may be served at the address for the filing of a tax return or protest in connection with such tax. (S. 256, Sec. 703)

Interest on Tax Claims. A new section 511 is added to the Code to govern the rate of interest in connection with tax claims. If the Code requires payment of interest on a tax claim or an administrative expense tax, or a determination of present value of an allowed amount of a tax claim, the rate of interest shall be the rate determined under applicable nonbankruptcy law. The interest rate to be paid on a tax claim paid under a confirmed plan shall be determined as of the calendar month in which the plan is confirmed. (S. 256, Sec. 704)

Suspension of Time Periods Relating to Priority Tax Claims. Section 507(a)(8) is amended to provide that the time periods specified in that paragraph with respect to priority tax claims are suspended for any period in which the taxing authority is prohibited under nonbankruptcy law from collecting the tax because of the debtor's request for a hearing and appeal regarding the tax, plus 90 days. Similarly, the time periods in section 507(a)(8) are suspended during the application of the automatic stay in a prior bankruptcy case, or while collection was precluded due to a plan confirmed in a prior case, plus 90 days. (S. 256, Sec. 705)

Priority Property Tax Claims. Section 507(a)(8) is amended so that property taxes incurred, whether or not assessed, before the commencement of the case and last payable without penalty within one year before the bankruptcy petition was filed, will be entitled to priority. (S. 256, Sec. 706)

Dischargeability of Taxes. Section 1328(a) is amended to provide that taxes required to be withheld or collected by the debtor that have priority under section 507(a)(8)(c) and debts described in section 523(a)(1)(B) or (C) are not dischargeable in chapter 13. (S. 256, Sec. 707)

No Discharge in Corporate Chapter 11 Cases for Governmental Claims Based on Fraud. A debt owed to a domestic governmental unit incurred by fraud is not dischargeable if the debtor is a corporation in chapter 11. In addition, a debt for a tax or customs duty is not discharged for a corporate debtor in chapter 11 if the debtor made a fraudulent return or willfully attempted to evade or defeat such tax or customs duty. (S. 256, Sec. 708)

Stay of Tax Proceedings. The automatic stay of the commencement or continuation of proceedings before the United States Tax Court under section 362(a)(8) is amended to limit it to a corporate debtor's tax liability for a taxable period the bankruptcy court may determine or, if the debtor is an individual, to a tax for a taxable period ending before the date of the order for relief. (S. 256, Sec. 709)

Payment of Tax Claims under a Chapter 11 Plan. Section 1129(a)(9) is amended to give greater rights to a governmental unit receiving payment of priority tax claims under a chapter 11 plan. First, the tax must be paid in regular installment payments. Second, it must be paid over a period ending not later than five years after the order for relief. Third, treatment of the tax claim under the plan may not be less favorable than the treatment of the most favored nonpriority unsecured claim, other than cash payments to an administrative convenience class under section 1122(b). In addition, if a tax claim is secured, but otherwise is the type of tax claim that would be entitled to priority under section 507(a)(8), the holder of the claim must receive cash payments in the same manner and over the same period as unsecured tax claims entitled to section 507(a)(8) priority. (S. 256, Sec. 710)

Avoidance of Statutory Tax Liens Limited. Current section 545(2) permits avoidance of statutory liens if the lien is not perfected or enforceable against an actual or hypothetical bona fide purchaser at the time the case was commenced. This provision is amended to provide that it is not applicable to a purchaser under a tax lien statute. (S. 256, Sec. 711)

Payment of Postpetition Taxes Incurred in the Conduct of Business. Section 960 of title 28 is amended to clarify that a trustee is required to pay taxes incurred in the conduct of business in a timely manner under applicable nonbankruptcy law, except for a property tax secured by a lien on property abandoned by a bankruptcy trustee within a reasonable time after the lien attaches, or if payment of the tax is excused under a specific provision of the Bankruptcy Code. Under certain situations, payment of the tax may be deferred in a chapter 7 case. Section 503(b) is amended to provide that an ad valorem tax, whether secured or unsecured, incurred by the estate is an administrative expense. (S. 256, Sec. 712)

Need to Request Payment of Governmental Administrative Expenses Eliminated. Section 503(b) is amended to provide that a governmental unit is not required to file a request for payment of an administrative expense for a tax or a tax penalty as a condition to allowance of an administrative expense. (S. 256, Sec. 712)

Secured Claims Entitled to Interest and Fees under State Statute. Section 506(b) is amended so that an oversecured creditor is entitled to interest and any reasonable fees, costs, or charges provided under a state statute. This provision will benefit state taxing authorities with oversecured claims. (S. 256, Sec. 712)

Surcharging Collateral for Ad Valorem Taxes. Section 506(c) is amended to clarify that the reasonable, necessary costs and expenses of preserving collateral for the benefit of a secured creditor, which may be recoverable from the collateral, include ad valorem taxes. (S. 256, Sec. 712)

Chapter 7 Distribution to Tardily Filed Priority Claims. Section 726(a)(1) is amended to provide that the trustee must make distributions to tardily filed priority claims along with timely filed priority claims if the tardily filed claims are filed before the earlier of 10 days after the mailing of a summary of the trustee's final report or the date the trustee commences final distribution. (S. 256, Sec. 713)

Tax Return Filed by Taxing Authority. Section 523(a) is amended to provide that the term "return" means a return that satisfies requirements of applicable nonbankruptcy law and does not include a return prepared by a taxing authority, except one based on information received from the person required to file a return and signed by that person. (S. 256, Sec. 714)

Discharge of Estate's Liability for Unpaid Taxes. The Code is amended to clarify that the bankruptcy estate is discharged from tax liability if the trustee has requested a determination of unpaid liability of the estate and certain requirements have been met in accordance with section 505(b)(2). (S. 256, Sec. 715)

Filing of Prepetition Tax Returns in Chapter 13 Cases. A new section 1308 requires a chapter 13 debtor to file with taxing authorities any unfiled tax returns that were required to have been filed in the four years before the petition by federal, state, or local law. The trustee may hold open the creditors' meeting for specified periods to allow the filing of such returns, and the court may extend such periods for specified reasons. If the debtor does not file such returns, the court must dismiss or convert the case on request of a party in interest or the United States trustee. A taxing authority's claim is deemed timely in a chapter 13 case if filed within 60 days of the filing of the return to which it relates. It is the sense of Congress that the Federal Rules of Bankruptcy Procedure should be amended to provide that no objection to confirmation need be filed by a taxing authority until 60 days after the filing of required tax returns and no objection to a tax claim may be filed, if a return is required with respect to the claim, until the tax return has been filed. (S. 256, Sec. 716)

Tax Information in Chapter 11 Disclosure Statements. Section 1125(a) is amended to require that disclosure statements include a discussion of the federal tax consequences of the chapter 11 plan to the debtor or any successor to the debtor, and to a hypothetical investor typical of the holders of the claims and interests in the case. (S. 256, Sec. 717)

Setoff of Tax Refunds. An exception to the automatic stay is added to permit the setoff of tax refunds for tax periods ending before the order for relief. If setoff is not permitted under applicable nonbankruptcy law because of a pending action disputing the tax, the taxing authority may hold a refund unless the court, on motion of the trustee after notice and a hearing, grants the taxing authority adequate protection. (S. 256, Sec. 718)

Special Provisions on the Treatment of State and Local Taxes. Section 346 is amended to add numerous provisions on state and local taxes, including provisions on separate taxable entities, taxation of partnerships, accounting methods, tax on transfers of property between the debtor and the estate, tax rates, withholding obligations, carryover or reduction of tax attributes, nonrealization of income from discharge of indebtedness, and the timing and manner of filing tax returns. (S. 256, Sec. 719)

Dismissal for Failure to File Tax Returns. A taxing authority may move for dismissal or conversion of a case if the debtor has not filed a tax return that becomes due after the petition or properly obtained an extension of time to file the return. If the debtor does not, within 90 days after such motion, file the return or obtain an extension of time to file the return, the case must be dismissed or converted. (S. 256, Sec. 720)

Ancillary and Other Cross-Border Cases
(Title VIII)

New Chapter 15 on Cross-Border Cases. A new chapter is added to the Code for the purpose of incorporating a model law on cross-border insolvency. The chapter is designed to provide efficient mechanisms for dealing with cross-border cases with objectives that include the cooperation of courts of different nations. This chapter, which provides for the filing of a petition for recognition of a foreign proceeding, replaces section 304 of the Code, which is repealed. (S. 256, Secs. 801–802)

Financial Contract Provisions
(Title IX)

Amendments to Nonbankruptcy Laws Relating to Insured Depository Institutions. Federal nonbankruptcy statutes, including the Federal Deposit Insurance Act and the Federal Credit Union Act, are amended with respect to the treatment of certain financial agreements by conservators or receivers of insured depository institutions, the treatment of master agreements, and the disaffirmance, repudiation, or transfer of qualified financial contracts. These federal statutes are also amended with respect to the authority of the FDIC and the National Credit Union Administration Board regarding failed or failing institutions, and with respect to record-keeping requirements. Many other changes in the law governing insured depository institutions are included in the legislation. (S. 256, Secs. 901–906, 908–909)

Financial Contracts and Master Netting Agreements. Many Code sections are amended, and several new sections are added, to clarify and expand the protection for certain financial contracts, including the right to liquidate, terminate, or accelerate securities contracts, forward contracts, commodities contracts, swap agreements, and repurchase agreements, in the event of a participant's bankruptcy. In addition, several sections are amended and a new section 561 is added to give effect to master netting agreements. A new section 562 is added to govern the timing of damage measurement in connection with the rejection of these types of financial contracts. (S. 256, Secs. 907, 910)

Exception to SIPC Stay for Exercising Rights in Connection with Certain Financial Contracts. The Securities Investor Protection Act is amended to provide that the exercise of a contractual right to liquidate, terminate, or accelerate a securities contract, commodity contract, forward contract, repurchase agreement, swap agreement, or master netting agreement is not stayed in a SIPC proceeding. (S. 256, Sec. 911)

Family Farmers and Family Fishermen
(Title X)

Chapter 12 Sunset Date Eliminated. Chapter 12 is reenacted without a sunset date. (S. 256, Sec. 1001)

Inflation Adjustments for Chapter 12 Debt Limits. Section 104(b) is amended to provide that the chapter 12 debt limits will be adjusted periodically for inflation. (S. 256, Sec. 1002)

Claims Arising from Transfer of a Farm Asset. A claim arising from the sale, transfer, exchange, or other disposition of a farm asset used in farming operations shall be treated as a nonpriority claim in a chapter 12 case, provided the debtor receives a discharge. (S. 256, Sec. 1003)

Debt Limit for Chapter 12. The debt limit in the definition of "family farmer" is increased from $1,500,000 to $3,237,000. (S. 256, Sec. 1004)

Farming Income Percentage Requirement. The definition of "family farmer" is changed to provide that a debtor may qualify if either 50% of the debtor's income was received from a farming operation in the tax year prior to the petition or 50% of the debtor's income was received from a farming operation in the each of the second and third years before the petition. (S. 256, Sec. 1005)

Retroactive Assessment of Disposable Income. Sections 1225 and 1229 are amended to provide that the disposable income provisions are based on projected disposable income and that plan payment amounts may not be modified after such payments are due and may not be modified in the last year of the plan in a way that leaves the debtor insufficient funds to carry on the farming operation after the plan is completed. (S. 256, Sec. 1006)

Family Fishermen. New definitions are added to section 101 for "commercial fishing operation," "commercial fishing vessel," "family fisherman," and "family fisherman with regular income." A family fisherman may be a debtor under chapter 12. (S. 256, Sec. 1007)

Health Care and Employee Benefits
(Title XI)

Patient Records of a Health Care Business. A new section 351 is added to the Code to protect patients of a health care business with respect to the maintenance or disposal of patient records. New definitions of "health care business," "patient," and "patient records" are added to section 101. (S. 256, Secs. 1101–1102)

Administrative Expense Priority for Costs of Closing a Health Care Business. Section 503(b) is amended to provide that the costs of closing a health care business incurred by a trustee or governmental agency, including expenses incurred in disposing of patient records or transferring patients from a closing health care business to another health care business, are administrative expenses. (S. 256, Sec. 1103)

Appointment of Patient Advocate. A new section is added to require the court, if the debtor is a health care business, to order the appointment of an ombudsman to monitor the quality of patient care and to represent the interests of patients unless the court finds that such an appointment is not necessary under the specific facts of the case. The ombudsman, who must be disinterested, is appointed by the United States trustee. The person appointed as ombudsman is compensated in the same manner as a professional person employed by the trustee. (S. 256, Sec. 1104)

Duty to Transfer Patients. Section 704 is amended to impose on the trustee the duty to use reasonable and best efforts to transfer patients from a debtor health care business that is in the process of being closed to an appropriate health care business that is in the vicinity of the debtor, provides patients with substantially the same services, and maintains a reasonable quality of care. (S. 256, Sec. 1105)

Exclusion from Health Care Program Participation Not Stayed. The debtor's exclusion by the Secretary of Health and Human Services from participation in the Medicare program or any other federal health care program is not subject to the automatic stay. (S. 256, Sec. 1106)

Other Amendments
(Title XII)

Amendments to Definitions. Amendments are made to definitions in section 101. Although most of these amendments are nonsubstantial, others are not. For example, the definition of "single asset real estate" in section 101 is amended to delete the $4 million debt limitation. (S. 256, Sec. 1201)

Inflation Adjustments. Section 104(b) is amended to add sections 101(19A), 522(f)(3) and (f)(4), 541(b), 547(c)(9), 1322(d), 1325(b), and 1326(b)(3) of title 11 and section 1409(b) of title 28 as sections with dollar amounts that are to be adjusted every three years for inflation. (S. 256, Sec. 1202)

Extension of Time. A technical amendment is made to section 108(c)(2). (S. 256, Sec. 1203)

Small Business Investment Companies. A technical amendment is made to section 109(b)(2) regarding small business investment companies that are ineligible for chapter 7 relief. (S. 256, Sec. 1204)

Postpetition Effect of Security Interest. A technical amendment is made to section 552(b). (S. 256, Sec. 1204)

Petition Preparers. A grammatical correction is made to section 110(j). (S. 256, Sec. 1205)

Compensation of Professional Persons. Section 330(a) is amended to clarify that the court may approve compensation for a professional person employed under section 327 or 1103 on a fixed or percentage fee basis. (S. 256, Sec. 1206)

Conversion. A technical clarification is made to section 348(f)(2). (S. 256, Sec. 1207)

Compensation for Professional Services Rendered to a Committee Member Not an Administrative Expense. Section 503(b)(4) is amended so that compensation for professional services rendered by an attorney or accountant for a member of a committee appointed under section 1102, and reimbursement of expenses incurred by such attorney or accountant, are not administrative expenses. (S. 256, Sec. 1208)

Drunk Boating or Flying. Section 523(a)(9) is amended to include operation of a vessel or aircraft. (S. 256, Sec. 1209)

Community Property Discharge. A stylistic change is made to section 524(a)(3). (S. 256, Sec. 1210)

Educational Loan or Grant Discrimination. A clarifying change is made to section 525(c). (S. 256, Sec. 1211)

Exclusion of Debtor's Interest in Liquid or Gaseous Hydrocarbons from Property of the Estate. A technical amendment is made to section 541(b)(4)(B)(ii). (S. 256, Sec. 1212)

Insider Preferences. Section 547 is amended to provide that if the trustee avoids a preference made between 90 days and one year before the commencement of the case to an entity that is not an insider, but for the benefit of a creditor that is an insider, the transfer shall be avoided only with respect to the creditor that is an insider. This amendment applies to cases pending or commenced on or after the date of enactment. (S. 256, Sec. 1213)

Postpetition Transactions. A technical amendment is made to section 549(c). (S. 256, Sec. 1214)

Distribution of Property. A technical correction is made to section 726(b). (S. 256, Sec. 1215)

Determination of Cure Amounts in Chapter 9 Cases. Section 901 is amended to make applicable to chapter 9 municipal debt adjustment cases section 1123(d), which provides that if a plan proposes to cure a default, the amount necessary to cure the default shall be determined in accordance with the underlying agreement and applicable nonbankruptcy law. (S. 256, Sec. 1216)

Abandonment of Railroad Line. A technical amendment is made to section 1170(e)(1). (S. 256, Sec. 1217)

Contents of Railroad Reorganization Plan. A technical amendment is made to section 1172(c)(1). (S. 256, Sec. 1218)

Nonreview of Abstention Decisions. Section 1334(d) of title 28 is amended to clarify that the prohibition on review by the court of appeals or the Supreme Court of a decision to abstain or not to abstain is applicable only with respect to discretionary abstention under section 1334(c)(1) and to a decision to abstain under the mandatory abstention provision in section 1334(c)(2). (S. 256, Sec. 1219)

Knowing Disregard of Bankruptcy Law or Rule. Technical changes and corrections are made to section 156 of title 18. (S. 256, Sec. 1220)

Transfers by a Nonprofit Charitable Organization. A transfer under section 363 of property by a nonprofit charitable corporation or trust must be made in accordance with applicable nonbankruptcy law that governs transfers by such entities. Similarly, Section 1129(a) is amended to require as a condition to confirmation of a chapter 11 plan that all property transferred under the plan be made in accordance with any applicable provisions of nonbankruptcy law that govern transfers by nonprofit charitable corporations or trusts. In addition, section 541 is amended to provide that property held by a debtor that is a nonprofit, tax-exempt corporation may be transferred to an entity that is not such a corporation, but only under the same conditions as would apply if the debtor had not been in bankruptcy. The legislation provides that none of these amendments shall be construed to require the bankruptcy court to refer or remand any proceeding to any other court or to require the approval of any other court for the transfer of property. (S. 256, Sec. 1221)

Protection of Purchase-Money Security Interests. Section 547(c)(3), which exempts from avoidance as a preference a purchase-money security interest if it is perfected within 20 days after the debtor receives possession of the property securing the debt, is amended to change the 20-day period to 30 days. (S. 256, Sec. 1222).

Additional Bankruptcy Judges. The legislation adds 28 new bankruptcy judgeships in 20 judicial districts. In five years, an equal number of judgeships in the same districts will not be filled after becoming vacant, so that the total number of judgeships in these districts will eventually return to its pre-2005 Act level unless Congress enacts further legislation. (S. 256, Sec. 1223)

Compensation of Chapter 7 Trustee in Chapter 13. Section 1326(b) is amended to provide that if a chapter 7 trustee has been allowed compensation due to the conversion or dismissal of a case under section 707(b) that has not been paid, such compensation may be paid in pro-rated amounts over the remaining duration of the plan. However, monthly payments of such compensation cannot exceed the greater of (1) $25 or (2) 5% of the total amount payable under the plan to nonpriority unsecured creditors divided by the number of months in the plan. Such compensation may be collected even if it was discharged in a prior case. (S. 256, Sec. 1224)

Automatic Stay and Real Property Tax Liens. Section 362(b)(18) is expanded so that the exception to the automatic stay for the creation or perfection of a statutory lien for an ad valorem property tax also applies to a special tax or special assessment on real property, whether or not ad valorem. (S. 256, Sec. 1225)

Judicial Education. The Director of the Federal Judicial Center, in consultation with the Director of the Executive Office for United States Trustees, is required to develop materials and conduct training useful to the courts in implementing the 2005 Act, including the means test under section 707(b) and reaffirmation agreements under section 524. (S. 256, Sec. 1226)

Reclamation. Section 546(c) is amended to alter the law on reclamation of goods by a seller. First, the right of reclamation is subject to prior rights of a holder of a security interest in the goods and the proceeds thereof. Second, the right of reclamation applies to goods received by the debtor within 45 days before bankruptcy. Third, the seller has until 45 days after receipt of the goods, or within 20 days after the commencement of the case if the 45-day period expires postpetition, to demand reclamation in writing. Fourth, the portion of section 546(c) that had given courts the discretion to deny a proper reclamation claim if it grants administrative priority to the seller has been deleted. If the seller does not make a timely demand for reclamation, the seller may have an administrative claim nonetheless with respect to goods delivered within 20 days before the commencement of the case. (S. 256, Sec. 1227)

Administrative Expense Treatment for Goods Sold Within 20 Days Before Bankruptcy. Section 503(b) is amended to include as an administrative expense the value of any goods received by the debtor within 20 days before the commencement of the case if the goods were sold to the debtor in the ordinary course of the debtor's business. (S. 256, Sec. 1227)

Provision of Documents to the Court. The court is not to grant a discharge under chapter 7 or confirm a plan in an individual chapter 11 or chapter 13 case if requested tax documents have not been filed with the court. The court is to destroy documents submitted in support of a bankruptcy claim not sooner than three years after an individual chapter 7, 11, or 13 case is concluded. The time may be extended if there is a pending audit or enforcement action. (S. 256, Sec. 1228)

Federal Reserve Board Study of Indiscriminate Extensions of Consumer Credit and Possible Regulations. The Federal Reserve Board is directed to conduct a study of consumer credit industry practices of soliciting and extending credit indiscriminately, without determining whether debtors can repay, in a manner that encourages accumulation of debt. The Board may then require additional disclosures to consumers or take other actions within its authority to ensure responsible lending and prevent consumer debt and insolvency. (S. 256, Sec. 1229)

Pawned Property. Section 541(b) is amended to exclude from the bankruptcy estate tangible personal property that has been pledged or sold as collateral for a loan to a person licensed to make such loans that is in the possession of the pledgee or transferee if the debtor has no obligation to repay the loan, redeem the property, or buy the property back at a stipulated price, and neither the trustee or debtor has exercised a right to redeem under applicable nonbankruptcy law that is timely under state law, as modified by section 108(b). (S. 256, Sec. 1230)

Judicial Review of Suspension or Termination of Panel and Standing Trustee. Section 586 of title 28 is amended to provide a chapter 7 panel trustee or a chapter 12 or chapter 13 standing trustee the opportunity for judicial review of an administrative decision to terminate the trustee's appointment or to cease assigning cases to the trustee. Judicial review is also provided with respect to a final agency decision denying a standing trustee's claim for actual, necessary expenses under section 586(e) of title 28. (S. 256, Sec. 1231)

Form for Means Test Calculations. The bankruptcy rules prescribed under section 2075 of title 28 are to prescribe a form for the calculations to determine whether a presumption of abuse arises under section 707(b). (S. 256, Sec. 1232)

Direct Appeals to the Court of Appeals. Section 158 of title 28 is amended to give the court of appeals jurisdiction to hear an appeal from a judgment or order of the bankruptcy court if certain conditions are satisfied. First, the bankruptcy court, district court, or bankruptcy appellate panel where the matter is pending, on request of a party or on its own motion, or all the appellants and appellees acting jointly, must certify that the judgment or order (a) involves a question of law as to which there is no controlling decision of the court of appeals for that circuit or the Supreme Court, or involves a matter of public importance; (b) involves a question of law requiring resolution of conflicting decisions; or that (c) an immediate appeal from the judgment or order may materially advance the progress of the case or proceeding in which the appeal is taken. In addition, the court of appeals must authorize the direct appeal after the certification is made. If the bankruptcy court, district court, or bankruptcy appellate panel, on its own motion or on a request for certification made within 60 days after entry of the judgment or order, determines that the above circumstances exist to warrant such certification, or within the 60-day period receives a request for certification made by a majority of the appellants and a majority of appellees, then the certification must be made by the bankruptcy court, district court, or bankruptcy appellate panel. Temporary procedural rules for direct appeals are also provided, including a provision that requires that a petition requesting permission to appeal based on a certification must be filed with the circuit clerk not later than 10 days after the certification is entered on the docket of the bankruptcy court, district court, or bankruptcy appellate panel. (S. 256, Sec. 1233)

Debts Subject to Bona Fide Dispute in Involuntary Cases. Sections 303(b) and 303(h) are amended to provide that a debt is subject to a bona fide dispute if there is a bona fide dispute as to liability or amount. (S. 256, Sec. 1234)

Dischargeability of Federal Election Fines and Penalties. Section 523 is amended to make fines and penalties imposed under federal election law nondischargeable. (S. 256, Sec. 1235)

Consumer Credit Law Changes
(Title XIII)

Disclosures Regarding Minimum Payment Consequences. The Truth in Lending Act is amended to provide that consumer creditors offering open-end credit plans give consumers minimal information about the consequences of making only the monthly minimum payments or a toll free number at which account holders may obtain such information. (S. 256, Sec. 1301)

Disclosure of Possible Nondeductibility of Mortgage Interest. Advertisements and disclosures with respect to mortgages that may exceed the market value of the homes securing them must inform consumers that the interest on the portion of the loan exceeding the market value of a home is not deductible and that they should consult a tax adviser for further information on deductibility of interest and charges. (S. 256, Sec. 1302)

Disclosure of Introductory Interest Rates. The Truth in Lending Act is amended to provide that applications and solicitations for credit card accounts with a "teaser" rate clearly and conspicuously disclose the rate as an introductory rate, disclose the time period the rate will be in effect, disclose the permanent rate applicable after that time period, and disclose under what conditions the introductory rate may be revoked. (S. 256, Sec. 1303)

Internet-Based Credit Card Solicitations. The Truth in Lending Act is amended to provide that Internet credit card solicitations include the disclosures required for other solicitations, updated regularly for changes in terms and fees, in close proximity to the solicitation. (S. 256, Sec. 1304)

Late Fee Disclosures. The Truth in Lending Act is amended to require clear and conspicuous disclosure on each billing statement of any late fee that will be applicable and the earliest date it would be imposed. (S. 256, Sec. 1305)

Prohibition of Account Termination for Failure to Incur Finance Charges. The Truth in Lending Act is amended to prohibit a creditor from terminating before its expiration a consumer credit account because the consumer pays off the total balance each month and thereby avoids finance charges. (S. 256, Sec. 1306)

Study of Unauthorized Use Liability on Dual Use Debit Cards. The Federal Reserve Board is to conduct a study of whether legislation is needed to limit the liability for unauthorized use of dual use debit cards. (S. 256, Sec. 1307)

Study of Credit Extended to Students. The Federal Reserve Board is to conduct a study of the impact of credit extended to high school and college students. (S. 256, Sec. 1308)

Regulations Defining "Clear and Conspicuous." The Federal Reserve Board is to promulgate regulations clarifying the meaning of "clear and conspicuous" in certain provisions of the Truth In Lending Act. (S. 256, Sec. 1309)

Provisions Relating to Fraudulent Transactions, Employee Claims, or Retiree Benefits
(Title XIV)

Employee Wage and Benefit Priorities. Section 507(a) is amended to increase the maximum priority for wages, salaries, and commissions from $4,950 to $10,000, and to extend the applicable prepetition time period from 90 days to 180 days. The maximum amount of the priority for contributions to employee benefit plans is increased from the number of employees multiplied by $4,950 to the number of employees multiplied by $10,000. (S. 256, Sec. 1401)

Fraudulent Transfers. Section 548 on fraudulent conveyances is amended in several respects. First, transfers made within two years, rather than only one year, before the petition date may be avoided under this section. Second, the section is amended to provide that transfers and obligations that are subject to avoidance include any transfer or obligation to or for the benefit of an insider under an employment contract. Third, a transfer or obligation is avoidable if the debtor received less than reasonably equivalent value in exchange for the transfer or obligation and the transfer or obligation was made for the benefit of an insider under an employment contract and not in the ordinary course of business. (S. 256, Sec. 1402)

Asset Protection Trusts. Section 548 is amended to provide that the trustee may avoid any transfer of the debtor's property that was made within 10 years before the commencement of the case if the transfer was made by the debtor to a self-settled trust or similar device, the debtor is the beneficiary of the trust or device, and the debtor made the transfer with actual intent to hinder, delay, or defraud any entity to which the debtor was or became indebted on or after the date of the transfer. The transfers covered by this provision include a transfer made in anticipation of any money judgment, settlement, civil penalty, equitable order, or criminal fine incurred by, or which the debtor believed would be incurred by, a violation of federal or state securities laws or by fraud or manipulation in a fiduciary capacity or in connection with the purchase or sale of a registered security. (S. 256, Sec. 1402)

Reinstatement of Prepetition Modification of Retiree Benefits. Section 1114 is amended to protect retirees from modification of benefits within 180 days before commencement of the bankruptcy case. If the debtor was insolvent at the time of the modification, the court, on motion of a party in interest, must order reinstatement, as of the date of the modification, of benefits in effect immediately before the modification, unless the court finds that the balance of the equities clearly favors such modification. (S. 256, Sec. 1403)

Nondischargeability of Debts Incurred by Securities Fraud. Section 523(a)(19), which renders debts nondischargeable if incurred in violation of securities fraud laws or for common law fraud in connection with the purchase or sale of a security, is amended so that it expressly applies regardless of whether the judgment, order, settlement agreement, or administrative order from which the claim resulted was issued before, on, or after the commencement of the case. (S. 256, Sec. 1404)

Request for Appointment of Trustee in Case of Suspected Fraud. Section 1104 is amended to require the United States trustee to move for the appointment of a trustee in a chapter 11 case if there are reasonable grounds to suspect that current members of the debtor's governing body, chief executive or chief financial officer, or members of the governing body who selected the debtor's chief executive, or chief financial officer, participated in actual fraud, dishonesty, or criminal conduct in the management of the debtor or the debtor's public financial reporting. (S. 256, Sec. 1405)

Effective Date of Amendments in Title XIV. The amendments included in title XIV of the 2005 Act are effective with respect to cases commenced on or after the date of enactment, except that the change in section 548 that extends the applicable time from one year to two years applies only in cases commenced more than one year after the enactment date. (S. 256, Sec. 1406)

General Effective Date; Application of Amendments
(Title XV)

General Effective Date. With certain specified exceptions, the 2005 Act and the amendments made by the Act are effective only in bankruptcy cases commenced at least 180 days after enactment. (S. 256, Sec. 1501)

TABLE OF AMENDMENTS

Bankruptcy Code	**S. 256**
341	402; 413
342	102(d); 104; 234(b); 315(a)
346	719(a)
348	309(a); 1207
351 (new)	1102(a)
362	106(f); 214; 224(b); 302; 303(a), (b); 305(1); 311(a), (b); 320; 401(b); 441; 444; 709; 718; 907(d)(1), (2), (o)(1), (2); 1106; 1225
363	204; 231(a); 1221(a)
365	309(b); 328(a); 404(a), (b)
366	417
501	702
502	201(a); 716(d); 910(b)
503	329; 331; 445; 712(b), (c); 1103; 1208; 1227(b)
504	326
505	701(b); 703; 715
506	327; 712(d)
507	212; 223; 705; 706; 1401; 1502(a)(1)
508	802(d)(7)
511 (new)	704(a)
521	106(d); 225(b); 304(1); 305(2); 315(b); 316; 446(a); 603(c); 720
522	216; 224(a), (e)(1); 307; 308; 313(a); 322(a)
523	215; 220; 224(c); 301; 310; 314(a); 412; 714; 1209; 1235; 1404(a); 1502(a)(2)

Bankruptcy Code	S. 256
524	202; 203(a); 1210
525	1211
526 (new)	227(a)
527 (new)	228(a)
528 (new)	229(a)
541	225(a); 323; 1212; 1221(c); 1230
545	711
546	406; 907(e), (o)(2), (3); 1227(a)
547	201(b); 217; 403; 409; 1213; 1222
548	907(f), (o)(4), (5), (6); 1402
549	1214
552	1204(2)
553	907(n)
555	907(g), (o)(7)
556	907(h), (o)(8)
559	907(i), (o)(9)
560	907(j), (o)(10)
561 (new)	907(k)(1)
562 (new)	910(a)(1)
704	102(c); 219(a); 446(b); 1105(a)
706	101
707	102(a), (f)
722	304(2)
724	701(a)
726	713; 1215
727	106(b); 312(1); 330(a); 603(d)
728 (deleted)	719(b)(1)
741	907(a)(2)
752	1502(a)(3)
753 (new)	907(m)
761	907(a)(3)
766	1502(a)(4)
767 (new)	907(l)
901	502; 1216; 1502(a)(5)
921	501(a)
943	1502(a)(6)
1102	405(a), (b); 432(b)
1104	416; 442(b); 1405
1106	219(b); 446(c); 1105(b)

41

Bankruptcy Code   **S. 256**

1112	442(a)
1114	447; 1403
1115 (new)	321(a)(1)
1116 (new)	436(a)
1121	411; 437
1123	321(b); 1502(a)(7)
1124	328(b)
1125	408; 431; 717
1127	321(e)
1129	213(1); 321(c)(1), (2); 438; 710; 1221(b); 1502(a)(8)
1141	321(d); 330(b); 708
1146	719(b)(3)
1170	1217
1172	1218
1202	219(c)
1203	1007(c)(2)
1206	1007(c)(3)
1208	213(2)
1222	213(3), (4); 1003(a)
1225	213(5); 218; 1006(a)
1226	1502(a)(9)
1228	213(6); 330(c)
1229	1006(b)
1231	719(b)(4); 1003(b)
1302	219(d)
1307	213(7); 716(c)
1308 (new)	716(b)
1322	213(8), (9); 224(d); 318(1)
1324	317
1325	102(g), (h); 213(10); 306(a), (b); 309(c)(1); 318(2), (3); 716(a)
1326	309(c)(2); 1224; 1502(a)(10)
1328	106(c); 213(11); 312(2); 314(b); 330(d); 707

Bankruptcy Code	**S. 256**
1329	102(i); 318(4)
1501–1532 (new Chapter 15)	801

12 USC	**S. 256**
12 USC 1787	901(a)(2), (b)(2), (c)(2), (d)(2), (e)(2), (f)(2), (g)(2), (h)(2), (i)(2); 902(b)(1), (2); 903(b)(1), (2), (3); 904(b); 905(b); 908(b)
12 USC 1821	901(a)(1), (b)(1), (c)(1), (d)(1), (e)(1), (f)(1), (g)(1), (h)(1), (i)(1); 902(a)(1), (2); 903(a)(1), (2), (3); 904(a); 905(a); 908(a)
12 USC 1823	909
12 USC 4402	906(a)
12 USC 4403	906(b)
12 USC 4404	906(c)
12 USC 4407	906(d)

15 USC	**S. 256**
15 USC 78eee	911
15 USC 78fff(e)	1502(b)
15 USC 1637	1301(a); 1303(a); 1304(a); 1305(a); 1306(a)
15 USC 1637a(a)(13)	1302(a)(1)
15 USC 1638	1302(b)(1)
15 USC 1664	1302(b)(2)
15 USC 1665b(b)	1302(a)(2)

18 USC	**S. 256**
18 USC 156(a)	1220
18 USC 157	332(c)
18 USC 158 (new)	203(b)

S. 256

109th Congress
1st Session

As passed by Congress on April 14, 2005*

An Act

To amend title 11 of the United States Code, and for other purposes.

Be it enacted by the Senate and House of Representatives of the United States of America in Congress assembled,

SECTION 1 Short Title; References; Table of Contents.

(a) Short Title—This Act may be cited as the "Bankruptcy Abuse Prevention and Consumer Protection Act of 2005".

(b) Table of Contents—The table of contents for this Act is as follows:

---

* The Public Law Number was not available at the time of publication.

TITLE IV—GENERAL AND SMALL BUSINESS
BANKRUPTCY PROVISIONS

Subtitle A—General Business Bankruptcy Provisions

TITLE I

NEEDS-BASED BANKRUPTCY

Sec. 101 CONVERSION.

Section 706(c) of title 11, United States Code, is amended by inserting "or consents to" after "requests".

Sec. 102 DISMISSAL OR CONVERSION.

(a) IN GENERAL—Section 707 of title 11, United States Code, is amended—

(1) by striking the section heading and inserting the following:

"§ 707. Dismissal of a case or conversion to a case under chapter 11 or 13";

and

(2) in subsection (b)—

(A) by inserting "(1)" after "(b)";

(B) in paragraph (1), as so redesignated by subparagraph (A) of this paragraph—

(i) in the first sentence—

(I) by striking "but not at the request or suggestion of" and inserting "trustee (or bankruptcy administrator, if any), or";

(II) by inserting ", or, with the debtor's consent, convert such a case to a case under chapter 11 or 13 of this title," after "consumer debts"; and

(III) by striking "a substantial abuse" and inserting "an abuse"; and

(ii) by striking the next to last sentence; and

(C) by adding at the end the following:

"(2)(A)(i) In considering under paragraph (1) whether the granting of relief would be an abuse of the provisions of this chapter, the court shall presume abuse exists if the debtor's current monthly income reduced by the amounts determined under clauses (ii), (iii), and (iv), and multiplied by 60 is not less than the lesser of—

"(I) 25 percent of the debtor's nonpriority unsecured claims in the case, or $6,000, whichever is greater; or

"(II) $10,000.

"(ii)(I) The debtor's monthly expenses shall be the debtor's applicable monthly expense amounts specified under the National Standards and Local Standards, and the debtor's actual monthly expenses for the categories specified as Other Necessary Expenses issued by the Internal Revenue Service for the area in which the debtor resides, as in effect on the date of the order for relief, for the debtor, the dependents of the debtor, and the spouse of the debtor in a joint case, if the spouse is not otherwise a dependent. Such expenses shall include reasonably necessary health insurance, disability insurance, and health savings account expenses for the debtor, the spouse of the debtor, or the dependents of the debtor. Notwithstanding any other provision of this clause, the monthly expenses of the debtor shall not include any payments for debts. In addition, the debtor's monthly expenses shall include the debtor's reasonably necessary expenses incurred to maintain the safety of the debtor and the family of the debtor from family violence as identified under section 309 of the Family Violence Prevention and Services Act, or other applicable Federal law. The expenses included in the debtor's monthly expenses described in the preceding sentence shall be kept confidential by the court. In addition, if it is demonstrated that it is reasonable and necessary, the debtor's monthly expenses may also include an additional allowance for food and clothing of up to 5 percent of the food and clothing categories as specified by the National Standards issued by the Internal Revenue Service.

"(II) In addition, the debtor's monthly expenses may include, if applicable, the continuation of actual expenses paid by the debtor that are reasonable and necessary for care and support of an elderly, chronically ill, or disabled household member or member of the debtor's immediate family (including parents, grandparents, siblings, children, and grandchildren of the debtor, the dependents of the debtor, and the spouse of the debtor in a joint case who is not a dependent) and who is unable to pay for such reasonable and necessary expenses.

"(III) In addition, for a debtor eligible for chapter 13, the debtor's monthly expenses may include the actual administrative expenses of administering a chapter 13 plan for the district in which the debtor resides, up to an amount of 10 percent of the projected plan payments, as determined under schedules issued by the Executive Office for United States Trustees.

"(IV) In addition, the debtor's monthly expenses may include the actual expenses for each dependent child less than 18 years of age, not to exceed $1,500 per year per child, to attend a private or public elementary or secondary school if the debtor provides documentation of such expenses and a detailed explanation of why such expenses are reasonable and necessary, and why such expenses are not already accounted for in the National Standards, Local Standards, or Other Necessary Expenses referred to in subclause (I).

"(V) In addition, the debtor's monthly expenses may include an allowance for housing and utilities, in excess of the allowance specified by the Local Standards for housing and utilities issued by the Internal Revenue Service, based on the actual expenses for home energy costs if the debtor provides documentation of such actual expenses and demonstrates that such actual expenses are reasonable and necessary.

"(iii) The debtor's average monthly payments on account of secured debts shall be calculated as the sum of—

"(I) the total of all amounts scheduled as contractually due to secured creditors in each month of the 60 months following the date of the petition; and

"(II) any additional payments to secured creditors necessary for the debtor, in filing a plan under chapter 13 of this title, to maintain possession of the debtor's primary residence, motor vehicle, or other property necessary for the support of the debtor and the debtor's dependents, that serves as collateral for secured debts;

divided by 60.

"(iv) The debtor's expenses for payment of all priority claims (including priority child support and alimony claims) shall be calculated as the total amount of debts entitled to priority, divided by 60.

"(B)(i) In any proceeding brought under this subsection, the presumption of abuse may only be rebutted by demonstrating special circumstances, such as a serious medical condition or a call or order to active duty in the Armed Forces, to the extent such special circumstances that justify additional expenses or adjustments of current monthly income for which there is no reasonable alternative.

"(ii) In order to establish special circumstances, the debtor shall be required to itemize each additional expense or adjustment of income and to provide—

"(I) documentation for such expense or adjustment to income; and

"(II) a detailed explanation of the special circumstances that make such expenses or adjustment to income necessary and reasonable.

"(iii) The debtor shall attest under oath to the accuracy of any information provided to demonstrate that additional expenses or adjustments to income are required.

"(iv) The presumption of abuse may only be rebutted if the additional expenses or adjustments to income referred to in clause (i) cause the product of the debtor's current monthly income reduced by the amounts determined under clauses (ii), (iii), and (iv) of subparagraph (A) when multiplied by 60 to be less than the lesser of—

"(I) 25 percent of the debtor's nonpriority unsecured claims, or $6,000, whichever is greater; or

"(II) $10,000.

"(C) As part of the schedule of current income and expenditures required under section 521, the debtor shall include a statement of the debtor's current monthly income, and the calculations that determine whether a presumption arises under subparagraph (A)(i), that show how each such amount is calculated.

"(D) Subparagraphs (A) through (C) shall not apply, and the court may not dismiss or convert a case based on any form of means testing, if the debtor is a disabled veteran (as defined in section 3741(1) of title 38), and the indebtedness occurred primarily during a period during which he or she was—

"(i) on active duty (as defined in section 101(d)(1) of title 10); or

"(ii) performing a homeland defense activity (as defined in section 901(1) of title 32).

"(3) In considering under paragraph (1) whether the granting of relief would be an abuse of the provisions of this chapter in a case in which the presumption in subparagraph (A)(i) of such paragraph does not arise or is rebutted, the court shall consider—

"(A) whether the debtor filed the petition in bad faith; or

"(B) the totality of the circumstances (including whether the debtor seeks to reject a personal services contract and the financial need for such rejection as sought by the debtor) of the debtor's financial situation demonstrates abuse.

"(4)(A) The court, on its own initiative or on the motion of a party in interest, in accordance with the procedures described in rule 9011 of the Federal Rules of Bankruptcy Procedure, may order the attorney for the debtor to reimburse the trustee for all reasonable costs in prosecuting a motion filed under section 707(b), including reasonable attorneys' fees, if—

"(i) a trustee files a motion for dismissal or conversion under this subsection; and

"(ii) the court—

"(I) grants such motion; and

"(II) finds that the action of the attorney for the debtor in filing a case under this chapter violated rule 9011 of the Federal Rules of Bankruptcy Procedure.

"(B) If the court finds that the attorney for the debtor violated rule 9011 of the Federal Rules of Bankruptcy Procedure, the court, on its own initiative or on the motion of a party in interest, in accordance with such procedures, may order—

"(i) the assessment of an appropriate civil penalty against the attorney for the debtor; and

"(ii) the payment of such civil penalty to the trustee, the United States trustee (or the bankruptcy administrator, if any).

"(C) The signature of an attorney on a petition, pleading, or written motion shall constitute a certification that the attorney has—

"(i) performed a reasonable investigation into the circumstances that gave rise to the petition, pleading, or written motion; and "(ii) determined that the petition, pleading, or written motion—

"(I) is well grounded in fact; and

"(II) is warranted by existing law or a good faith argument for the extension, modification, or reversal of existing law and does not constitute an abuse under paragraph (1).

"(D) The signature of an attorney on the petition shall constitute a certification that the attorney has no knowledge after an inquiry that the information in the schedules filed with such petition is incorrect.

"(5)(A) Except as provided in subparagraph (B) and subject to paragraph (6), the court, on its own initiative or on the motion of a party in interest, in accordance with the procedures described in rule 9011 of the Federal Rules of Bankruptcy Procedure, may award a debtor all reasonable costs (including reasonable attorneys' fees) in contesting a motion filed by a party in interest (other than a trustee or United States trustee (or bankruptcy administrator, if any)) under this subsection if—

"(i) the court does not grant the motion; and

"(ii) the court finds that—

"(I) the position of the party that filed the motion violated rule 9011 of the Federal Rules of Bankruptcy Procedure; or

"(II) the attorney (if any) who filed the motion did not comply with the requirements of clauses (i) and (ii) of paragraph (4)(C), and the motion was made solely for the purpose of coercing a debtor into waiving a right guaranteed to the debtor under this title.

"(B) A small business that has a claim of an aggregate amount less than $1,000 shall not be subject to subparagraph (A)(ii)(I).

"(C) For purposes of this paragraph—

"(i) the term 'small business' means an unincorporated business, partnership, corporation, association, or organization that—

"(I) has fewer than 25 full-time employees as determined on the date on which the motion is filed; and

"(II) is engaged in commercial or business activity; and

"(ii) the number of employees of a wholly owned subsidiary of a corporation includes the employees of—

"(I) a parent corporation; and

"(II) any other subsidiary corporation of the parent corporation.

"(6) Only the judge or United States trustee (or bankruptcy administrator, if any) may file a motion under section 707(b), if the current monthly income of the debtor, or in a joint case, the debtor and the debtor's spouse, as of the date of the order for relief, when multiplied by 12, is equal to or less than—

"(A) in the case of a debtor in a household of 1 person, the median family income of the applicable State for 1 earner;

"(B) in the case of a debtor in a household of 2, 3, or 4 individuals, the highest median family income of the applicable State for a family of the same number or fewer individuals; or

"(C) in the case of a debtor in a household exceeding 4 individuals, the highest median family income of the applicable State for a family of 4 or fewer individuals, plus $525 per month for each individual in excess of 4.

"(7)(A) No judge, United States trustee (or bankruptcy administrator, if any), trustee, or other party in interest may file a motion under paragraph (2) if the current monthly income of the debtor, including a veteran (as that term is defined in section 101 of title 38), and the debtor's spouse combined, as of the date of the order for relief when multiplied by 12, is equal to or less than—

"(i) in the case of a debtor in a household of 1 person, the median family income of the applicable State for 1 earner;

"(ii) in the case of a debtor in a household of 2, 3, or 4 individuals, the highest median family income of the applicable State for a family of the same number or fewer individuals; or

"(iii) in the case of a debtor in a household exceeding 4 individuals, the highest median family income of the applicable State for a family of 4 or fewer individuals, plus $525 per month for each individual in excess of 4.

"(B) In a case that is not a joint case, current monthly income of the debtor's spouse shall not be considered for purposes of subparagraph (A) if—

"(i)(I) the debtor and the debtor's spouse are separated under applicable nonbankruptcy law; or

"(II) the debtor and the debtor's spouse are living separate and apart, other than for the purpose of evading subparagraph (A); and

"(ii) the debtor files a statement under penalty of perjury—

"(I) specifying that the debtor meets the requirement of subclause (I) or (II) of clause (i); and

"(II) disclosing the aggregate, or best estimate of the aggregate, amount of any cash or money payments received from the debtor's spouse attributed to the debtor's current monthly income.".

(b) DEFINITION—Section 101 of title 11, United States Code, is amended by inserting after paragraph (10) the following:

"(10A) 'current monthly income'—

"(A) means the average monthly income from all sources that the debtor receives (or in a joint case the debtor and the debtor's spouse receive) without regard to whether such income is taxable income, derived during the 6-month period ending on—

"(i) the last day of the calendar month immediately preceding the date of the commencement of the case if the debtor files the schedule of current income required by section 521(a)(1)(B)(ii); or "(ii) the date on which current income is determined by the court for purposes of this title if the debtor does not file the schedule of current income required by section 521(a)(1)(B)(ii); and

"(B) includes any amount paid by any entity other than the debtor (or in a joint case the debtor and the debtor's spouse), on a regular basis for the household expenses of the debtor or the debtor's dependents (and in a joint case the debtor's spouse if not otherwise a dependent), but excludes benefits received under the Social Security Act, payments to victims of war crimes or crimes against humanity on account of their status as victims of such crimes, and payments to victims of international terrorism (as defined in section 2331 of title 18) or domestic terrorism (as defined in section 2331 of title 18) on account of their status as victims of such terrorism;".

(c) UNITED STATES TRUSTEE AND BANKRUPTCY ADMINISTRATOR DUTIES— Section 704 of title 11, United States Code, is amended—

(1) by inserting "(a)" before "The trustee shall—"; and

(2) by adding at the end the following:

"(b)(1) With respect to a debtor who is an individual in a case under this chapter—

"(A) the United States trustee (or the bankruptcy administrator, if any) shall review all materials filed by the debtor and, not later than 10 days after the date of the first meeting of creditors, file with the court a statement as to whether the debtor's case would be presumed to be an abuse under section 707(b); and

"(B) not later than 5 days after receiving a statement under subparagraph (A), the court shall provide a copy of the statement to all creditors.

"(2) The United States trustee (or bankruptcy administrator, if any) shall, not later than 30 days after the date of filing a statement under paragraph (1), either file a motion to dismiss or convert under section 707(b) or file a statement setting forth the reasons the United States trustee (or the bankruptcy administrator, if any) does not consider such a motion to be appropriate, if the United States trustee (or the bankruptcy administrator, if any) determines that the debtor's case should be presumed to be an abuse under section 707(b) and the product of the debtor's current monthly income, multiplied by 12 is not less than—

"(A) in the case of a debtor in a household of 1 person, the median family income of the applicable State for 1 earner; or

"(B) in the case of a debtor in a household of 2 or more individuals, the highest median family income of the applicable State for a family of the same number or fewer individuals.".

(d) NOTICE—Section 342 of title 11, United States Code, is amended by adding at the end the following:

"(d) In a case under chapter 7 of this title in which the debtor is an individual and in which the presumption of abuse arises under section

707(b), the clerk shall give written notice to all creditors not later than 10 days after the date of the filing of the petition that the presumption of abuse has arisen.".

(e) NONLIMITATION OF INFORMATION—Nothing in this title shall limit the ability of a creditor to provide information to a judge (except for information communicated ex parte, unless otherwise permitted by applicable law), United States trustee (or bankruptcy administrator, if any), or trustee.

(f) DISMISSAL FOR CERTAIN CRIMES—Section 707 of title 11, United States Code, is amended by adding at the end the following:

"(c)(1) In this subsection—

"(A) the term 'crime of violence' has the meaning given such term in section 16 of title 18; and

"(B) the term 'drug trafficking crime' has the meaning given such term in section 924(c)(2) of title 18.

"(2) Except as provided in paragraph (3), after notice and a hearing, the court, on a motion by the victim of a crime of violence or a drug trafficking crime, may when it is in the best interest of the victim dismiss a voluntary case filed under this chapter by a debtor who is an individual if such individual was convicted of such crime.

"(3) The court may not dismiss a case under paragraph (2) if the debtor establishes by a preponderance of the evidence that the filing of a case under this chapter is necessary to satisfy a claim for a domestic support obligation.".

(g) CONFIRMATION OF PLAN—Section 1325(a) of title 11, United States Code, is amended—

(1) in paragraph (5), by striking "and" at the end;

(2) in paragraph (6), by striking the period and inserting a semicolon; and

(3) by inserting after paragraph (6) the following:

"(7) the action of the debtor in filing the petition was in good faith;".

(h) APPLICABILITY OF MEANS TEST TO CHAPTER 13—Section 1325(b) of title 11, United States Code, is amended—

(1) in paragraph (1)(B), by inserting "to unsecured creditors" after "to make payments"; and

(2) by striking paragraph (2) and inserting the following:

"(2) For purposes of this subsection, the term 'disposable income' means current monthly income received by the debtor (other than child support payments, foster care payments, or disability payments for a dependent child made in accordance with applicable nonbankruptcy law to the extent reasonably necessary to be expended for such child) less amounts reasonably necessary to be expended—

"(A)(i) for the maintenance or support of the debtor or a dependent of the debtor, or for a domestic support obligation, that first becomes payable after the date the petition is filed; and "(ii) for charitable contributions (that meet the definition of "charitable contribution" under section 548(d)(3) to a qualified religious or charitable entity or organization (as defined in section 548(d)(4)) in an amount not to exceed 15 percent of gross income of the debtor for the year in which the contributions are made; and

"(B) if the debtor is engaged in business, for the payment of expenditures necessary for the continuation, preservation, and operation of such business.

"(3) Amounts reasonably necessary to be expended under paragraph (2) shall be determined in accordance with subparagraphs (A) and (B) of section 707(b)(2), if the debtor has current monthly income, when multiplied by 12, greater than—

"(A) in the case of a debtor in a household of 1 person, the median family income of the applicable State for 1 earner;

"(B) in the case of a debtor in a household of 2, 3, or 4 individuals, the highest median family income of the applicable State for a family of the same number or fewer individuals; or

"(C) in the case of a debtor in a household exceeding 4 individuals, the highest median family income of the applicable State for a family of 4 or fewer individuals, plus $525 per month for each individual in excess of 4.".

(i) SPECIAL ALLOWANCE FOR HEALTH INSURANCE—Section 1329(a) of title 11, United States Code, is amended—

(1) in paragraph (2) by striking "or" at the end;

(2) in paragraph (3) by striking the period at the end and inserting "; or"; and

(3) by adding at the end the following:

"(4) reduce amounts to be paid under the plan by the actual amount expended by the debtor to purchase health insurance for the debtor (and for any dependent of the debtor if such dependent does not otherwise have health insurance coverage) if the debtor documents the cost of such insurance and demonstrates that—

"(A) such expenses are reasonable and necessary;

"(B)(i) if the debtor previously paid for health insurance, the amount is not materially larger than the cost the debtor previously paid or the cost necessary to maintain the lapsed policy; or

"(ii) if the debtor did not have health insurance, the amount is not materially larger than the reasonable cost that would be incurred by a debtor who purchases health insurance, who has similar income, expenses, age, and health status, and who lives in the same geographical location with the same number of dependents who do not otherwise have health insurance coverage; and

"(C) the amount is not otherwise allowed for purposes of determining disposable income under section 1325(b) of this title;

and upon request of any party in interest, files proof that a health insurance policy was purchased.".

(j) ADJUSTMENT OF DOLLAR AMOUNTS—Section 104(b) of title 11, United States Code, is amended by striking "and 523(a)(2)(C)" each place it appears and inserting "523(a)(2)(C), 707(b), and 1325(b)(3)".

(k) DEFINITION OF "MEDIAN FAMILY INCOME"—Section 101 of title 11, United States Code, is amended by inserting after paragraph (39) the following:

"(39A) 'median family income' means for any year—

"(A) the median family income both calculated and reported by the Bureau of the Census in the then most recent year; and

"(B) if not so calculated and reported in the then current year, adjusted annually after such most recent year until the next year in which median family income is both calculated and reported by the Bureau of the Census, to reflect the percentage change in the Consumer Price Index for All Urban Consumers during the period of years occurring after such most recent year and before such current year;".

(k) CLERICAL AMENDMENT—The table of sections for chapter 7 of title 11, United States Code, is amended by striking the item relating to section 707 and inserting the following:

"707. Dismissal of a case or conversion to a case under chapter 11 or 13.".

Sec. 103 SENSE OF CONGRESS AND STUDY.

(a) SENSE OF CONGRESS—It is the sense of Congress that the Secretary of the Treasury has the authority to alter the Internal Revenue Service standards established to set guidelines for repayment plans as needed to accommodate their use under section 707(b) of title 11, United States Code.

(b) STUDY—

(1) IN GENERAL—Not later than 2 years after the date of enactment of this Act, the Director of the Executive Office for United States Trustees shall submit a report to the Committee on the Judiciary of the Senate and the Committee on the Judiciary of the House of Representatives containing the findings of the Director regarding the utilization of Internal Revenue Service standards for determining—

(A) the current monthly expenses of a debtor under section 707(b) of title 11, United States Code; and

(B) the impact that the application of such standards has had on debtors and on the bankruptcy courts.

(2) RECOMMENDATION—The report under paragraph (1) may include recommendations for amendments to title 11, United States Code, that are consistent with the findings of the Director under paragraph (1).

Sec. 104 NOTICE OF ALTERNATIVES.

Section 342(b) of title 11, United States Code, is amended to read as follows:

"(b) Before the commencement of a case under this title by an individual whose debts are primarily consumer debts, the clerk shall give to such individual written notice containing—

"(1) a brief description of—

"(A) chapters 7, 11, 12, and 13 and the general purpose, benefits, and costs of proceeding under each of those chapters; and

"(B) the types of services available from credit counseling agencies; and

"(2) statements specifying that—

"(A) a person who knowingly and fraudulently conceals assets or makes a false oath or statement under penalty of perjury in connection with a case under this title shall be subject to fine, imprisonment, or both; and

"(B) all information supplied by a debtor in connection with a case under this title is subject to examination by the Attorney General.".

Sec. 105 DEBTOR FINANCIAL MANAGEMENT TRAINING TEST PROGRAM.

(a) DEVELOPMENT OF FINANCIAL MANAGEMENT AND TRAINING CURRICU-LUM AND MATERIALS—The Director of the Executive Office for United States Trustees (in this section referred to as the "Director") shall consult with a wide range of individuals who are experts in the field of debtor education, including trustees who serve in cases under chapter 13 of title 11, United States Code, and who operate financial management education programs for debtors, and shall develop a financial management training curriculum and materials that can be used to educate debtors who are individuals on how to better manage their finances.

(b) TEST—

(1) SELECTION OF DISTRICTS—The Director shall select 6 judicial districts of the United States in which to test the effectiveness of the financial management training curriculum and materials developed under subsection (a).

(2) USE—For an 18-month period beginning not later than 270 days after the date of the enactment of this Act, such curriculum and materials shall be, for the 6 judicial districts selected under paragraph (1), used as the instructional course concerning personal financial management for purposes of section 111 of title 11, United States Code.

(c) EVALUATION—

(1) IN GENERAL—During the 18-month period referred to in subsection (b), the Director shall evaluate the effectiveness of—

(A) the financial management training curriculum and materials developed under subsection (a); and

(B) a sample of existing consumer education programs such as those described in the Report of the National Bankruptcy Review

Commission (October 20, 1997) that are representative of consumer education programs carried out by the credit industry, by trustees serving under chapter 13 of title 11, United States Code, and by consumer counseling groups.

(2) REPORT—Not later than 3 months after concluding such evaluation, the Director shall submit a report to the Speaker of the House of Representatives and the President pro tempore of the Senate, for referral to the appropriate committees of the Congress, containing the findings of the Director regarding the effectiveness of such curriculum, such materials, and such programs and their costs.

Sec. 106 CREDIT COUNSELING.

(a) WHO MAY BE A DEBTOR—Section 109 of title 11, United States Code, is amended by adding at the end the following:

"(h)(1) Subject to paragraphs (2) and (3), and notwithstanding any other provision of this section, an individual may not be a debtor under this title unless such individual has, during the 180-day period preceding the date of filing of the petition by such individual, received from an approved nonprofit budget and credit counseling agency described in section 111(a) an individual or group briefing (including a briefing conducted by telephone or on the Internet) that outlined the opportunities for available credit counseling and assisted such individual in performing a related budget analysis.

"(2)(A) Paragraph (1) shall not apply with respect to a debtor who resides in a district for which the United States trustee (or the bankruptcy administrator, if any) determines that the approved nonprofit budget and credit counseling agencies for such district are not reasonably able to provide adequate services to the additional individuals who would other-wise seek credit counseling from such agencies by reason of the require-ments of paragraph (1).

"(B) The United States trustee (or the bankruptcy administrator, if any) who makes a determination described in subparagraph (A) shall review such determination not later than 1 year after the date of such determina-tion, and not less frequently than annually thereafter. Notwithstanding the preceding sentence, a nonprofit budget and credit counseling agency may be disapproved by the United States trustee (or the bankruptcy administra-tor, if any) at any time.

"(3)(A) Subject to subparagraph (B), the requirements of paragraph (1) shall not apply with respect to a debtor who submits to the court a certification that—

"(i) describes exigent circumstances that merit a waiver of the require-ments of paragraph (1);

"(ii) states that the debtor requested credit counseling services from an approved nonprofit budget and credit counseling agency, but was unable to obtain the services referred to in paragraph (1) during the 5-day period beginning on the date on which the debtor made that request; and "(iii) is satisfactory to the court.

"(B) With respect to a debtor, an exemption under subparagraph (A) shall cease to apply to that debtor on the date on which the debtor meets the requirements of paragraph (1), but in no case may the exemption apply to that debtor after the date that is 30 days after the debtor files a petition, except that the court, for cause, may order an additional 15 days.

"(4) The requirements of paragraph (1) shall not apply with respect to a debtor whom the court determines, after notice and hearing, is unable to complete those requirements because of incapacity, disability, or active military duty in a military combat zone. For the purposes of this paragraph, incapacity means that the debtor is impaired by reason of mental illness or mental deficiency so that he is incapable of realizing and making rational decisions with respect to his financial responsibilities; and "disability" means that the debtor is so physically impaired as to be unable, after reasonable effort, to participate in an in person, telephone, or Internet briefing required under paragraph (1).".

(b) CHAPTER 7 DISCHARGE—Section 727(a) of title 11, United States Code, is amended—

(1) in paragraph (9), by striking "or" at the end;

(2) in paragraph (10), by striking the period and inserting "; or"; and

(3) by adding at the end the following:

"(11) after filing the petition, the debtor failed to complete an instructional course concerning personal financial management described in section 111, except that this paragraph shall not apply with respect to a debtor who is a person described in section 109(h)(4) or who resides in a district for which the United States trustee (or the bankruptcy administrator, if any) determines that the approved instructional courses are not adequate to service the additional individuals who would otherwise be required to complete such instructional courses under this section (The United States trustee (or the bankruptcy administrator, if any) who makes a determination described in this paragraph shall review such determination not later than 1 year after the date of such determination, and not less frequently than annually thereafter.).".

(c) CHAPTER 13 DISCHARGE—Section 1328 of title 11, United States Code, is amended by adding at the end the following:

"(g)(1) The court shall not grant a discharge under this section to a debtor unless after filing a petition the debtor has completed an instructional course concerning personal financial management described in section 111.

"(2) Paragraph (1) shall not apply with respect to a debtor who is a person described in section 109(h)(4) or who resides in a district for which the United States trustee (or the bankruptcy administrator, if any) determines that the approved instructional courses are not adequate to service the additional individuals who would otherwise be required to complete such instructional course by reason of the requirements of paragraph (1).

"(3) The United States trustee (or the bankruptcy administrator, if any) who makes a determination described in paragraph (2) shall review such determination not later than 1 year after the date of such determination, and not less frequently than annually thereafter.".

(d) DEBTOR'S DUTIES—Section 521 of title 11, United States Code, is amended—

(1) by inserting "(a)" before "The debtor shall—"; and

(2) by adding at the end the following:

"(b) In addition to the requirements under subsection (a), a debtor who is an individual shall file with the court—

"(1) a certificate from the approved nonprofit budget and credit counseling agency that provided the debtor services under section 109(h) describing the services provided to the debtor; and

"(2) a copy of the debt repayment plan, if any, developed under section 109(h) through the approved nonprofit budget and credit counseling agency referred to in paragraph (1).".

(e) GENERAL PROVISIONS—

(1) IN GENERAL—Chapter 1 of title 11, United States Code, is amended by adding at the end the following:

"§ 111. Nonprofit budget and credit counseling agencies; financial management instructional courses

"(a) The clerk shall maintain a publicly available list of—

"(1) nonprofit budget and credit counseling agencies that provide 1 or more services described in section 109(h) currently approved by the United States trustee (or the bankruptcy administrator, if any); and

"(2) instructional courses concerning personal financial management currently approved by the United States trustee (or the bankruptcy administrator, if any), as applicable.

"(b) The United States trustee (or bankruptcy administrator, if any) shall only approve a nonprofit budget and credit counseling agency or an instructional course concerning personal financial management as follows:

"(1) The United States trustee (or bankruptcy administrator, if any) shall have thoroughly reviewed the qualifications of the nonprofit budget and credit counseling agency or of the provider of the instructional course under the standards set forth in this section, and the services or instructional courses that will be offered by such agency or such provider, and may require such agency or such provider that has sought approval to provide information with respect to such review.

"(2) The United States trustee (or bankruptcy administrator, if any) shall have determined that such agency or such instructional course fully satisfies the applicable standards set forth in this section.

"(3) If a nonprofit budget and credit counseling agency or instructional course did not appear on the approved list for the district under subsection (a) immediately before approval under this section, approval under this subsection of such agency or such instructional course shall be for a probationary period not to exceed 6 months.

"(4) At the conclusion of the applicable probationary period under paragraph (3), the United States trustee (or bankruptcy administrator, if any) may only approve for an additional 1-year period, and for successive 1-year periods thereafter, an agency or instructional course that has demonstrated during the probationary or applicable subsequent period of approval that such agency or instructional course—

"(A) has met the standards set forth under this section during such period; and

"(B) can satisfy such standards in the future.

"(5) Not later than 30 days after any final decision under paragraph (4), an interested person may seek judicial review of such decision in the appropriate district court of the United States.

"(c)(1) The United States trustee (or the bankruptcy administrator, if any) shall only approve a nonprofit budget and credit counseling agency that demonstrates that it will provide qualified counselors, maintain adequate provision for safekeeping and payment of client funds, provide adequate counseling with respect to client credit problems, and deal responsibly and effectively with other matters relating to the quality, effectiveness, and financial security of the services it provides.

"(2) To be approved by the United States trustee (or the bankruptcy administrator, if any), a nonprofit budget and credit counseling agency shall, at a minimum—

"(A) have a board of directors the majority of which—

"(i) are not employed by such agency; and

"(ii) will not directly or indirectly benefit financially from the outcome of the counseling services provided by such agency;

"(B) if a fee is charged for counseling services, charge a reasonable fee, and provide services without regard to ability to pay the fee;

"(C) provide for safekeeping and payment of client funds, including an annual audit of the trust accounts and appropriate employee bonding;

"(D) provide full disclosures to a client, including funding sources, counselor qualifications, possible impact on credit reports, and any costs of such program that will be paid by such client and how such costs will be paid;

"(E) provide adequate counseling with respect to a client's credit problems that includes an analysis of such client's current financial condition, factors that caused such financial condition, and how such client can develop a plan to respond to the problems without incurring negative amortization of debt;

"(F) provide trained counselors who receive no commissions or bonuses based on the outcome of the counseling services provided by such agency, and who have adequate experience, and have been adequately trained to provide counseling services to individuals in financial difficulty, including the matters described in subparagraph (E);

"(G) demonstrate adequate experience and background in providing credit counseling; and

"(H) have adequate financial resources to provide continuing support services for budgeting plans over the life of any repayment plan.

"(d) The United States trustee (or the bankruptcy administrator, if any) shall only approve an instructional course concerning personal financial management—

"(1) for an initial probationary period under subsection (b)(3) if the course will provide at a minimum—

"(A) trained personnel with adequate experience and training in providing effective instruction and services;

"(B) learning materials and teaching methodologies designed to assist debtors in understanding personal financial management and that are consistent with stated objectives directly related to the goals of such instructional course;

"(C) adequate facilities situated in reasonably convenient locations at which such instructional course is offered, except that such facilities may include the provision of such instructional course by telephone or through the Internet, if such instructional course is effective;

"(D) the preparation and retention of reasonable records (which shall include the debtor's bankruptcy case number) to permit evaluation of the effectiveness of such instructional course, including any evaluation of satisfaction of instructional course requirements for each debtor attending such instructional course, which shall be available for inspection and evaluation by the Executive Office for United States Trustees, the United States trustee (or the bankruptcy administrator, if any), or the chief bankruptcy judge for the district in which such instructional course is offered; and

"(E) if a fee is charged for the instructional course, charge a reasonable fee, and provide services without regard to ability to pay the fee.

"(2) for any 1-year period if the provider thereof has demonstrated that the course meets the standards of paragraph (1) and, in addition—

"(A) has been effective in assisting a substantial number of debtors to understand personal financial management; and

"(B) is otherwise likely to increase substantially the debtor's understanding of personal financial management.

"(e) The district court may, at any time, investigate the qualifications of a nonprofit budget and credit counseling agency referred to in subsection (a), and request production of documents to ensure the integrity and effectiveness of such agency. The district court may, at any time, remove from the approved list under subsection (a) a nonprofit budget and credit counseling agency upon finding such agency does not meet the qualifications of subsection (b).

"(f) The United States trustee (or the bankruptcy administrator, if any) shall notify the clerk that a nonprofit budget and credit counseling agency or an instructional course is no longer approved, in which case the clerk shall remove it from the list maintained under subsection (a).

"(g)(1) No nonprofit budget and credit counseling agency may provide to a credit reporting agency information concerning whether a debtor has received or sought instruction concerning personal financial management from such agency.

"(2) A nonprofit budget and credit counseling agency that willfully or negligently fails to comply with any requirement under this title with respect to a debtor shall be liable for damages in an amount equal to the sum of—

"(A) any actual damages sustained by the debtor as a result of the violation; and

"(B) any court costs or reasonable attorneys' fees (as determined by the court) incurred in an action to recover those damages.".

(2) CLERICAL AMENDMENT—The table of sections for chapter 1 of title 11, United States Code, is amended by adding at the end the following:

"111. Nonprofit budget and credit counseling agencies; financial management instructional courses.".

(f) LIMITATION—Section 362 of title 11, United States Code, is amended by adding at the end the following:

"(i) If a case commenced under chapter 7, 11, or 13 is dismissed due to the creation of a debt repayment plan, for purposes of subsection (c)(3), any subsequent case commenced by the debtor under any such chapter shall not be presumed to be filed not in good faith.

"(j) On request of a party in interest, the court shall issue an order under subsection (c) confirming that the automatic stay has been terminated.".

Sec. 107 SCHEDULES OF REASONABLE AND NECESSARY EXPENSES.

For purposes of section 707(b) of title 11, United States Code, as amended by this Act, the Director of the Executive Office for United States Trustees shall, not later than 180 days after the date of enactment of this Act, issue schedules of reasonable and necessary administrative expenses of administering a chapter 13 plan for each judicial district of the United States.

TITLE II

ENHANCED CONSUMER PROTECTION

Subtitle A   Penalties for Abusive Creditor Practices

Sec. 201 PROMOTION OF ALTERNATIVE DISPUTE RESOLUTION.

(a) REDUCTION OF CLAIM—Section 502 of title 11, United States Code, is amended by adding at the end the following:

"(k)(1) The court, on the motion of the debtor and after a hearing, may reduce a claim filed under this section based in whole on an unsecured consumer debt by not more than 20 percent of the claim, if—

"(A) the claim was filed by a creditor who unreasonably refused to negotiate a reasonable alternative repayment schedule proposed on behalf of the debtor by an approved nonprofit budget and credit counseling agency described in section 111;

"(B) the offer of the debtor under subparagraph (A)—

"(i) was made at least 60 days before the date of the filing of the petition; and

"(ii) provided for payment of at least 60 percent of the amount of the debt over a period not to exceed the repayment period of the loan, or a reasonable extension thereof; and

"(C) no part of the debt under the alternative repayment schedule is nondischargeable.

"(2) The debtor shall have the burden of proving, by clear and convincing evidence, that—

"(A) the creditor unreasonably refused to consider the debtor's proposal; and

"(B) the proposed alternative repayment schedule was made prior to expiration of the 60-day period specified in paragraph (1)(B)(i).".

(b) LIMITATION ON AVOIDABILITY—Section 547 of title 11, United States Code, is amended by adding at the end the following:

"(h) The trustee may not avoid a transfer if such transfer was made as a part of an alternative repayment schedule between the debtor and any creditor of the debtor created by an approved nonprofit budget and credit counseling agency.".

Sec. 202 EFFECT OF DISCHARGE.

Section 524 of title 11, United States Code, is amended by adding at the end the following:

"(i) The willful failure of a creditor to credit payments received under a plan confirmed under this title, unless the order confirming the plan is revoked, the plan is in default, or the creditor has not received payments required to be made under the plan in the manner required by the plan (including crediting the amounts required under the plan), shall constitute a violation of an injunction under subsection (a)(2) if the act of the creditor to collect and failure to credit payments in the manner required by the plan caused material injury to the debtor.

"(j) Subsection (a)(2) does not operate as an injunction against an act by a creditor that is the holder of a secured claim, if—

"(1) such creditor retains a security interest in real property that is the principal residence of the debtor;

"(2) such act is in the ordinary course of business between the creditor and the debtor; and

"(3) such act is limited to seeking or obtaining periodic payments associated with a valid security interest in lieu of pursuit of in rem relief to enforce the lien.".

Sec. 203 Discouraging Abuse of Reaffirmation Agreement Practices.

(a) In General—Section 524 of title 11, United States Code, as amended section 202, is amended—

(1) in subsection (c), by striking paragraph (2) and inserting the following:

"(2) the debtor received the disclosures described in subsection (k) at or before the time at which the debtor signed the agreement;"; and

(2) by adding at the end the following:

"(k)(1) The disclosures required under subsection (c)(2) shall consist of the disclosure statement described in paragraph (3), completed as required in that paragraph, together with the agreement specified in subsection (c), statement, declaration, motion and order described, respectively, in paragraphs (4) through (8), and shall be the only disclosures required in connection with entering into such agreement.

"(2) Disclosures made under paragraph (1) shall be made clearly and conspicuously and in writing. The terms 'Amount Reaffirmed' and 'Annual Percentage Rate' shall be disclosed more conspicuously than other terms, data or information provided in connection with this disclosure, except that the phrases 'Before agreeing to reaffirm a debt, review these important disclosures' and 'Summary of Reaffirmation Agreement' may be equally conspicuous. Disclosures may be made in a different order and may use terminology different from that set forth in paragraphs (2) through (8), except that the terms 'Amount Reaffirmed' and 'Annual Percentage Rate' must be used where indicated.

"(3) The disclosure statement required under this paragraph shall consist of the following:

"(A) The statement: 'Part A: Before agreeing to reaffirm a debt, review these important disclosures:';

"(B) Under the heading 'Summary of Reaffirmation Agreement', the statement: 'This Summary is made pursuant to the requirements of the Bankruptcy Code';

"(C) The 'Amount Reaffirmed', using that term, which shall be—

"(i) the total amount of debt that the debtor agrees to reaffirm by entering into an agreement of the kind specified in subsection (c), and

"(ii) the total of any fees and costs accrued as of the date of the disclosure statement, related to such total amount.

"(D) In conjunction with the disclosure of the 'Amount Reaffirmed', the statements—

"(i) 'The amount of debt you have agreed to reaffirm'; and

"(ii) 'Your credit agreement may obligate you to pay additional amounts which may come due after the date of this disclosure. Consult your credit agreement.'.

"(E) The 'Annual Percentage Rate', using that term, which shall be disclosed as—

"(i) if, at the time the petition is filed, the debt is an extension of credit under an open end credit plan, as the terms 'credit' and 'open end credit plan' are defined in section 103 of the Truth in Lending Act, then—

"(I) the annual percentage rate determined under paragraphs (5) and (6) of section 127(b) of the Truth in Lending Act, as applicable, as disclosed to the debtor in the most recent periodic statement prior to entering into an agreement of the kind specified in subsection (c) or, if no such periodic statement has been given to the debtor during the prior 6 months, the annual percentage rate as it would have been so disclosed at the time the disclosure statement is given to the debtor, or to the extent this annual percentage rate is not readily available or not applicable, then

"(II) the simple interest rate applicable to the amount reaffirmed as of the date the disclosure statement is given to the debtor, or if different simple interest rates apply to different balances, the simple interest rate applicable to each such balance, identifying the amount of each such balance included in the amount reaffirmed, or

"(III) if the entity making the disclosure elects, to disclose the annual percentage rate under subclause (I) and the simple interest rate under subclause (II); or

"(ii) if, at the time the petition is filed, the debt is an extension of credit other than under an open end credit plan, as the terms 'credit' and 'open end credit plan' are defined in section 103 of the Truth in Lending Act, then—

"(I) the annual percentage rate under section 128(a)(4) of the Truth in Lending Act, as disclosed to the debtor in the most recent disclosure statement given to the debtor prior to the entering into an agreement of the kind specified in subsection (c) with respect to the debt, or, if no such disclosure statement was given to the debtor, the annual percentage rate as it would have been so disclosed at the time the disclosure statement is given to the debtor, or to the extent this annual percentage rate is not readily available or not applicable, then

"(II) the simple interest rate applicable to the amount reaffirmed as of the date the disclosure statement is given to the debtor, or if different simple interest rates apply to different balances, the simple interest rate applicable to each such balance, identifying the amount of such balance included in the amount reaffirmed, or

"(III) if the entity making the disclosure elects, to disclose the annual percentage rate under (I) and the simple interest rate under (II).

"(F) If the underlying debt transaction was disclosed as a variable rate transaction on the most recent disclosure given under the Truth in Lending Act, by stating 'The interest rate on your loan may be a variable interest rate which changes from time to time, so that the annual percentage rate disclosed here may be higher or lower.'.

"(G) If the debt is secured by a security interest which has not been waived in whole or in part or determined to be void by a final order of the court at the time of the disclosure, by disclosing that a security interest or lien in goods or property is asserted over some or all of the debts the debtor is reaffirming and listing the items and their original purchase price that are subject to the asserted security interest, or if not a purchase-money security interest then listing by items or types and the original amount of the loan.

"(H) At the election of the creditor, a statement of the repayment schedule using 1 or a combination of the following—

"(i) by making the statement: 'Your first payment in the amount of $__ is due on __ but the future payment amount may be different. Consult your reaffirmation agreement or credit agreement, as applicable.', and stating the amount of the first payment and the due date of that payment in the places provided;

"(ii) by making the statement: 'Your payment schedule will be:', and describing the repayment schedule with the number, amount, and due dates or period of payments scheduled to repay the debts reaffirmed to the extent then known by the disclosing party; or

"(iii) by describing the debtor's repayment obligations with reasonable specificity to the extent then known by the disclosing party.

"(I) The following statement: 'Note: When this disclosure refers to what a creditor "may" do, it does not use the word "may" to give the creditor specific permission. The word "may" is used to tell you what might occur if the law permits the creditor to take the action. If you have questions about your reaffirming a debt or what the law requires, consult with the attorney who helped you negotiate this agreement reaffirming a debt. If you don't have an attorney helping you, the judge will explain the effect of your reaffirming a debt when the hearing on the reaffirmation agreement is held.'.

"(J)(i) The following additional statements:

"Reaffirming a debt is a serious financial decision. The law requires you to take certain steps to make sure the decision is in your best interest. If these steps are not completed, the reaffirmation agreement is not effective, even though you have signed it.

" '1. Read the disclosures in this Part A carefully. Consider the decision to reaffirm carefully. Then, if you want to reaffirm, sign the reaffirmation agreement in Part B (or you may use a separate agreement you and your creditor agree on).

" '2. Complete and sign Part D and be sure you can afford to make the payments you are agreeing to make and have received a copy of the disclosure statement and a completed and signed reaffirmation agreement.

" '3. If you were represented by an attorney during the negotiation of your reaffirmation agreement, the attorney must have signed the certification in Part C.

" '4. If you were not represented by an attorney during the negotiation of your reaffirmation agreement, you must have completed and signed Part E.

" '5. The original of this disclosure must be filed with the court by you or your creditor. If a separate reaffirmation agreement (other than the one in Part B) has been signed, it must be attached.

" '6. If you were represented by an attorney during the negotiation of your reaffirmation agreement, your reaffirmation agreement becomes effective upon filing with the court unless the reaffirmation is presumed to be an undue hardship as explained in Part D.

" '7. If you were not represented by an attorney during the negotiation of your reaffirmation agreement, it will not be effective unless the court approves it. The court will notify you of the hearing on your reaffirmation agreement. You must attend this hearing in bankruptcy court where the judge will review your reaffirmation agreement. The bankruptcy court must approve your reaffirmation agreement as consistent with your best interests, except that no court approval is required if your reaffirmation agreement is for a consumer debt secured by a mortgage, deed of trust, security deed, or other lien on your real property, like your home.

" 'Your right to rescind (cancel) your reaffirmation agreement. You may rescind (cancel) your reaffirmation agreement at any time before the bankruptcy court enters a discharge order, or before the expiration of the 60-day period that begins on the date your reaffirmation agreement is filed with the court, whichever occurs later. To rescind (cancel) your reaffirmation agreement, you must notify the creditor that your reaffirmation agreement is rescinded (or canceled).

" 'What are your obligations if you reaffirm the debt? A reaffirmed debt remains your personal legal obligation. It is not discharged in your bankruptcy case. That means that if you default on your reaffirmed debt after your bankruptcy case is over, your creditor may be able to take your property or your wages. Otherwise, your obligations will be determined by the reaffirmation agreement which may have changed the terms of the original agreement. For example, if you are reaffirming an open end credit agreement, the creditor may be permitted by that agreement or applicable law to change the terms of that agreement in the future under certain conditions.

" 'Are you required to enter into a reaffirmation agreement by any law? No, you are not required to reaffirm a debt by any law. Only agree to reaffirm a debt if it is in your best interest. Be sure you can afford the payments you agree to make.

" 'What if your creditor has a security interest or lien? Your bankruptcy discharge does not eliminate any lien on your property. A "lien" is often referred to as a security interest, deed of trust, mortgage or security deed. Even if you do not reaffirm and your personal liability on the debt is discharged, because of the lien your creditor may still have the right to take the security property if you do not pay the debt or default on it. If the lien is on an item of personal property that is exempt under your State's law or that the trustee has abandoned, you may be able to redeem the item rather than reaffirm the debt. To redeem, you make a single payment to the creditor equal to the current value of the security property, as agreed by the parties or determined by the court.'.

"(ii) In the case of a reaffirmation under subsection (m)(2), numbered paragraph 6 in the disclosures required by clause (i) of this subparagraph shall read as follows:

" '6. If you were represented by an attorney during the negotiation of your reaffirmation agreement, your reaffirmation agreement becomes effective upon filing with the court.'.

"(4) The form of such agreement required under this paragraph shall consist of the following:

" 'Part B: Reaffirmation Agreement. I (we) agree to reaffirm the debts arising under the credit agreement described below.

" 'Brief description of credit agreement:

" 'Description of any changes to the credit agreement made as part of this reaffirmation agreement:

" 'Signature: Date:

" 'Borrower:

" 'Co-borrower, if also reaffirming these debts:

" 'Accepted by creditor:

" 'Date of creditor acceptance:'.

"(5) The declaration shall consist of the following:

"(A) The following certification:

" 'Part C: Certification by Debtor's Attorney (If Any).

" 'I hereby certify that (1) this agreement represents a fully informed and voluntary agreement by the debtor; (2) this agreement does not impose an undue hardship on the debtor or any dependent of the debtor; and (3) I have fully advised the debtor of the legal effect and consequences of this agreement and any default under this agreement.

" 'Signature of Debtor's Attorney: Date:'.

"(B) If a presumption of undue hardship has been established with respect to such agreement, such certification shall state that in the opinion of the attorney, the debtor is able to make the payment.

"(C) In the case of a reaffirmation agreement under subsection (m)(2), subparagraph (B) is not applicable.

"(6)(A) The statement in support of such agreement, which the debtor shall sign and date prior to filing with the court, shall consist of the following:

" 'Part D: Debtor's Statement in Support of Reaffirmation Agreement.

" '1. I believe this reaffirmation agreement will not impose an undue hardship on my dependents or me. I can afford to make the payments on the reaffirmed debt because my monthly income (take home pay plus any other income received) is $__, and my actual current monthly expenses including monthly payments on post-bankruptcy debt and other reaffirmation agreements total $__, leaving $__ to make the required payments on this reaffirmed debt. I understand that if my income less my monthly expenses does not leave enough to make the payments, this reaffirmation agreement is presumed to be an undue hardship on me and must be reviewed by the court. However, this presumption may be overcome if I explain to the satisfaction of the court how I can afford to make the payments here: __.

" '2. I received a copy of the Reaffirmation Disclosure Statement in Part A and a completed and signed reaffirmation agreement.'.

"(B) Where the debtor is represented by an attorney and is reaffirming a debt owed to a creditor defined in section 19(b)(1)(A)(iv) of the Federal Reserve Act, the statement of support of the reaffirmation agreement, which the debtor shall sign and date prior to filing with the court, shall consist of the following:

" 'I believe this reaffirmation agreement is in my financial interest. I can afford to make the payments on the reaffirmed debt. I received a copy of the Reaffirmation Disclosure Statement in Part A and a completed and signed reaffirmation agreement.'.

"(7) The motion that may be used if approval of such agreement by the court is required in order for it to be effective, shall be signed and dated by the movant and shall consist of the following:

" 'Part E: Motion for Court Approval (To be completed only if the debtor is not represented by an attorney.). I (we), the debtor(s), affirm the following to be true and correct:

" 'I am not represented by an attorney in connection with this reaffirmation agreement.

" 'I believe this reaffirmation agreement is in my best interest based on the income and expenses I have disclosed in my Statement in Support of this reaffirmation agreement, and because (provide any additional relevant reasons the court should consider):

" 'Therefore, I ask the court for an order approving this reaffirmation agreement.'.

"(8) The court order, which may be used to approve such agreement, shall consist of the following:

" 'Court Order: The court grants the debtor's motion and approves the reaffirmation agreement described above.'.

"(l) Notwithstanding any other provision of this title the following shall apply:

"(1) A creditor may accept payments from a debtor before and after the filing of an agreement of the kind specified in subsection (c) with the court.

"(2) A creditor may accept payments from a debtor under such agreement that the creditor believes in good faith to be effective.

"(3) The requirements of subsections (c)(2) and (k) shall be satisfied if disclosures required under those subsections are given in good faith.

"(m)(1) Until 60 days after an agreement of the kind specified in subsection (c) is filed with the court (or such additional period as the court, after notice and a hearing and for cause, orders before the expiration of such period), it shall be presumed that such agreement is an undue hardship on the debtor if the debtor's monthly income less the debtor's monthly expenses as shown on the debtor's completed and signed statement in support of such agreement required under subsection (k)(6)(A) is less than the scheduled payments on the reaffirmed debt. This presumption shall be reviewed by the court. The presumption may be rebutted in writing by the debtor if the statement includes an explanation that identifies additional sources of funds to make the payments as agreed upon under the terms of such agreement. If the presumption is not rebutted to the satisfaction of the court, the court may disapprove such agreement. No agreement shall be disapproved without notice and a hearing to the debtor and creditor, and such hearing shall be concluded before the entry of the debtor's discharge.

"(2) This subsection does not apply to reaffirmation agreements where the creditor is a credit union, as defined in section 19(b)(1)(A)(iv) of the Federal Reserve Act.".

(b) LAW ENFORCEMENT—

(1) IN GENERAL—Chapter 9 of title 18, United States Code, is amended by adding at the end the following:

"§ 158. Designation of United States attorneys and agents of the Federal Bureau of Investigation to address abusive reaffirmations of debt and materially fraudulent statements in bankruptcy schedules

"(a) IN GENERAL—The Attorney General of the United States shall designate the individuals described in subsection (b) to have primary responsibility in carrying out enforcement activities in addressing violations of section 152 or 157 relating to abusive reaffirmations of debt. In addition to addressing the violations referred to in the preceding sentence, the individuals described under subsection (b) shall address violations of section 152 or 157 relating to materially fraudulent statements in bankruptcy schedules that are intentionally false or intentionally misleading.

"(b) UNITED STATES ATTORNEYS AND AGENTS OF THE FEDERAL BUREAU OF INVESTIGATION—The individuals referred to in subsection (a) are—

"(1) the United States attorney for each judicial district of the United States; and

"(2) an agent of the Federal Bureau of Investigation for each field office of the Federal Bureau of Investigation.

"(c) BANKRUPTCY INVESTIGATIONS—Each United States attorney designated under this section shall, in addition to any other responsibilities, have primary responsibility for carrying out the duties of a United States attorney under section 3057.

"(d) BANKRUPTCY PROCEDURES—The bankruptcy courts shall establish procedures for referring any case that may contain a materially fraudulent statement in a bankruptcy schedule to the individuals designated under this section.".

(2) CLERICAL AMENDMENT—The table of sections for chapter 9 of title 18, United States Code, is amended by adding at the end the following:

"158. Designation of United States attorneys and agents of the Federal Bureau of Investigation to address abusive reaffirmations of debt and materially fraudulent statements in bankruptcy schedules.".

Sec. 204 PRESERVATION OF CLAIMS AND DEFENSES UPON SALE OF PREDATORY LOANS.

Section 363 of title 11, United States Code, is amended—

(1) by redesignating subsection (o) as subsection (p), and

(2) by inserting after subsection (n) the following:

"(o) Notwithstanding subsection (f), if a person purchases any interest in a consumer credit transaction that is subject to the Truth in Lending Act or any interest in a consumer credit contract (as defined in section 433.1 of title 16 of the Code of Federal Regulations (January 1, 2004), as amended from time to time), and if such interest is purchased through a sale under this section, then such person shall remain subject to all claims and defenses that are related to such consumer credit transaction or such consumer credit contract, to the same extent as such person would be subject to such claims and defenses of the consumer had such interest been purchased at a sale not under this section.".

Sec. 205 GAO STUDY AND REPORT ON REAFFIRMATION AGREEMENT PROCESS.

(a) STUDY—The Comptroller General of the United States shall conduct a study of the reaffirmation agreement process that occurs under title 11 of the United States Code, to determine the overall treatment of consumers within the context of such process, and shall include in such study consideration of—

(1) the policies and activities of creditors with respect to reaffirmation agreements; and

(2) whether consumers are fully, fairly, and consistently informed of their rights pursuant to such title.

(b) REPORT TO THE CONGRESS—Not later than 18 months after the date of the enactment of this Act, the Comptroller General shall submit to the President pro tempore of the Senate and the Speaker of the House of Representatives a report on the results of the study conducted under subsection (a), together with recommendations for legislation (if any) to address any abusive or coercive tactics found in connection with the reaffirmation agreement process that occurs under title 11 of the United States Code.

Subtitle B Priority Child Support

Sec. 211 DEFINITION OF DOMESTIC SUPPORT OBLIGATION.

Section 101 of title 11, United States Code, is amended—

(1) by striking paragraph (12A); and

(2) by inserting after paragraph (14) the following:

"(14A) 'domestic support obligation' means a debt that accrues before, on, or after the date of the order for relief in a case under this title, including interest that accrues on that debt as provided under applicable nonbankruptcy law notwithstanding any other provision of this title, that is—

"(A) owed to or recoverable by—

"(i) a spouse, former spouse, or child of the debtor or such child's parent, legal guardian, or responsible relative; or

"(ii) a governmental unit;

"(B) in the nature of alimony, maintenance, or support (including assistance provided by a governmental unit) of such spouse, former spouse, or child of the debtor or such child's parent, without regard to whether such debt is expressly so designated;

"(C) established or subject to establishment before, on, or after the date of the order for relief in a case under this title, by reason of applicable provisions of—

"(i) a separation agreement, divorce decree, or property settlement agreement;

"(ii) an order of a court of record; or

"(iii) a determination made in accordance with applicable non-bankruptcy law by a governmental unit; and

"(D) not assigned to a nongovernmental entity, unless that obligation is assigned voluntarily by the spouse, former spouse, child of the debtor, or such child's parent, legal guardian, or responsible relative for the purpose of collecting the debt;".

Sec. 212 PRIORITIES FOR CLAIMS FOR DOMESTIC SUPPORT OBLIGATIONS.

Section 507(a) of title 11, United States Code, is amended—

(1) by striking paragraph (7);

(2) by redesignating paragraphs (1) through (6) as paragraphs (2) through (7), respectively;

(3) in paragraph (2), as so redesignated, by striking "First" and inserting "Second";

(4) in paragraph (3), as so redesignated, by striking "Second" and inserting "Third";

(5) in paragraph (4), as so redesignated—

(A) by striking "Third" and inserting "Fourth"; and

(B) by striking the semicolon at the end and inserting a period;

(6) in paragraph (5), as so redesignated, by striking "Fourth" and inserting "Fifth";

(7) in paragraph (6), as so redesignated, by striking "Fifth" and inserting "Sixth";

(8) in paragraph (7), as so redesignated, by striking "Sixth" and inserting "Seventh"; and

(9) by inserting before paragraph (2), as so redesignated, the following:

"(1) First:

"(A) Allowed unsecured claims for domestic support obligations that, as of the date of the filing of the petition in a case under this title, are owed to or recoverable by a spouse, former spouse, or child of the debtor, or such child's parent, legal guardian, or responsible relative, without regard to whether the claim is filed by such person or is filed by a governmental unit on behalf of such person, on the condition that funds received under this paragraph by a governmental unit under this title after the date of the filing of the petition shall be applied and distributed in accordance with applicable nonbankruptcy law.

"(B) Subject to claims under subparagraph (A), allowed unsecured claims for domestic support obligations that, as of the date of the filing of the petition, are assigned by a spouse, former spouse, child of the debtor, or such child's parent, legal guardian, or responsible relative to a governmental unit (unless such obligation is assigned voluntarily by the spouse, former spouse, child, parent, legal guardian, or responsible relative of the child for the purpose of collecting the debt) or are owed directly to or recoverable by a governmental unit under applicable nonbankruptcy law, on the condition that funds received under this paragraph by a governmental unit under this title after the date of the filing of the petition be applied and distributed in accordance with applicable nonbankruptcy law.

"(C) If a trustee is appointed or elected under section 701, 702, 703, 1104, 1202, or 1302, the administrative expenses of the trustee allowed under paragraphs (1)(A), (2), and (6) of section 503(b) shall be paid before payment of claims under subparagraphs (A) and (B), to the extent that the trustee administers assets that are otherwise available for the payment of such claims.".

Sec. 213 REQUIREMENTS TO OBTAIN CONFIRMATION AND DISCHARGE IN CASES INVOLVING DOMESTIC SUPPORT OBLIGATIONS.

Title 11, United States Code, is amended—

(1) in section 1129(a), by adding at the end the following:

"(14) If the debtor is required by a judicial or administrative order, or by statute, to pay a domestic support obligation, the debtor has paid all amounts payable under such order or such statute for such obligation that first become payable after the date of the filing of the petition.";

(2) in section 1208(c)—

(A) in paragraph (8), by striking "or" at the end;

(B) in paragraph (9), by striking the period at the end and inserting "; and"; and

(C) by adding at the end the following:

"(10) failure of the debtor to pay any domestic support obligation that first becomes payable after the date of the filing of the petition.";

(3) in section 1222(a)—

(A) in paragraph (2), by striking "and" at the end;

(B) in paragraph (3), by striking the period at the end and inserting "; and"; and

(C) by adding at the end the following:

"(4) notwithstanding any other provision of this section, a plan may provide for less than full payment of all amounts owed for a claim entitled to priority under section 507(a)(1)(B) only if the plan provides that all of the debtor's projected disposable income for a 5-year period beginning on the date that the first payment is due under the plan will be applied to make payments under the plan.";

(4) in section 1222(b)—

(A) in paragraph (10), by striking "and" at the end;

(B) by redesignating paragraph (11) as paragraph (12); and

(C) by inserting after paragraph (10) the following:

"(11) provide for the payment of interest accruing after the date of the filing of the petition on unsecured claims that are nondischargeable under section 1228(a), except that such interest may be paid only to the extent that the debtor has disposable income available to pay such interest after making provision for full payment of all allowed claims; and';

(5) in section 1225(a)—

(A) in paragraph (5), by striking "and" at the end;

(B) in paragraph (6), by striking the period at the end and inserting "; and"; and

(C) by adding at the end the following:

"(7) the debtor has paid all amounts that are required to be paid under a domestic support obligation and that first become payable after the date of the filing of the petition if the debtor is required by a judicial or administrative order, or by statute, to pay such domestic support obligation.";

(6) in section 1228(a), in the matter preceding paragraph (1), by inserting ", and in the case of a debtor who is required by a judicial or administrative order, or by statute, to pay a domestic support obligation, after such debtor certifies that all amounts payable under such order or such statute that are due on or before the date of the certification (including amounts due before the petition was filed, but only to the extent provided for by the plan) have been paid" after "completion by the debtor of all payments under the plan";

(7) in section 1307(c)—

(A) in paragraph (9), by striking "or" at the end;

(B) in paragraph (10), by striking the period at the end and inserting "; or"; and

(C) by adding at the end the following:

"(11) failure of the debtor to pay any domestic support obligation that first becomes payable after the date of the filing of the petition.";

(8) in section 1322(a)—

(A) in paragraph (2), by striking "and" at the end;

(B) in paragraph (3), by striking the period at the end and inserting "; and"; and

(C) by adding at the end the following:

"(4) notwithstanding any other provision of this section, a plan may provide for less than full payment of all amounts owed for a claim entitled to priority under section 507(a)(1)(B) only if the plan provides that all of the debtor's projected disposable income for a 5-year period beginning on the date that the first payment is due under the plan will be applied to make payments under the plan.";

(9) in section 1322(b)—

(A) in paragraph (9), by striking "; and" and inserting a semicolon;

(B) by redesignating paragraph (10) as paragraph (11); and

(C) inserting after paragraph (9) the following:

"(10) provide for the payment of interest accruing after the date of the filing of the petition on unsecured claims that are nondischargeable under section 1328(a), except that such interest may be paid only to the extent that the debtor has disposable income available to pay such interest after making provision for full payment of all allowed claims; and";

(10) in section 1325(a), as amended by section 102, by inserting after paragraph (7) the following:

"(8) the debtor has paid all amounts that are required to be paid under a domestic support obligation and that first become payable after the date of the filing of the petition if the debtor is required by a judicial or administrative order, or by statute, to pay such domestic support obligation; and";

(11) in section 1328(a), in the matter preceding paragraph (1), by inserting ", and in the case of a debtor who is required by a judicial or administrative order, or by statute, to pay a domestic support obligation, after such debtor certifies that all amounts payable under such order or such statute that are due on or before the date of the certification (including amounts due before the petition was filed, but only to the extent provided for by the plan) have been paid" after "completion by the debtor of all payments under the plan".

Sec. 214 EXCEPTIONS TO AUTOMATIC STAY IN DOMESTIC SUPPORT OBLIGATION PROCEEDINGS.

Section 362(b) of title 11, United States Code, is amended by striking paragraph (2) and inserting the following:

"(2) under subsection (a)—

"(A) of the commencement or continuation of a civil action or proceeding—

"(i) for the establishment of paternity;

"(ii) for the establishment or modification of an order for domestic support obligations;

"(iii) concerning child custody or visitation;

"(iv) for the dissolution of a marriage, except to the extent that such proceeding seeks to determine the division of property that is property of the estate; or

"(v) regarding domestic violence;

"(B) of the collection of a domestic support obligation from property that is not property of the estate;

"(C) with respect to the withholding of income that is property of the estate or property of the debtor for payment of a domestic support obligation under a judicial or administrative order or a statute;

"(D) of the withholding, suspension, or restriction of a driver's license, a professional or occupational license, or a recreational license, under State law, as specified in section 466(a)(16) of the Social Security Act;

"(E) of the reporting of overdue support owed by a parent to any consumer reporting agency as specified in section 466(a)(7) of the Social Security Act;

"(F) of the interception of a tax refund, as specified in sections 464 and 466(a)(3) of the Social Security Act or under an analogous State law; or

"(G) of the enforcement of a medical obligation, as specified under title IV of the Social Security Act;".

Sec. 215 NONDISCHARGEABILITY OF CERTAIN DEBTS FOR ALIMONY, MAINTENANCE, AND SUPPORT.

Section 523 of title 11, United States Code, is amended—

(1) in subsection (a)—

(A) by striking paragraph (5) and inserting the following:

"(5) for a domestic support obligation;"; and

(B) by striking paragraph (18);

(2) in subsection (c), by striking "(6), or (15)" each place it appears and inserting "or (6)"; and

(3) in paragraph (15), as added by Public Law 103-394 (108 Stat. 4133)—

(A) by inserting "to a spouse, former spouse, or child of the debtor and" before "not of the kind";

(B) by inserting "or" after "court of record,"; and

(C) by striking "unless—" and all that follows through the end of the paragraph and inserting a semicolon.

Sec. 216 CONTINUED LIABILITY OF PROPERTY.

Section 522 of title 11, United States Code, is amended—

(1) in subsection (c), by striking paragraph (1) and inserting the following:

"(1) a debt of a kind specified in paragraph (1) or (5) of section 523(a) (in which case, notwithstanding any provision of applicable nonbankruptcy law to the contrary, such property shall be liable for a debt of a kind specified in section 523(a)(5));";

(2) in subsection (f)(1)(A), by striking the dash and all that follows through the end of the subparagraph and inserting "of a kind that is specified in section 523(a)(5); or"; and

(3) in subsection (g)(2), by striking "subsection (f)(2)" and inserting "subsection (f)(1)(B)".

Sec. 217 PROTECTION OF DOMESTIC SUPPORT CLAIMS AGAINST PREFERENTIAL TRANSFER MOTIONS.

Section 547(c)(7) of title 11, United States Code, is amended to read as follows:

"(7) to the extent such transfer was a bona fide payment of a debt for a domestic support obligation;".

Sec. 218 DISPOSABLE INCOME DEFINED.

Section 1225(b)(2)(A) of title 11, United States Code, is amended by inserting "or for a domestic support obligation that first becomes payable after the date of the filing of the petition" after "dependent of the debtor".

Sec. 219 COLLECTION OF CHILD SUPPORT.

(a) DUTIES OF TRUSTEE UNDER CHAPTER 7—Section 704 of title 11, United States Code, as amended by section 102, is amended—

(1) in subsection (a)—

(A) in paragraph (8), by striking "and" at the end;

(B) in paragraph (9), by striking the period and inserting a semicolon; and

(C) by adding at the end the following:

"(10) if with respect to the debtor there is a claim for a domestic support obligation, provide the applicable notice specified in subsection (c); and'; and

(2) by adding at the end the following:

"(c)(1) In a case described in subsection (a)(10) to which subsection (a)(10) applies, the trustee shall—

"(A)(i) provide written notice to the holder of the claim described in subsection (a)(10) of such claim and of the right of such holder to use the services of the State child support enforcement agency established under sections 464 and 466 of the Social Security Act for the State in which such holder resides, for assistance in collecting child support during and after the case under this title;

"(ii) include in the notice provided under clause (i) the address and telephone number of such State child support enforcement agency; and

"(iii) include in the notice provided under clause (i) an explanation of the rights of such holder to payment of such claim under this chapter;

"(B)(i) provide written notice to such State child support enforcement agency of such claim; and

"(ii) include in the notice provided under clause (i) the name, address, and telephone number of such holder; and

"(C) at such time as the debtor is granted a discharge under section 727, provide written notice to such holder and to such State child support enforcement agency of—

"(i) the granting of the discharge;

"(ii) the last recent known address of the debtor;

"(iii) the last recent known name and address of the debtor's employer; and

"(iv) the name of each creditor that holds a claim that—

"(I) is not discharged under paragraph (2), (4), or (14A) of section 523(a); or

"(II) was reaffirmed by the debtor under section 524(c).

"(2)(A) The holder of a claim described in subsection (a)(10) or the State child support enforcement agency of the State in which such holder resides may request from a creditor described in paragraph (1)(C)(iv) the last known address of the debtor.

"(B) Notwithstanding any other provision of law, a creditor that makes a disclosure of a last known address of a debtor in connection with a request made under subparagraph (A) shall not be liable by reason of making such disclosure.".

(b) DUTIES OF TRUSTEE UNDER CHAPTER 11—Section 1106 of title 11, United States Code, is amended—

(1) in subsection (a)—

(A) in paragraph (6), by striking "and" at the end;

(B) in paragraph (7), by striking the period and inserting "; and"; and

(C) by adding at the end the following:

"(8) if with respect to the debtor there is a claim for a domestic support obligation, provide the applicable notice specified in subsection (c)."; and

(2) by adding at the end the following:

"(c)(1) In a case described in subsection (a)(8) to which subsection (a)(8) applies, the trustee shall—

"(A)(i) provide written notice to the holder of the claim described in subsection (a)(8) of such claim and of the right of such holder to use the services of the State child support enforcement agency established under sections 464 and 466 of the Social Security Act for the State in which such holder resides, for assistance in collecting child support during and after the case under this title; and

"(ii) include in the notice required by clause (i) the address and telephone number of such State child support enforcement agency;

"(B)(i) provide written notice to such State child support enforcement agency of such claim; and

"(ii) include in the notice required by clause (i) the name, address, and telephone number of such holder; and

"(C) at such time as the debtor is granted a discharge under section 1141, provide written notice to such holder and to such State child support enforcement agency of—

"(i) the granting of the discharge;

"(ii) the last recent known address of the debtor;

"(iii) the last recent known name and address of the debtor's employer; and

"(iv) the name of each creditor that holds a claim that—

"(I) is not discharged under paragraph (2), (4), or (14A) of section 523(a); or

"(II) was reaffirmed by the debtor under section 524(c).

"(2)(A) The holder of a claim described in subsection (a)(8) or the State child enforcement support agency of the State in which such holder resides may request from a creditor described in paragraph (1)(C)(iv) the last known address of the debtor.

"(B) Notwithstanding any other provision of law, a creditor that makes a disclosure of a last known address of a debtor in connection with a request made under subparagraph (A) shall not be liable by reason of making such disclosure.".

(c) Duties of Trustee Under Chapter 12—Section 1202 of title 11, United States Code, is amended—

(1) in subsection (b)—

(A) in paragraph (4), by striking "and" at the end;

(B) in paragraph (5), by striking the period and inserting "; and"; and

(C) by adding at the end the following:

"(6) if with respect to the debtor there is a claim for a domestic support obligation, provide the applicable notice specified in subsection (c)."; and

(2) by adding at the end the following:

"(c)(1) In a case described in subsection (b)(6) to which subsection (b)(6) applies, the trustee shall—

"(A)(i) provide written notice to the holder of the claim described in subsection (b)(6) of such claim and of the right of such holder to use the services of the State child support enforcement agency established under sections 464 and 466 of the Social Security Act for the State in which such holder resides, for assistance in collecting child support during and after the case under this title; and

"(ii) include in the notice provided under clause (i) the address and telephone number of such State child support enforcement agency;

"(B)(i) provide written notice to such State child support enforcement agency of such claim; and

"(ii) include in the notice provided under clause (i) the name, address, and telephone number of such holder; and

"(C) at such time as the debtor is granted a discharge under section 1228, provide written notice to such holder and to such State child support enforcement agency of—

"(i) the granting of the discharge;

"(ii) the last recent known address of the debtor;

"(iii) the last recent known name and address of the debtor's employer; and

"(iv) the name of each creditor that holds a claim that—

"(I) is not discharged under paragraph (2), (4), or (14A) of section 523(a); or

"(II) was reaffirmed by the debtor under section 524(c).

"(2)(A) The holder of a claim described in subsection (b)(6) or the State child support enforcement agency of the State in which such holder resides may request from a creditor described in paragraph (1)(C)(iv) the last known address of the debtor.

"(B) Notwithstanding any other provision of law, a creditor that makes a disclosure of a last known address of a debtor in connection with a request made under subparagraph (A) shall not be liable by reason of making that disclosure.".

(d) DUTIES OF TRUSTEE UNDER CHAPTER 13—Section 1302 of title 11, United States Code, is amended—

(1) in subsection (b)—

(A) in paragraph (4), by striking "and" at the end;

(B) in paragraph (5), by striking the period and inserting "; and"; and

(C) by adding at the end the following:

"(6) if with respect to the debtor there is a claim for a domestic support obligation, provide the applicable notice specified in subsection (d).";and

(2) by adding at the end the following:

"(d)(1) In a case described in subsection (b)(6) to which subsection (b)(6) applies, the trustee shall—

"(A)(i) provide written notice to the holder of the claim described in subsection (b)(6) of such claim and of the right of such holder to use the services of the State child support enforcement agency established under sections 464 and 466 of the Social Security Act for the State in which such holder resides, for assistance in collecting child support during and after the case under this title; and

"(ii) include in the notice provided under clause (i) the address and telephone number of such State child support enforcement agency;

"(B)(i) provide written notice to such State child support enforcement agency of such claim; and

"(ii) include in the notice provided under clause (i) the name, address, and telephone number of such holder; and

"(C) at such time as the debtor is granted a discharge under section 1328, provide written notice to such holder and to such State child support enforcement agency of—

"(i) the granting of the discharge;

"(ii) the last recent known address of the debtor;

"(iii) the last recent known name and address of the debtor's employer; and

"(iv) the name of each creditor that holds a claim that—

"(I) is not discharged under paragraph (2) or (4) of section 523(a); or

"(II) was reaffirmed by the debtor under section 524(c).

"(2)(A) The holder of a claim described in subsection (b)(6) or the State child support enforcement agency of the State in which such holder resides may request from a creditor described in paragraph (1)(C)(iv) the last known address of the debtor.

"(B) Notwithstanding any other provision of law, a creditor that makes a disclosure of a last known address of a debtor in connection with a request made under subparagraph (A) shall not be liable by reason of making that disclosure.".

Sec. 220 NONDISCHARGEABILITY OF CERTAIN EDUCATIONAL BENEFITS AND LOANS.

Section 523(a) of title 11, United States Code, is amended by striking paragraph (8) and inserting the following:

"(8) unless excepting such debt from discharge under this paragraph would impose an undue hardship on the debtor and the debtor's dependents, for—

"(A)(i) an educational benefit overpayment or loan made, insured, or guaranteed by a governmental unit, or made under any program funded in whole or in part by a governmental unit or nonprofit institution; or

"(ii) an obligation to repay funds received as an educational benefit, scholarship, or stipend; or

"(B) any other educational loan that is a qualified education loan, as defined in section 221(d)(1) of the Internal Revenue Code of 1986, incurred by a debtor who is an individual;".

Subtitle C   Other Consumer Protections

Sec. 221 AMENDMENTS TO DISCOURAGE ABUSIVE BANKRUPTCY FILINGS.

Section 110 of title 11, United States Code, is amended—

(1) in subsection (a)(1), by striking "or an employee of an attorney" and inserting "for the debtor or an employee of such attorney under the direct supervision of such attorney";

(2) in subsection (b)—

(A) in paragraph (1), by adding at the end the following: "If a bankruptcy petition preparer is not an individual, then an officer, principal, responsible person, or partner of the bankruptcy petition preparer shall be required to—

"(A) sign the document for filing; and

"(B) print on the document the name and address of that officer, principal, responsible person, or partner."; and

(B) by striking paragraph (2) and inserting the following:

"(2)(A) Before preparing any document for filing or accepting any fees from a debtor, the bankruptcy petition preparer shall provide to the debtor a written notice which shall be on an official form prescribed by the Judicial Conference of the United States in accordance with rule 9009 of the Federal Rules of Bankruptcy Procedure.

"(B) The notice under subparagraph (A)—

"(i) shall inform the debtor in simple language that a bankruptcy petition preparer is not an attorney and may not practice law or give legal advice;

"(ii) may contain a description of examples of legal advice that a bankruptcy petition preparer is not authorized to give, in addition to any advice that the preparer may not give by reason of subsection (e)(2); and

"(iii) shall—

"(I) be signed by the debtor and, under penalty of perjury, by the bankruptcy petition preparer; and

"(II) be filed with any document for filing.";

(3) in subsection (c)—

(A) in paragraph (2)—

(i) by striking "(2) For purposes" and inserting "(2)(A) Subject to subparagraph (B), for purposes"; and

(ii) by adding at the end the following:

"(B) If a bankruptcy petition preparer is not an individual, the identifying number of the bankruptcy petition preparer shall be the Social Security account number of the officer, principal, responsible person, or partner of the bankruptcy petition preparer."; and

(B) by striking paragraph (3);

(4) in subsection (d)—

(A) by striking "(d)(1)" and inserting "(d)"; and

(B) by striking paragraph (2);

(5) in subsection (e)—

(A) by striking paragraph (2); and

(B) by adding at the end the following:

"(2)(A) A bankruptcy petition preparer may not offer a potential bankruptcy debtor any legal advice, including any legal advice described in subparagraph (B).

"(B) The legal advice referred to in subparagraph (A) includes advising the debtor—

"(i) whether—

"(I) to file a petition under this title; or

"(II) commencing a case under chapter 7, 11, 12, or 13 is appropriate;

"(ii) whether the debtor's debts will be discharged in a case under this title;

"(iii) whether the debtor will be able to retain the debtor's home, car, or other property after commencing a case under this title;

"(iv) concerning—

"(I) the tax consequences of a case brought under this title; or

"(II) the dischargeability of tax claims;

"(v) whether the debtor may or should promise to repay debts to a creditor or enter into a reaffirmation agreement with a creditor to reaffirm a debt;

"(vi) concerning how to characterize the nature of the debtor's interests in property or the debtor's debts; or

"(vii) concerning bankruptcy procedures and rights.";

(6) in subsection (f)—

(A) by striking "(f)(1)" and inserting "(f)"; and

(B) by striking paragraph (2);

(7) in subsection (g)—

(A) by striking "(g)(1)" and inserting "(g)"; and

(B) by striking paragraph (2);

(8) in subsection (h)—

(A) by redesignating paragraphs (1) through (4) as paragraphs (2) through (5), respectively;

(B) by inserting before paragraph (2), as so redesignated, the following:

"(1) The Supreme Court may promulgate rules under section 2075 of title 28, or the Judicial Conference of the United States may prescribe guidelines, for setting a maximum allowable fee chargeable by a bankruptcy petition preparer. A bankruptcy petition preparer shall notify the debtor of any such maximum amount before preparing any document for filing for a debtor or accepting any fee from the debtor.";

(C) in paragraph (2), as so redesignated—

(i) by striking "Within 10 days after the date of the filing of a petition, a bankruptcy petition preparer shall file a" and inserting "A";

(ii) by inserting "by the bankruptcy petition preparer shall be filed together with the petition," after "perjury"; and

(iii) by adding at the end the following: "If rules or guidelines setting a maximum fee for services have been promulgated or prescribed under paragraph (1), the declaration under this paragraph shall include a certification that the bankruptcy petition preparer complied with the notification requirement under paragraph (1).";

(D) by striking paragraph (3), as so redesignated, and inserting the following:

"(3)(A) The court shall disallow and order the immediate turnover to the bankruptcy trustee any fee referred to in paragraph (2) found to be in excess of the value of any services—

"(i) rendered by the bankruptcy petition preparer during the 12-month period immediately preceding the date of the filing of the petition; or

"(ii) found to be in violation of any rule or guideline promulgated or prescribed under paragraph (1).

"(B) All fees charged by a bankruptcy petition preparer may be forfeited in any case in which the bankruptcy petition preparer fails to comply with this subsection or subsection (b), (c), (d), (e), (f), or (g).

"(C) An individual may exempt any funds recovered under this paragraph under section 522(b)."; and

(E) in paragraph (4), as so redesignated, by striking "or the United States trustee" and inserting "the United States trustee (or the bankruptcy administrator, if any) or the court, on the initiative of the court,";

(9) in subsection (i)(1), by striking the matter preceding subparagraph (A) and inserting the following:

"(i)(1) If a bankruptcy petition preparer violates this section or commits any act that the court finds to be fraudulent, unfair, or deceptive, on the motion of the debtor, trustee, United States trustee (or the bankruptcy administrator, if any), and after notice and a hearing, the court shall order the bankruptcy petition preparer to pay to the debtor—";

(10) in subsection (j)—

(A) in paragraph (2)—

(i) in subparagraph (A)(i)(I), by striking "a violation of which subjects a person to criminal penalty";

(ii) in subparagraph (B)—

(I) by striking "or has not paid a penalty" and inserting "has not paid a penalty"; and

(II) by inserting "or failed to disgorge all fees ordered by the court" after "a penalty imposed under this section,";

(B) by redesignating paragraph (3) as paragraph (4); and

(C) by inserting after paragraph (2) the following:

"(3) The court, as part of its contempt power, may enjoin a bankruptcy petition preparer that has failed to comply with a previous order issued under this section. The injunction under this paragraph may be issued on the motion of the court, the trustee, or the United States trustee (or the bankruptcy administrator, if any)."; and

(11) by adding at the end the following:

"(l)(1) A bankruptcy petition preparer who fails to comply with any provision of subsection (b), (c), (d), (e), (f), (g), or (h) may be fined not more than $500 for each such failure.

"(2) The court shall triple the amount of a fine assessed under paragraph (1) in any case in which the court finds that a bankruptcy petition preparer—

"(A) advised the debtor to exclude assets or income that should have been included on applicable schedules;

"(B) advised the debtor to use a false Social Security account number;

"(C) failed to inform the debtor that the debtor was filing for relief under this title; or

"(D) prepared a document for filing in a manner that failed to disclose the identity of the bankruptcy petition preparer.

"(3) A debtor, trustee, creditor, or United States trustee (or the bankruptcy administrator, if any) may file a motion for an order imposing a fine on the bankruptcy petition preparer for any violation of this section.

"(4)(A) Fines imposed under this subsection in judicial districts served by United States trustees shall be paid to the United States trustee, who shall deposit an amount equal to such fines in a special account of the United States Trustee System Fund referred to in section 586(e)(2) of title 28. Amounts deposited under this subparagraph shall be available to fund the enforcement of this section on a national basis.

"(B) Fines imposed under this subsection in judicial districts served by bankruptcy administrators shall be deposited as offsetting receipts to the fund established under section 1931 of title 28, and shall remain available until expended to reimburse any appropriation for the amount paid out of such appropriation for expenses of the operation and maintenance of the courts of the United States.".

Sec. 222 SENSE OF CONGRESS.

It is the sense of Congress that States should develop curricula relating to the subject of personal finance, designed for use in elementary and secondary schools.

Sec. 223 ADDITIONAL AMENDMENTS TO TITLE 11, UNITED STATES CODE.

Section 507(a) of title 11, United States Code, as amended by section 212, is amended by inserting after paragraph (9) the following:

"(10) Tenth, allowed claims for death or personal injury resulting from the operation of a motor vehicle or vessel if such operation was unlawful because the debtor was intoxicated from using alcohol, a drug, or another substance.".

Sec. 224 PROTECTION OF RETIREMENT SAVINGS IN BANKRUPTCY.

(a) IN GENERAL—Section 522 of title 11, United States Code, is amended—

(1) in subsection (b)—

(A) in paragraph (2)—

(i) in subparagraph (A), by striking "and" at the end;

(ii) in subparagraph (B), by striking the period at the end and inserting "; and";

(iii) by adding at the end the following:

"(C) retirement funds to the extent that those funds are in a fund or account that is exempt from taxation under section 401, 403, 408, 408A, 414, 457, or 501(a) of the Internal Revenue Code of 1986."; and

(iv) by striking "(2)(A) any property" and inserting:

"(3) Property listed in this paragraph is—

"(A) any property';

(B) by striking paragraph (1) and inserting:

"(2) Property listed in this paragraph is property that is specified under subsection (d), unless the State law that is applicable to the debtor under paragraph (3)(A) specifically does not so authorize.";

(C) by striking "(b) Notwithstanding" and inserting "(b)(1) Notwithstanding";

(D) by striking "paragraph (2)" each place it appears and inserting "paragraph (3)";

(E) by striking "paragraph (1)" each place it appears and inserting "paragraph (2)";

(F) by striking "Such property is—"; and

(G) by adding at the end the following:

"(4) For purposes of paragraph (3)(C) and subsection (d)(12), the following shall apply:

"(A) If the retirement funds are in a retirement fund that has received a favorable determination under section 7805 of the Internal Revenue Code of 1986, and that determination is in effect as of the date of the filing of the petition in a case under this title, those funds shall be presumed to be exempt from the estate.

"(B) If the retirement funds are in a retirement fund that has not received a favorable determination under such section 7805, those funds are exempt from the estate if the debtor demonstrates that—

"(i) no prior determination to the contrary has been made by a court or the Internal Revenue Service; and

"(ii)(I) the retirement fund is in substantial compliance with the applicable requirements of the Internal Revenue Code of 1986; or

"(II) the retirement fund fails to be in substantial compliance with the applicable requirements of the Internal Revenue Code of 1986 and the debtor is not materially responsible for that failure.

"(C) A direct transfer of retirement funds from 1 fund or account that is exempt from taxation under section 401, 403, 408, 408A, 414, 457, or 501(a) of the Internal Revenue Code of 1986, under section 401(a)(31) of the Internal Revenue Code of 1986, or otherwise, shall not cease to qualify for exemption under paragraph (3)(C) or subsection (d)(12) by reason of such direct transfer.

"(D)(i) Any distribution that qualifies as an eligible rollover distribution within the meaning of section 402(c) of the Internal Revenue Code of 1986 or that is described in clause (ii) shall not cease to qualify for exemption under paragraph (3)(C) or subsection (d)(12) by reason of such distribution.

"(ii) A distribution described in this clause is an amount that—

"(I) has been distributed from a fund or account that is exempt from taxation under section 401, 403, 408, 408A, 414, 457, or 501(a) of the Internal Revenue Code of 1986; and

"(II) to the extent allowed by law, is deposited in such a fund or account not later than 60 days after the distribution of such amount."; and

(2) in subsection (d)—

(A) in the matter preceding paragraph (1), by striking "subsection (b)(1)" and inserting "subsection (b)(2)"; and

(B) by adding at the end the following:

"(12) Retirement funds to the extent that those funds are in a fund or account that is exempt from taxation under section 401, 403, 408, 408A, 414, 457, or 501(a) of the Internal Revenue Code of 1986.".

(b) AUTOMATIC STAY—Section 362(b) of title 11, United States Code, is amended—

(1) in paragraph (17), by striking "or" at the end;

(2) in paragraph (18), by striking the period and inserting a semicolon; and

(3) by inserting after paragraph (18) the following:

"(19) under subsection (a), of withholding of income from a debtor's wages and collection of amounts withheld, under the debtor's agreement authorizing that withholding and collection for the benefit of a pension, profit-sharing, stock bonus, or other plan established under section 401, 403, 408, 408A, 414, 457, or 501(c) of the Internal Revenue Code of 1986, that is sponsored by the employer of the debtor, or an affiliate, successor, or predecessor of such employer—

"(A) to the extent that the amounts withheld and collected are used solely for payments relating to a loan from a plan under section 408(b)(1) of the Employee Retirement Income Security Act of 1974 or is subject to section 72(p) of the Internal Revenue Code of 1986; or

"(B) a loan from a thrift savings plan permitted under subchapter III of chapter 84 of title 5, that satisfies the requirements of section 8433(g) of such title;

but nothing in this paragraph may be construed to provide that any loan made under a governmental plan under section 414(d), or a contract or account under section 403(b), of the Internal Revenue Code of 1986 constitutes a claim or a debt under this title;".

(c) EXCEPTIONS TO DISCHARGE—Section 523(a) of title 11, United States Code, as amended by section 215, is amended by inserting after paragraph (17) the following:

"(18) owed to a pension, profit-sharing, stock bonus, or other plan established under section 401, 403, 408, 408A, 414, 457, or 501(c) of the Internal Revenue Code of 1986, under—

"(A) a loan permitted under section 408(b)(1) of the Employee Retirement Income Security Act of 1974, or subject to section 72(p) of the Internal Revenue Code of 1986; or

"(B) a loan from a thrift savings plan permitted under subchapter III of chapter 84 of title 5, that satisfies the requirements of section 8433(g) of such title;

but nothing in this paragraph may be construed to provide that any loan made under a governmental plan under section 414(d), or a contract or account under section 403(b), of the Internal Revenue Code of 1986 constitutes a claim or a debt under this title; or".

(d) PLAN CONTENTS—Section 1322 of title 11, United States Code, is amended by adding at the end the following:

"(f) A plan may not materially alter the terms of a loan described in section 362(b)(19) and any amounts required to repay such loan shall not constitute "disposable income" under section 1325.".

(e) ASSET LIMITATION—

(1) LIMITATION—Section 522 of title 11, United States Code, is amended by adding at the end the following:

"(n) For assets in individual retirement accounts described in section 408 or 408A of the Internal Revenue Code of 1986, other than a simplified employee pension under section 408(k) of such Code or a simple retirement account under section 408(p) of such Code, the aggregate value of such assets exempted under this section, without regard to amounts attributable to rollover contributions under section 402(c), 402(e)(6), 403(a)(4), 403(a)(5), and 403(b)(8) of the Internal Revenue Code of 1986, and earnings thereon, shall not exceed $1,000,000 in a case filed by a debtor who is an individual, except that such amount may be increased if the interests of justice so require.".

(2) ADJUSTMENT OF DOLLAR AMOUNTS—Paragraphs (1) and (2) of section 104(b) of title 11, United States Code, are amended by inserting "522(n)," after "522(d),".

Sec. 225 PROTECTION OF EDUCATION SAVINGS IN BANKRUPTCY.

(a) EXCLUSIONS—Section 541 of title 11, United States Code, is amended—

(1) in subsection (b)—

(A) in paragraph (4), by striking "or" at the end;

(B) by redesignating paragraph (5) as paragraph (9); and

(C) by inserting after paragraph (4) the following:

"(5) funds placed in an education individual retirement account (as defined in section 530(b)(1) of the Internal Revenue Code of 1986) not later than 365 days before the date of the filing of the petition in a case under this title, but—

"(A) only if the designated beneficiary of such account was a child, stepchild, grandchild, or stepgrandchild of the debtor for the taxable year for which funds were placed in such account;

"(B) only to the extent that such funds—

"(i) are not pledged or promised to any entity in connection with any extension of credit; and

"(ii) are not excess contributions (as described in section 4973(e) of the Internal Revenue Code of 1986); and

"(C) in the case of funds placed in all such accounts having the same designated beneficiary not earlier than 720 days nor later than 365 days before such date, only so much of such funds as does not exceed $5,000;

"(6) funds used to purchase a tuition credit or certificate or contributed to an account in accordance with section 529(b)(1)(A) of the Internal Revenue Code of 1986 under a qualified State tuition program (as defined in section 529(b)(1) of such Code) not later than 365 days before the date of the filing of the petition in a case under this title, but—

"(A) only if the designated beneficiary of the amounts paid or contributed to such tuition program was a child, stepchild, grandchild, or stepgrandchild of the debtor for the taxable year for which funds were paid or contributed;

"(B) with respect to the aggregate amount paid or contributed to such program having the same designated beneficiary, only so much of such amount as does not exceed the total contributions permitted under section 529(b)(7) of such Code with respect to such beneficiary, as adjusted beginning on the date of the filing of the petition in a case under this title by the annual increase or decrease (rounded to the nearest tenth of 1 percent) in the education expenditure category of the Consumer Price Index prepared by the Department of Labor; and

"(C) in the case of funds paid or contributed to such program having the same designated beneficiary not earlier than 720 days nor later than 365 days before such date, only so much of such funds as does not exceed $5,000;"; and

(2) by adding at the end the following:

"(e) In determining whether any of the relationships specified in paragraph (5)(A) or (6)(A) of subsection (b) exists, a legally adopted child of an individual (and a child who is a member of an individual's household, if placed with such individual by an authorized placement agency for legal adoption by such individual), or a foster child of an individual (if such child has as the child's principal place of abode the home of the debtor and is a member of the debtor's household) shall be treated as a child of such individual by blood.".

(b) DEBTOR'S DUTIES—Section 521 of title 11, United States Code, as amended by section 106, is amended by adding at the end the following:

"(c) In addition to meeting the requirements under subsection (a), a debtor shall file with the court a record of any interest that a debtor has in an education individual retirement account (as defined in section 530(b)(1) of the Internal Revenue Code of 1986) or under a qualified State tuition program (as defined in section 529(b)(1) of such Code).".

Sec. 226 DEFINITIONS.

(a) DEFINITIONS—Section 101 of title 11, United States Code, is amended—

(1) by inserting after paragraph (2) the following:

"(3) 'assisted person' means any person whose debts consist primarily of consumer debts and the value of whose nonexempt property is less than $150,000;";

(2) by inserting after paragraph (4) the following:

"(4A) 'bankruptcy assistance' means any goods or services sold or otherwise provided to an assisted person with the express or implied purpose of providing information, advice, counsel, document preparation, or filing, or attendance at a creditors' meeting or appearing in a case or proceeding on behalf of another or providing legal representation with respect to a case or proceeding under this title;"; and

(3) by inserting after paragraph (12) the following:

"(12A) 'debt relief agency' means any person who provides any bankruptcy assistance to an assisted person in return for the payment of money or other valuable consideration, or who is a bankruptcy petition preparer under section 110, but does not include—

"(A) any person who is an officer, director, employee, or agent of a person who provides such assistance or of the bankruptcy petition preparer;

"(B) a nonprofit organization that is exempt from taxation under section 501(c)(3) of the Internal Revenue Code of 1986;

"(C) a creditor of such assisted person, to the extent that the creditor is assisting such assisted person to restructure any debt owed by such assisted person to the creditor;

"(D) a depository institution (as defined in section 3 of the Federal Deposit Insurance Act) or any Federal credit union or State credit union (as those terms are defined in section 101 of the Federal Credit Union Act), or any affiliate or subsidiary of such depository institution or credit union; or

"(E) an author, publisher, distributor, or seller of works subject to copyright protection under title 17, when acting in such capacity.".

(b) CONFORMING AMENDMENT—Section 104(b) of title 11, United States Code, is amended by inserting "101(3)," after "sections" each place it appears.

Sec. 227 RESTRICTIONS ON DEBT RELIEF AGENCIES.

(a) ENFORCEMENT—Subchapter II of chapter 5 of title 11, United States Code, is amended by adding at the end the following:

"§ 526. Restrictions on debt relief agencies

"(a) A debt relief agency shall not—

"(1) fail to perform any service that such agency informed an assisted person or prospective assisted person it would provide in connection with a case or proceeding under this title;

"(2) make any statement, or counsel or advise any assisted person or prospective assisted person to make a statement in a document filed in a case or proceeding under this title, that is untrue and misleading, or that upon the exercise of reasonable care, should have been known by such agency to be untrue or misleading;

"(3) misrepresent to any assisted person or prospective assisted person, directly or indirectly, affirmatively or by material omission, with respect to—

"(A) the services that such agency will provide to such person; or

"(B) the benefits and risks that may result if such person becomes a debtor in a case under this title; or

"(4) advise an assisted person or prospective assisted person to incur more debt in contemplation of such person filing a case under this title or to pay an attorney or bankruptcy petition preparer fee or charge for services performed as part of preparing for or representing a debtor in a case under this title.

"(b) Any waiver by any assisted person of any protection or right provided under this section shall not be enforceable against the debtor by any Federal or State court or any other person, but may be enforced against a debt relief agency.

"(c)(1) Any contract for bankruptcy assistance between a debt relief agency and an assisted person that does not comply with the material requirements of this section, section 527, or section 528 shall be void and may not be enforced by any Federal or State court or by any other person, other than such assisted person.

"(2) Any debt relief agency shall be liable to an assisted person in the amount of any fees or charges in connection with providing bankruptcy assistance to such person that such debt relief agency has received, for actual damages, and for reasonable attorneys' fees and costs if such agency is found, after notice and a hearing, to have—

"(A) intentionally or negligently failed to comply with any provision of this section, section 527, or section 528 with respect to a case or proceeding under this title for such assisted person;

"(B) provided bankruptcy assistance to an assisted person in a case or proceeding under this title that is dismissed or converted to a case under another chapter of this title because of such agency's intentional or negligent failure to file any required document including those specified in section 521; or

"(C) intentionally or negligently disregarded the material requirements of this title or the Federal Rules of Bankruptcy Procedure applicable to such agency.

"(3) In addition to such other remedies as are provided under State law, whenever the chief law enforcement officer of a State, or an official or agency designated by a State, has reason to believe that any person has violated or is violating this section, the State—

"(A) may bring an action to enjoin such violation;

"(B) may bring an action on behalf of its residents to recover the actual damages of assisted persons arising from such violation, including any liability under paragraph (2); and

"(C) in the case of any successful action under subparagraph (A) or (B), shall be awarded the costs of the action and reasonable attorneys' fees as determined by the court.

"(4) The district courts of the United States for districts located in the State shall have concurrent jurisdiction of any action under subparagraph (A) or (B) of paragraph (3).

"(5) Notwithstanding any other provision of Federal law and in addition to any other remedy provided under Federal or State law, if the court, on its own motion or on the motion of the United States trustee or the debtor, finds that a person intentionally violated this section, or engaged in a clear and consistent pattern or practice of violating this section, the court may—

"(A) enjoin the violation of such section; or

"(B) impose an appropriate civil penalty against such person.

"(d) No provision of this section, section 527, or section 528 shall—

"(1) annul, alter, affect, or exempt any person subject to such sections from complying with any law of any State except to the extent that such law is inconsistent with those sections, and then only to the extent of the inconsistency; or

"(2) be deemed to limit or curtail the authority or ability—

"(A) of a State or subdivision or instrumentality thereof, to determine and enforce qualifications for the practice of law under the laws of that State; or

"(B) of a Federal court to determine and enforce the qualifications for the practice of law before that court.".

(b) CONFORMING AMENDMENT—The table of sections for chapter 5 of title 11, United States Code, is amended by inserting after the item relating to section 525, the following:

"526. Restrictions on debt relief agencies.".

Sec. 228 Disclosures.

(a) Disclosures—Subchapter II of chapter 5 of title 11, United States Code, as amended by section 227, is amended by adding at the end the following:

"§ 527. Disclosures

"(a) A debt relief agency providing bankruptcy assistance to an assisted person shall provide—

"(1) the written notice required under section 342(b)(1); and

"(2) to the extent not covered in the written notice described in paragraph (1), and not later than 3 business days after the first date on which a debt relief agency first offers to provide any bankruptcy assistance services to an assisted person, a clear and conspicuous written notice advising assisted persons that—

"(A) all information that the assisted person is required to provide with a petition and thereafter during a case under this title is required to be complete, accurate, and truthful;

"(B) all assets and all liabilities are required to be completely and accurately disclosed in the documents filed to commence the case, and the replacement value of each asset as defined in section 506 must be stated in those documents where requested after reasonable inquiry to establish such value;

"(C) current monthly income, the amounts specified in section 707(b)(2), and, in a case under chapter 13 of this title, disposable income (determined in accordance with section 707(b)(2)), are required to be stated after reasonable inquiry; and

"(D) information that an assisted person provides during their case may be audited pursuant to this title, and that failure to provide such information may result in dismissal of the case under this title or other sanction, including a criminal sanction.

"(b) A debt relief agency providing bankruptcy assistance to an assisted person shall provide each assisted person at the same time as the notices required under subsection (a)(1) the following statement, to the extent applicable, or one substantially similar. The statement shall be clear and conspicuous and shall be in a single document separate from other documents or notices provided to the assisted person:

"IMPORTANT INFORMATION ABOUT BANKRUPTCY ASSISTANCE SERVICES FROM AN ATTORNEY OR BANKRUPTCY PETITION PREPARER.

"If you decide to seek bankruptcy relief, you can represent yourself, you can hire an attorney to represent you, or you can get help in some localities from a bankruptcy petition preparer who is not an attorney. THE LAW REQUIRES AN ATTORNEY OR BANKRUPTCY PETITION PREPARER TO GIVE YOU A WRITTEN CONTRACT SPECIFYING WHAT THE ATTORNEY OR BANKRUPTCY PETITION PREPARER WILL DO FOR

YOU AND HOW MUCH IT WILL COST. Ask to see the contract before you hire anyone.

"The following information helps you understand what must be done in a routine bankruptcy case to help you evaluate how much service you need. Although bankruptcy can be complex, many cases are routine.

"Before filing a bankruptcy case, either you or your attorney should analyze your eligibility for different forms of debt relief available under the Bankruptcy Code and which form of relief is most likely to be beneficial for you. Be sure you understand the relief you can obtain and its limitations. To file a bankruptcy case, documents called a Petition, Schedules and Statement of Financial Affairs, as well as in some cases a Statement of Intention need to be prepared correctly and filed with the bankruptcy court. You will have to pay a filing fee to the bankruptcy court. Once your case starts, you will have to attend the required first meeting of creditors where you may be questioned by a court official called a 'trustee' and by creditors.

"If you choose to file a chapter 7 case, you may be asked by a creditor to reaffirm a debt. You may want help deciding whether to do so. A creditor is not permitted to coerce you into reaffirming your debts.

"If you choose to file a chapter 13 case in which you repay your creditors what you can afford over 3 to 5 years, you may also want help with preparing your chapter 13 plan and with the confirmation hearing on your plan which will be before a bankruptcy judge.

"If you select another type of relief under the Bankruptcy Code other than chapter 7 or chapter 13, you will want to find out what should be done from someone familiar with that type of relief.

"Your bankruptcy case may also involve litigation. You are generally permitted to represent yourself in litigation in bankruptcy court, but only attorneys, not bankruptcy petition preparers, can give you legal advice.".

"(c) Except to the extent the debt relief agency provides the required information itself after reasonably diligent inquiry of the assisted person or others so as to obtain such information reasonably accurately for inclusion on the petition, schedules or statement of financial affairs, a debt relief agency providing bankruptcy assistance to an assisted person, to the extent permitted by nonbankruptcy law, shall provide each assisted person at the time required for the notice required under subsection (a)(1) reasonably sufficient information (which shall be provided in a clear and conspicuous writing) to the assisted person on how to provide all the information the assisted person is required to provide under this title pursuant to section 521, including—

"(1) how to value assets at replacement value, determine current monthly income, the amounts specified in section 707(b)(2) and, in a chapter 13 case, how to determine disposable income in accordance with section 707(b)(2) and related calculations;

"(2) how to complete the list of creditors, including how to determine what amount is owed and what address for the creditor should be shown; and

"(3) how to determine what property is exempt and how to value exempt property at replacement value as defined in section 506.

"(d) A debt relief agency shall maintain a copy of the notices required under subsection (a) of this section for 2 years after the date on which the notice is given the assisted person.".

(b) CONFORMING AMENDMENT—The table of sections for chapter 5 of title 11, United States Code, as amended by section 227, is amended by inserting after the item relating to section 526 the following:

"527. Disclosures.".

Sec. 229 REQUIREMENTS FOR DEBT RELIEF AGENCIES.

(a) ENFORCEMENT—Subchapter II of chapter 5 of title 11, United States Code, as amended by sections 227 and 228, is amended by adding at the end the following:

"§ 528. Requirements for debt relief agencies

"(a) A debt relief agency shall—

"(1) not later than 5 business days after the first date on which such agency provides any bankruptcy assistance services to an assisted person, but prior to such assisted person's petition under this title being filed, execute a written contract with such assisted person that explains clearly and conspicuously—

"(A) the services such agency will provide to such assisted person; and

"(B) the fees or charges for such services, and the terms of payment;

"(2) provide the assisted person with a copy of the fully executed and completed contract;

"(3) clearly and conspicuously disclose in any advertisement of bankruptcy assistance services or of the benefits of bankruptcy directed to the general public (whether in general media, seminars or specific mailings, telephonic or electronic messages, or otherwise) that the services or benefits are with respect to bankruptcy relief under this title; and

"(4) clearly and conspicuously use the following statement in such advertisement: 'We are a debt relief agency. We help people file for bankruptcy relief under the Bankruptcy Code.' or a substantially similar statement.

"(b)(1) An advertisement of bankruptcy assistance services or of the benefits of bankruptcy directed to the general public includes—

"(A) descriptions of bankruptcy assistance in connection with a chapter 13 plan whether or not chapter 13 is specifically mentioned in such advertisement; and

"(B) statements such as 'federally supervised repayment plan' or 'Federal debt restructuring help' or other similar statements that could lead a reasonable consumer to believe that debt counseling was being offered when in fact the services were directed to providing bankruptcy assistance with a chapter 13 plan or other form of bankruptcy relief under this title.

"(2) An advertisement, directed to the general public, indicating that the debt relief agency provides assistance with respect to credit defaults, mortgage foreclosures, eviction proceedings, excessive debt, debt collection pressure, or inability to pay any consumer debt shall—

"(A) disclose clearly and conspicuously in such advertisement that the assistance may involve bankruptcy relief under this title; and

"(B) include the following statement: 'We are a debt relief agency. We help people file for bankruptcy relief under the Bankruptcy Code.' or a substantially similar statement.".

(b) CONFORMING AMENDMENT—The table of sections for chapter 5 of title 11, United States Code, as amended by section 227 and 228, is amended by inserting after the item relating to section 527, the following:

"528. Requirements for debt relief agencies.".

Sec. 230 GAO STUDY.

(a) STUDY—Not later than 270 days after the date of enactment of this Act, the Comptroller General of the United States shall conduct a study of the feasibility, effectiveness, and cost of requiring trustees appointed under title 11, United States Code, or the bankruptcy courts, to provide to the Office of Child Support Enforcement promptly after the commencement of cases by debtors who are individuals under such title, the names and social security account numbers of such debtors for the purposes of allowing such Office to determine whether such debtors have outstanding obligations for child support (as determined on the basis of information in the Federal Case Registry or other national database).

(b) REPORT—Not later than 300 days after the date of enactment of this Act, the Comptroller General shall submit to the President pro tempore of the Senate and the Speaker of the House of Representatives a report containing the results of the study required by subsection (a).

Sec. 231 PROTECTION OF PERSONALLY IDENTIFIABLE INFORMATION.

(a) LIMITATION—Section 363(b)(1) of title 11, United States Code, is amended by striking the period at the end and inserting the following:

", except that if the debtor in connection with offering a product or a service discloses to an individual a policy prohibiting the transfer of personally identifiable information about individuals to persons that are not affiliated with the debtor and if such policy is in effect on the date of the commencement of the case, then the trustee may not sell or lease personally identifiable information to any person unless—

"(A) such sale or such lease is consistent with such policy; or

"(B) after appointment of a consumer privacy ombudsman in accordance with section 332, and after notice and a hearing, the court approves such sale or such lease—

"(i) giving due consideration to the facts, circumstances, and conditions of such sale or such lease; and

"(ii) finding that no showing was made that such sale or such lease would violate applicable nonbankruptcy law.".

(b) DEFINITION—Section 101 of title 11, United States Code, is amended by inserting after paragraph (41) the following:

"(41A) 'personally identifiable information' means—

"(A) if provided by an individual to the debtor in connection with obtaining a product or a service from the debtor primarily for personal, family, or household purposes—

"(i) the first name (or initial) and last name of such individual, whether given at birth or time of adoption, or resulting from a lawful change of name;

"(ii) the geographical address of a physical place of residence of such individual;

"(iii) an electronic address (including an e-mail address) of such individual;

"(iv) a telephone number dedicated to contacting such individual at such physical place of residence;

"(v) a social security account number issued to such individual; or

"(vi) the account number of a credit card issued to such individual; or

"(B) if identified in connection with 1 or more of the items of information specified in subparagraph (A)—

"(i) a birth date, the number of a certificate of birth or adoption, or a place of birth; or

"(ii) any other information concerning an identified individual that, if disclosed, will result in contacting or identifying such individual physically or electronically;".

Sec. 232 CONSUMER PRIVACY OMBUDSMAN.

(a) CONSUMER PRIVACY OMBUDSMAN—Title 11 of the United States Code is amended by inserting after section 331 the following:

"§ 332. Consumer privacy ombudsman

"(a) If a hearing is required under section 363(b)(1)(B), the court shall order the United States trustee to appoint, not later than 5 days before the commencement of the hearing, 1 disinterested person (other than the United States trustee) to serve as the consumer privacy ombudsman in the case and shall require that notice of such hearing be timely given to such ombudsman.

"(b) The consumer privacy ombudsman may appear and be heard at such hearing and shall provide to the court information to assist the court in its consideration of the facts, circumstances, and conditions of the proposed sale or lease of personally identifiable information under section 363(b)(1)(B). Such information may include presentation of—

"(1) the debtor's privacy policy;

"(2) the potential losses or gains of privacy to consumers if such sale or such lease is approved by the court;

"(3) the potential costs or benefits to consumers if such sale or such lease is approved by the court; and

"(4) the potential alternatives that would mitigate potential privacy losses or potential costs to consumers.

"(c) A consumer privacy ombudsman shall not disclose any personally identifiable information obtained by the ombudsman under this title.".

(b) COMPENSATION OF CONSUMER PRIVACY OMBUDSMAN—Section 330(a)(1) of title 11, United States Code, is amended in the matter preceding subparagraph (A), by inserting "a consumer privacy ombudsman appointed under section 332," before "an examiner".

(c) CONFORMING AMENDMENT—The table of sections for subchapter II of chapter 3 of title 11, United States Code, is amended by adding at the end the following:

"332. Consumer privacy ombudsman.".

Sec. 233 PROHIBITION ON DISCLOSURE OF NAME OF MINOR CHILDREN.

(a) PROHIBITION—Title 11 of the United States Code, as amended by section 106, is amended by inserting after section 111 the following:

"§ 112. Prohibition on disclosure of name of minor children

"The debtor may be required to provide information regarding a minor child involved in matters under this title but may not be required to disclose in the public records in the case the name of such minor child. The debtor may be required to disclose the name of such minor child in a nonpublic record that is maintained by the court and made available by the court for examination by the United States trustee, the trustee, and the auditor (if any) serving under section 586(f) of title 28, in the case. The court, the United States trustee, the trustee, and such auditor shall not disclose the name of such minor child maintained in such nonpublic record.".

(b) CLERICAL AMENDMENT—The table of sections for chapter 1 of title 11, United States Code, as amended by section 106, is amended by inserting after the item relating to section 111 the following:

"112. Prohibition on disclosure of name of minor children.".

(c) CONFORMING AMENDMENT—Section 107(a) of title 11, United States Code, is amended by inserting "and subject to section 112" after "section".

Sec. 234 PROTECTION OF PERSONAL INFORMATION.

(a) RESTRICTION OF PUBLIC ACCESS TO CERTAIN INFORMATION CONTAINED IN BANKRUPTCY CASE FILES—Section 107 of title 11, United States Code, is amended by adding at the end the following:

"(c)(1) The bankruptcy court, for cause, may protect an individual, with respect to the following types of information to the extent the court finds that disclosure of such information would create undue risk of identity theft or other unlawful injury to the individual or the individual's property:

"(A) Any means of identification (as defined in section 1028(d) of title 18) contained in a paper filed, or to be filed, in a case under this title.

"(B) Other information contained in a paper described in subparagraph (A).

"(2) Upon ex parte application demonstrating cause, the court shall provide access to information protected pursuant to paragraph (1) to an entity acting pursuant to the police or regulatory power of a domestic governmental unit.

"(3) The United States trustee, bankruptcy administrator, trustee, and any auditor serving under section 586(f) of title 28—

"(A) shall have full access to all information contained in any paper filed or submitted in a case under this title; and

"(B) shall not disclose information specifically protected by the court under this title.".

(b) SECURITY OF SOCIAL SECURITY ACCOUNT NUMBER OF DEBTOR IN NOTICE TO CREDITOR—Section 342(c) of title 11, United States Code, is amended—

(1) by inserting "last 4 digits of the" before "taxpayer identification number"; and

(2) by adding at the end the following: "If the notice concerns an amendment that adds a creditor to the schedules of assets and liabilities, the debtor shall include the full taxpayer identification number in the notice sent to that creditor, but the debtor shall include only the last 4 digits of the taxpayer identification number in the copy of the notice filed with the court.".

(c) Conforming Amendment—Section 107(a) of title 11, United States Code, is amended by striking "subsection (b)," and inserting "subsections (b) and (c),".

TITLE III

DISCOURAGING BANKRUPTCY ABUSE

Sec. 301 TECHNICAL AMENDMENTS.

Section 523(a)(17) of title 11, United States Code, is amended—

(1) by striking "by a court" and inserting "on a prisoner by any court";

(2) by striking "section 1915(b) or (f)" and inserting "subsection (b) or (f)(2) of section 1915"; and

(3) by inserting "(or a similar non-Federal law)" after "title 28" each place it appears.

Sec. 302 DISCOURAGING BAD FAITH REPEAT FILINGS.

Section 362(c) of title 11, United States Code, is amended—

(1) in paragraph (1), by striking "and" at the end;

(2) in paragraph (2), by striking the period at the end and inserting a semicolon; and

(3) by adding at the end the following:

"(3) if a single or joint case is filed by or against debtor who is an individual in a case under chapter 7, 11, or 13, and if a single or joint case of the debtor was pending within the preceding 1-year period but was dismissed, other than a case refiled under a chapter other than chapter 7 after dismissal under section 707(b)—

"(A) the stay under subsection (a) with respect to any action taken with respect to a debt or property securing such debt or with respect to any lease shall terminate with respect to the debtor on the 30th day after the filing of the later case;

"(B) on the motion of a party in interest for continuation of the automatic stay and upon notice and a hearing, the court may extend the stay in particular cases as to any or all creditors (subject to such conditions or limitations as the court may then impose) after notice and a hearing completed before the expiration of the 30-day period only if the party in interest demonstrates that the filing of the later case is in good faith as to the creditors to be stayed; and

"(C) for purposes of subparagraph (B), a case is presumptively filed not in good faith (but such presumption may be rebutted by clear and convincing evidence to the contrary)—

"(i) as to all creditors, if—

"(I) more than 1 previous case under any of chapters 7, 11, and 13 in which the individual was a debtor was pending within the preceding 1-year period;

"(II) a previous case under any of chapters 7, 11, and 13 in which the individual was a debtor was dismissed within such 1-year period, after the debtor failed to—

"(aa) file or amend the petition or other documents as required by this title or the court without substantial excuse (but mere inadvertence or negligence shall not be a substantial excuse unless the dismissal was caused by the negligence of the debtor's attorney);

"(bb) provide adequate protection as ordered by the court; or

"(cc) perform the terms of a plan confirmed by the court; or

"(III) there has not been a substantial change in the financial or personal affairs of the debtor since the dismissal of the next most previous case under chapter 7, 11, or 13 or any other reason to conclude that the later case will be concluded—

"(aa) if a case under chapter 7, with a discharge; or

"(bb) if a case under chapter 11 or 13, with a confirmed plan that will be fully performed; and

"(ii) as to any creditor that commenced an action under subsection (d) in a previous case in which the individual was a debtor if, as of the date of dismissal of such case, that action was still pending or had been resolved by terminating, conditioning, or limiting the stay as to actions of such creditor; and

"(4)(A)(i) if a single or joint case is filed by or against a debtor who is an individual under this title, and if 2 or more single or joint cases of the debtor were pending within the previous year but were dismissed, other than a case refiled under section 707(b), the stay under subsection (a) shall not go into effect upon the filing of the later case; and

"(ii) on request of a party in interest, the court shall promptly enter an order confirming that no stay is in effect;

"(B) if, within 30 days after the filing of the later case, a party in interest requests the court may order the stay to take effect in the case as to any or all creditors (subject to such conditions or limitations as the court may impose), after notice and a hearing, only if the party in interest demonstrates that the filing of the later case is in good faith as to the creditors to be stayed;

"(C) a stay imposed under subparagraph (B) shall be effective on the date of the entry of the order allowing the stay to go into effect; and

"(D) for purposes of subparagraph (B), a case is presumptively filed not in good faith (but such presumption may be rebutted by clear and convincing evidence to the contrary)—

"(i) as to all creditors if—

"(I) 2 or more previous cases under this title in which the individual was a debtor were pending within the 1-year period;

"(II) a previous case under this title in which the individual was a debtor was dismissed within the time period stated in this paragraph after the debtor failed to file or amend the petition or other documents as required by this title or the court without substantial excuse (but mere inadvertence or negligence shall not be substantial excuse unless the dismissal was caused by the negligence of the debtor's attorney), failed to provide adequate protection as ordered by the court, or failed to perform the terms of a plan confirmed by the court; or

"(III) there has not been a substantial change in the financial or personal affairs of the debtor since the dismissal of the next most previous case under this title, or any other reason to conclude that the later case will not be concluded, if a case under chapter 7, with a discharge, and if a case under chapter 11 or 13, with a confirmed plan that will be fully performed; or

"(ii) as to any creditor that commenced an action under subsection (d) in a previous case in which the individual was a debtor if, as of the date of dismissal of such case, such action was still pending or had been resolved by terminating, conditioning, or limiting the stay as to such action of such creditor.".

Sec. 303 CURBING ABUSIVE FILINGS.

(a) IN GENERAL—Section 362(d) of title 11, United States Code, is amended—

(1) in paragraph (2), by striking "or" at the end;

(2) in paragraph (3), by striking the period at the end and inserting "; or"; and

(3) by adding at the end the following:

"(4) with respect to a stay of an act against real property under subsection (a), by a creditor whose claim is secured by an interest in such real property, if the court finds that the filing of the petition was part of a scheme to delay, hinder, and defraud creditors that involved either—

"(A) transfer of all or part ownership of, or other interest in, such real property without the consent of the secured creditor or court approval; or

"(B) multiple bankruptcy filings affecting such real property.

If recorded in compliance with applicable State laws governing notices of interests or liens in real property, an order entered under paragraph (4) shall be binding in any other case under this title purporting to affect such real property filed not later than 2 years after the date of the entry of such order by the court, except that a debtor in a subsequent case under this title may move for relief from such order based upon changed circumstances or for good cause shown, after notice and a hearing. Any Federal, State, or local governmental unit that accepts notices of interests or liens in real property shall accept any certified copy of an order described in this subsection for indexing and recording.".

(b) AUTOMATIC STAY—Section 362(b) of title 11, United States Code, as amended by section 224, is amended by inserting after paragraph (19), the following:

"(20) under subsection (a), of any act to enforce any lien against or security interest in real property following entry of the order under subsection (d)(4) as to such real property in any prior case under this title, for a period of 2 years after the date of the entry of such an order, except that the debtor, in a subsequent case under this title, may move for relief from such order based upon changed circumstances or for other good cause shown, after notice and a hearing;

"(21) under subsection (a), of any act to enforce any lien against or security interest in real property—

"(A) if the debtor is ineligible under section 109(g) to be a debtor in a case under this title; or

"(B) if the case under this title was filed in violation of a bankruptcy court order in a prior case under this title prohibiting the debtor from being a debtor in another case under this title;".

Sec. 304 DEBTOR RETENTION OF PERSONAL PROPERTY SECURITY.

Title 11, United States Code, is amended—

(1) in section 521(a), as so designated by section 106—

(A) in paragraph (4), by striking ", and" at the end and inserting a semicolon;

(B) in paragraph (5), by striking the period at the end and inserting "; and"; and

(C) by adding at the end the following:

"(6) in a case under chapter 7 of this title in which the debtor is an individual, not retain possession of personal property as to which a creditor has an allowed claim for the purchase price secured in whole or in part by an interest in such personal property unless the debtor, not later than 45 days after the first meeting of creditors under section 341(a), either—

"(A) enters into an agreement with the creditor pursuant to section 524(c) with respect to the claim secured by such property; or

"(B) redeems such property from the security interest pursuant to section 722.

If the debtor fails to so act within the 45-day period referred to in paragraph (6), the stay under section 362(a) is terminated with respect to the personal property of the estate or of the debtor which is affected, such property shall no longer be property of the estate, and the creditor may take whatever action as to such property as is permitted by applicable nonbankruptcy law, unless the court determines on the motion of the trustee filed before the expiration of such 45-day period, and after notice and a hearing, that such property is of consequential value or benefit to the estate, orders appropriate adequate protection of the creditor's interest, and orders the debtor to deliver any collateral in the debtor's possession to the trustee."; and

(2) in section 722, by inserting "in full at the time of redemption" before the period at the end.

Sec. 305 Relief From the Automatic Stay When the Debtor Does Not Complete Intended Surrender of Consumer Debt Collateral.

Title 11, United States Code, is amended—

(1) in section 362, as amended by section 106—

(A) in subsection (c), by striking "(e), and (f)" and inserting "(e), (f), and (h)";

(B) by redesignating subsection (h) as subsection (k) and transferring such subsection so as to insert it after subsection (j) as added by section 106; and

(C) by inserting after subsection (g) the following:

"(h)(1) In a case in which the debtor is an individual, the stay provided by subsection (a) is terminated with respect to personal property of the estate or of the debtor securing in whole or in part a claim, or subject to an unexpired lease, and such personal property shall no longer be property of the estate if the debtor fails within the applicable time set by section 521(a)(2)—

"(A) to file timely any statement of intention required under section 521(a)(2) with respect to such personal property or to indicate in such statement that the debtor will either surrender such personal property or retain it and, if retaining such personal property, either redeem such personal property pursuant to section 722, enter into an agreement of the kind specified in section 524(c) applicable to the debt secured by such personal property, or assume such unexpired lease pursuant to section 365(p) if the trustee does not do so, as applicable; and

"(B) to take timely the action specified in such statement, as it may be amended before expiration of the period for taking action, unless such statement specifies the debtor's intention to reaffirm such debt on the original contract terms and the creditor refuses to agree to the reaffirmation on such terms.

"(2) Paragraph (1) does not apply if the court determines, on the motion of the trustee filed before the expiration of the applicable time set by section

521(a)(2), after notice and a hearing, that such personal property is of consequential value or benefit to the estate, and orders appropriate adequate protection of the creditor's interest, and orders the debtor to deliver any collateral in the debtor's possession to the trustee. If the court does not so determine, the stay provided by subsection (a) shall terminate upon the conclusion of the hearing on the motion."; and

(2) in section 521, as amended by sections 106 and 225—

(A) in subsection (a)(2) by striking "consumer";

(B) in subsection (a)(2)(B)—

(i) by striking "forty-five days after the filing of a notice of intent under this section" and inserting "30 days after the first date set for the meeting of creditors under section 341(a)"; and

(ii) by striking "forty-five day" and inserting "30-day";

(C) in subsection (a)(2)(C) by inserting ", except as provided in section 362(h)" before the semicolon; and

(D) by adding at the end the following:

"(d) If the debtor fails timely to take the action specified in subsection (a)(6) of this section, or in paragraphs (1) and (2) of section 362(h), with respect to property which a lessor or bailor owns and has leased, rented, or bailed to the debtor or as to which a creditor holds a security interest not otherwise voidable under section 522(f), 544, 545, 547, 548, or 549, nothing in this title shall prevent or limit the operation of a provision in the underlying lease or agreement that has the effect of placing the debtor in default under such lease or agreement by reason of the occurrence, pendency, or existence of a proceeding under this title or the insolvency of the debtor. Nothing in this subsection shall be deemed to justify limiting such a provision in any other circumstance.".

Sec. 306 GIVING SECURED CREDITORS FAIR TREATMENT IN CHAPTER 13.

(a) IN GENERAL—Section 1325(a)(5)(B)(i) of title 11, United States Code, is amended to read as follows:

"(i) the plan provides that—

"(I) the holder of such claim retain the lien securing such claim until the earlier of—

"(aa) the payment of the underlying debt determined under nonbankruptcy law; or

"(bb) discharge under section 1328; and

"(II) if the case under this chapter is dismissed or converted without completion of the plan, such lien shall also be retained by such holder to the extent recognized by applicable nonbankruptcy law; and".

(b) RESTORING THE FOUNDATION FOR SECURED CREDIT—Section 1325(a) of title 11, United States Code, is amended by adding at the end the following:

"For purposes of paragraph (5), section 506 shall not apply to a claim described in that paragraph if the creditor has a purchase money security interest securing the debt that is the subject of the claim, the debt was incurred within the 910-day preceding the date of the filing of the petition, and the collateral for that debt consists of a motor vehicle (as defined in section 30102 of title 49) acquired for the personal use of the debtor, or if collateral for that debt consists of any other thing of value, if the debt was incurred during the 1-year period preceding that filing.".

(c) DEFINITIONS—Section 101 of title 11, United States Code, is amended—

(1) by inserting after paragraph (13) the following:

"(13A) 'debtor's principal residence'—

"(A) means a residential structure, including incidental property, without regard to whether that structure is attached to real property; and

"(B) includes an individual condominium or cooperative unit, a mobile or manufactured home, or trailer;"; and

(2) by inserting after paragraph (27), the following:

"(27A) 'incidental property' means, with respect to a debtor's principal residence—

"(A) property commonly conveyed with a principal residence in the area where the real property is located;

"(B) all easements, rights, appurtenances, fixtures, rents, royalties, mineral rights, oil or gas rights or profits, water rights, escrow funds, or insurance proceeds; and

"(C) all replacements or additions;".

Sec. 307 DOMICILIARY REQUIREMENTS FOR EXEMPTIONS.

Section 522(b)(3) of title 11, United States Code, as so designated by section 106, is amended—

(1) in subparagraph (A)—

(A) by striking "180 days" and inserting "730 days"; and

(B) by striking ", or for a longer portion of such 180-day period than in any other place" and inserting "or if the debtor's domicile has not been located at a single State for such 730-day period, the place in which the debtor's domicile was located for 180 days immediately preceding the 730-day period or for a longer portion of such 180-day period than in any other place"; and

(2) by adding at the end the following:

"If the effect of the domiciliary requirement under subparagraph (A) is to render the debtor ineligible for any exemption, the debtor may elect to exempt property that is specified under subsection (d).".

Sec. 308 Reduction of Homestead Exemption for Fraud.

Section 522 of title 11, United States Code, as amended by section 224, is amended—

(1) in subsection (b)(3)(A), as so designated by this Act, by inserting "subject to subsections (o) and (p)," before "any property"; and

(2) by adding at the end the following:

"(o) For purposes of subsection (b)(3)(A), and notwithstanding subsection (a), the value of an interest in—

"(1) real or personal property that the debtor or a dependent of the debtor uses as a residence;

"(2) a cooperative that owns property that the debtor or a dependent of the debtor uses as a residence;

"(3) a burial plot for the debtor or a dependent of the debtor; or

"(4) real or personal property that the debtor or a dependent of the debtor claims as a homestead;

shall be reduced to the extent that such value is attributable to any portion of any property that the debtor disposed of in the 10-year period ending on the date of the filing of the petition with the intent to hinder, delay, or defraud a creditor and that the debtor could not exempt, or that portion that the debtor could not exempt, under subsection (b), if on such date the debtor had held the property so disposed of.".

Sec. 309 Protecting Secured Creditors in Chapter 13 Cases.

(a) Stopping Abusive Conversions from Chapter 13—Section 348(f)(1) of title 11, United States Code, is amended—

(1) in subparagraph (A), by striking "and" at the end;

(2) in subparagraph (B)—

(A) by striking "in the converted case, with allowed secured claims" and inserting "only in a case converted to a case under chapter 11 or 12, but not in a case converted to a case under chapter 7, with allowed secured claims in cases under chapters 11 and 12"; and

(B) by striking the period and inserting "; and"; and

(3) by adding at the end the following:

"(C) with respect to cases converted from chapter 13—

"(i) the claim of any creditor holding security as of the date of the petition shall continue to be secured by that security unless the full amount of such claim determined under applicable nonbankruptcy law has been paid in full as of the date of conversion, notwithstanding any valuation or determination of the amount of an allowed secured claim made for the purposes of the case under chapter 13; and "(ii) unless a prebankruptcy default has been fully cured under the plan at the time of conversion, in any proceeding under this title or otherwise, the default shall have the effect given under applicable nonbankruptcy law.".

(b) Giving Debtors the Ability to Keep Leased Personal Property by Assumption—Section 365 of title 11, United States Code, is amended by adding at the end the following:

"(p)(1) If a lease of personal property is rejected or not timely assumed by the trustee under subsection (d), the leased property is no longer property of the estate and the stay under section 362(a) is automatically terminated.

"(2)(A) If the debtor in a case under chapter 7 is an individual, the debtor may notify the creditor in writing that the debtor desires to assume the lease. Upon being so notified, the creditor may, at its option, notify the debtor that it is willing to have the lease assumed by the debtor and may condition such assumption on cure of any outstanding default on terms set by the contract.

"(B) If, not later than 30 days after notice is provided under subparagraph (A), the debtor notifies the lessor in writing that the lease is assumed, the liability under the lease will be assumed by the debtor and not by the estate.

"(C) The stay under section 362 and the injunction under section 524(a)(2) shall not be violated by notification of the debtor and negotiation of cure under this subsection.

"(3) In a case under chapter 11 in which the debtor is an individual and in a case under chapter 13, if the debtor is the lessee with respect to personal property and the lease is not assumed in the plan confirmed by the court, the lease is deemed rejected as of the conclusion of the hearing on confirmation. If the lease is rejected, the stay under section 362 and any stay under section 1301 is automatically terminated with respect to the property subject to the lease.".

(c) Adequate Protection of Lessors and Purchase Money Secured Creditors—

(1) Confirmation of Plan—Section 1325(a)(5)(B) of title 11, United States Code, as amended by section 306, is amended—

(A) in clause (i), by striking "and" at the end;

(B) in clause (ii), by striking "or" at the end and inserting "and"; and

(C) by adding at the end the following:

"(iii) if—

"(I) property to be distributed pursuant to this subsection is in the form of periodic payments, such payments shall be in equal monthly amounts; and

"(II) the holder of the claim is secured by personal property, the amount of such payments shall not be less than an amount sufficient to provide to the holder of such claim adequate protection during the period of the plan; or".

(2) PAYMENTS—Section 1326(a) of title 11, United States Code, is amended to read as follows:

"(a)(1) Unless the court orders otherwise, the debtor shall commence making payments not later than 30 days after the date of the filing of the plan or the order for relief, whichever is earlier, in the amount—

"(A) proposed by the plan to the trustee;

"(B) scheduled in a lease of personal property directly to the lessor for that portion of the obligation that becomes due after the order for relief, reducing the payments under subparagraph (A) by the amount so paid and providing the trustee with evidence of such payment, including the amount and date of payment; and

"(C) that provides adequate protection directly to a creditor holding an allowed claim secured by personal property to the extent the claim is attributable to the purchase of such property by the debtor for that portion of the obligation that becomes due after the order for relief, reducing the payments under subparagraph (A) by the amount so paid and providing the trustee with evidence of such payment, including the amount and date of payment.

"(2) A payment made under paragraph (1)(A) shall be retained by the trustee until confirmation or denial of confirmation. If a plan is confirmed, the trustee shall distribute any such payment in accordance with the plan as soon as is practicable. If a plan is not confirmed, the trustee shall return any such payments not previously paid and not yet due and owing to creditors pursuant to paragraph (3) to the debtor, after deducting any unpaid claim allowed under section 503(b).

"(3) Subject to section 363, the court may, upon notice and a hearing, modify, increase, or reduce the payments required under this subsection pending confirmation of a plan.

"(4) Not later than 60 days after the date of filing of a case under this chapter, a debtor retaining possession of personal property subject to a lease or securing a claim attributable in whole or in part to the purchase price of such property shall provide the lessor or secured creditor reasonable evidence of the maintenance of any required insurance coverage with respect to the use or ownership of such property and continue to do so for so long as the debtor retains possession of such property.".

Sec. 310 LIMITATION ON LUXURY GOODS.

Section 523(a)(2)(C) of title 11, United States Code, is amended to read as follows:

"(C)(i) for purposes of subparagraph (A)—

"(I) consumer debts owed to a single creditor and aggregating more than $500 for luxury goods or services incurred by an individual debtor on or within 90 days before the order for relief under this title are presumed to be nondischargeable; and

"(II) cash advances aggregating more than $750 that are extensions of consumer credit under an open end credit plan obtained by an individual debtor on or within 70 days before the order for relief under this title, are presumed to be nondischargeable; and

"(ii) for purposes of this subparagraph—

"(I) the terms 'consumer', 'credit', and 'open end credit plan' have the same meanings as in section 103 of the Truth in Lending Act; and

"(II) the term 'luxury goods or services' does not include goods or services reasonably necessary for the support or maintenance of the debtor or a dependent of the debtor.".

Sec. 311 AUTOMATIC STAY.

(a) IN GENERAL—Section 362(b) of title 11, United States Code, as amended by sections 224 and 303, is amended by inserting after paragraph (21), the following:

"(22) subject to subsection (l), under subsection (a)(3), of the continuation of any eviction, unlawful detainer action, or similar proceeding by a lessor against a debtor involving residential property in which the debtor resides as a tenant under a lease or rental agreement and with respect to which the lessor has obtained before the date of the filing of the bankruptcy petition, a judgment for possession of such property against the debtor;

"(23) subject to subsection (m), under subsection (a)(3), of an eviction action that seeks possession of the residential property in which the debtor resides as a tenant under a lease or rental agreement based on endangerment of such property or the illegal use of controlled substances on such property, but only if the lessor files with the court, and serves upon the debtor, a certification under penalty of perjury that such an eviction action has been filed, or that the debtor, during the 30-day period preceding the date of the filing of the certification, has endangered property or illegally used or allowed to be used a controlled substance on the property;

"(24) under subsection (a), of any transfer that is not avoidable under section 544 and that is not avoidable under section 549;".

(b) LIMITATIONS—Section 362 of title 11, United States Code, as amended by sections 106 and 305, is amended by adding at the end the following:

"(l)(1) Except as otherwise provided in this subsection, subsection (b)(22) shall apply on the date that is 30 days after the date on which the bankruptcy petition is filed, if the debtor files with the petition and serves upon the lessor a certification under penalty of perjury that—

"(A) under nonbankruptcy law applicable in the jurisdiction, there are circumstances under which the debtor would be permitted to cure the entire monetary default that gave rise to the judgment for possession, after that judgment for possession was entered; and

"(B) the debtor (or an adult dependent of the debtor) has deposited with the clerk of the court, any rent that would become due during the 30-day period after the filing of the bankruptcy petition.

"(2) If, within the 30-day period after the filing of the bankruptcy petition, the debtor (or an adult dependent of the debtor) complies with paragraph (1) and files with the court and serves upon the lessor a further certification under penalty of perjury that the debtor (or an adult dependent of the debtor) has cured, under nonbankrupcty law applicable in the jurisdiction, the entire monetary default that gave rise to the judgment under which possession is sought by the lessor, subsection (b)(22) shall not apply, unless ordered to apply by the court under paragraph (3).

"(3)(A) If the lessor files an objection to any certification filed by the debtor under paragraph (1) or (2), and serves such objection upon the debtor, the court shall hold a hearing within 10 days after the filing and service of such objection to determine if the certification filed by the debtor under paragraph (1) or (2) is true.

"(B) If the court upholds the objection of the lessor filed under subparagraph (A)—

"(i) subsection (b)(22) shall apply immediately and relief from the stay provided under subsection (a)(3) shall not be required to enable the lessor to complete the process to recover full possession of the property; and

"(ii) the clerk of the court shall immediately serve upon the lessor and the debtor a certified copy of the court's order upholding the lessor's objection.

"(4) If a debtor, in accordance with paragraph (5), indicates on the petition that there was a judgment for possession of the residential rental property in which the debtor resides and does not file a certification under paragraph (1) or (2)—

"(A) subsection (b)(22) shall apply immediately upon failure to file such certification, and relief from the stay provided under subsection (a)(3) shall not be required to enable the lessor to complete the process to recover full possession of the property; and

"(B) the clerk of the court shall immediately serve upon the lessor and the debtor a certified copy of the docket indicating the absence of a filed certification and the applicability of the exception to the stay under subsection (b)(22).

"(5)(A) Where a judgment for possession of residential property in which the debtor resides as a tenant under a lease or rental agreement has been obtained by the lessor, the debtor shall so indicate on the bankruptcy petition and shall provide the name and address of the lessor that obtained that pre-petition judgment on the petition and on any certification filed under this subsection.

"(B) The form of certification filed with the petition, as specified in this subsection, shall provide for the debtor to certify, and the debtor shall certify—

"(i) whether a judgment for possession of residential rental housing in which the debtor resides has been obtained against the debtor before the date of the filing of the petition; and

"(ii) whether the debtor is claiming under paragraph (1) that under nonbankruptcy law applicable in the jurisdiction, there are circumstances under which the debtor would be permitted to cure the entire monetary default that gave rise to the judgment for possession, after that judgment of possession was entered, and has made the appropriate deposit with the court.

"(C) The standard forms (electronic and otherwise) used in a bankruptcy proceeding shall be amended to reflect the requirements of this subsection.

"(D) The clerk of the court shall arrange for the prompt transmittal of the rent deposited in accordance with paragraph (1)(B) to the lessor.

"(m)(1) Except as otherwise provided in this subsection, subsection (b)(23) shall apply on the date that is 15 days after the date on which the lessor files and serves a certification described in subsection (b)(23).

"(2)(A) If the debtor files with the court an objection to the truth or legal sufficiency of the certification described in subsection (b)(23) and serves such objection upon the lessor, subsection (b)(23) shall not apply, unless ordered to apply by the court under this subsection.

"(B) If the debtor files and serves the objection under subparagraph (A), the court shall hold a hearing within 10 days after the filing and service of such objection to determine if the situation giving rise to the lessor's certification under paragraph (1) existed or has been remedied.

"(C) If the debtor can demonstrate to the satisfaction of the court that the situation giving rise to the lessor's certification under paragraph (1) did not exist or has been remedied, the stay provided under subsection (a)(3) shall remain in effect until the termination of the stay under this section.

"(D) If the debtor cannot demonstrate to the satisfaction of the court that the situation giving rise to the lessor's certification under paragraph (1) did not exist or has been remedied—

"(i) relief from the stay provided under subsection (a)(3) shall not be required to enable the lessor to proceed with the eviction; and

"(ii) the clerk of the court shall immediately serve upon the lessor and the debtor a certified copy of the court's order upholding the lessor's certification.

"(3) If the debtor fails to file, within 15 days, an objection under paragraph (2)(A)—

"(A) subsection (b)(23) shall apply immediately upon such failure and relief from the stay provided under subsection (a)(3) shall not be required to enable the lessor to complete the process to recover full possession of the property; and

"(B) the clerk of the court shall immediately serve upon the lessor and the debtor a certified copy of the docket indicating such failure.".

Sec. 312 EXTENSION OF PERIOD BETWEEN BANKRUPTCY DISCHARGES.

Title 11, United States Code, is amended—

(1) in section 727(a)(8), by striking "six" and inserting "8"; and

(2) in section 1328, by inserting after subsection (e) the following:

"(f) Notwithstanding subsections (a) and (b), the court shall not grant a discharge of all debts provided for in the plan or disallowed under section 502, if the debtor has received a discharge—

"(1) in a case filed under chapter 7, 11, or 12 of this title during the 4-year period preceding the date of the order for relief under this chapter, or

"(2) in a case filed under chapter 13 of this title during the 2-year period preceding the date of such order.".

Sec. 313 DEFINITION OF HOUSEHOLD GOODS AND ANTIQUES.

(a) DEFINITION—Section 522(f) of title 11, United States Code, is amended by adding at the end the following:

"(4)(A) Subject to subparagraph (B), for purposes of paragraph (1)(B), the term 'household goods' means—

"(i) clothing;

"(ii) furniture;

"(iii) appliances;

"(iv) 1 radio;

"(v) 1 television;

"(vi) 1 VCR;

"(vii) linens;

"(viii) china;

"(ix) crockery;

"(x) kitchenware;

"(xi) educational materials and educational equipment primarily for the use of minor dependent children of the debtor;

"(xii) medical equipment and supplies;

"(xiii) furniture exclusively for the use of minor children, or elderly or disabled dependents of the debtor;

"(xiv) personal effects (including the toys and hobby equipment of minor dependent children and wedding rings) of the debtor and the dependents of the debtor; and "(xv) 1 personal computer and related equipment.

"(B) The term 'household goods' does not include—

"(i) works of art (unless by or of the debtor, or any relative of the debtor);

"(ii) electronic entertainment equipment with a fair market value of more than $500 in the aggregate (except 1 television, 1 radio, and 1 VCR);

"(iii) items acquired as antiques with a fair market value of more than $500 in the aggregate;

"(iv) jewelry with a fair market value of more than $500 in the aggregate (except wedding rings); and

"(v) a computer (except as otherwise provided for in this section), motor vehicle (including a tractor or lawn tractor), boat, or a motorized recreational device, conveyance, vehicle, watercraft, or aircraft.".

(b) STUDY—Not later than 2 years after the date of enactment of this Act, the Director of the Executive Office for United States Trustees shall submit a report to the Committee on the Judiciary of the Senate and the Committee on the Judiciary of the House of Representatives containing its findings regarding utilization of the definition of household goods, as defined in section 522(f)(4) of title 11, United States Code, as added by subsection (a), with respect to the avoidance of nonpossessory, nonpurchase money security interests in household goods under section 522(f)(1)(B) of title 11, United States Code, and the impact such section 522(f)(4) has had on debtors and on the bankruptcy courts. Such report may include recommendations for amendments to such section 522(f)(4) consistent with the Director's findings.

Sec. 314 DEBT INCURRED TO PAY NONDISCHARGEABLE DEBTS.

(a) IN GENERAL—Section 523(a) of title 11, United States Code, is amended by inserting after paragraph (14) the following:

"(14A) incurred to pay a tax to a governmental unit, other than the United States, that would be nondischargeable under paragraph (1);".

(b) DISCHARGE UNDER CHAPTER 13—Section 1328(a) of title 11, United States Code, is amended by striking paragraphs (1) through (3) and inserting the following:

"(1) provided for under section 1322(b)(5);

"(2) of the kind specified in paragraph (2), (3), (4), (5), (8), or (9) of section 523(a);

"(3) for restitution, or a criminal fine, included in a sentence on the debtor's conviction of a crime; or

"(4) for restitution, or damages, awarded in a civil action against the debtor as a result of willful or malicious injury by the debtor that caused personal injury to an individual or the death of an individual.".

Sec. 315 GIVING CREDITORS FAIR NOTICE IN CHAPTERS 7 AND 13 CASES.

(a) NOTICE—Section 342 of title 11, United States Code, as amended by section 102, is amended—

(1) in subsection (c)—

(A) by inserting "(1)" after "(c)";

(B) by striking ", but the failure of such notice to contain such information shall not invalidate the legal effect of such notice"; and

(C) by adding at the end the following:

"(2)(A) If, within the 90 days before the commencement of a voluntary case, a creditor supplies the debtor in at least 2 communications sent to the debtor with the current account number of the debtor and the address at which such creditor requests to receive correspondence, then any notice required by this title to be sent by the debtor to such creditor shall be sent to such address and shall include such account number.

"(B) If a creditor would be in violation of applicable nonbankruptcy law by sending any such communication within such 90-day period and if such creditor supplies the debtor in the last 2 communications with the current account number of the debtor and the address at which such creditor requests to receive correspondence, then any notice required by this title to be sent by the debtor to such creditor shall be sent to such address and shall include such account number."; and

(2) by adding at the end the following:

"(e)(1) In a case under chapter 7 or 13 of this title of a debtor who is an individual, a creditor at any time may both file with the court and serve on the debtor a notice of address to be used to provide notice in such case to such creditor.

"(2) Any notice in such case required to be provided to such creditor by the debtor or the court later than 5 days after the court and the debtor receive such creditor's notice of address, shall be provided to such address.

"(f)(1) An entity may file with any bankruptcy court a notice of address to be used by all the bankruptcy courts or by particular bankruptcy courts, as so specified by such entity at the time such notice is filed, to provide notice to such entity in all cases under chapters 7 and 13 pending in the courts with respect to which such notice is filed, in which such entity is a creditor.

"(2) In any case filed under chapter 7 or 13, any notice required to be provided by a court with respect to which a notice is filed under paragraph (1), to such entity later than 30 days after the filing of such notice under paragraph (1) shall be provided to such address unless with respect to a particular case a different address is specified in a notice filed and served in accordance with subsection (e).

"(3) A notice filed under paragraph (1) may be withdrawn by such entity.

"(g)(1) Notice provided to a creditor by the debtor or the court other than in accordance with this section (excluding this subsection) shall not be effective notice until such notice is brought to the attention of such creditor. If such creditor designates a person or an organizational subdivision of such creditor to be responsible for receiving notices under this title and establishes reasonable procedures so that such notices receivable by such creditor are to be delivered to such person or such subdivision, then a notice provided to such creditor other than in accordance with this section (excluding this subsection) shall not be considered to have been brought to the attention of such creditor until such notice is received by such person or such subdivision.

"(2) A monetary penalty may not be imposed on a creditor for a violation of a stay in effect under section 362(a) (including a monetary penalty imposed under section 362(k)) or for failure to comply with section 542 or 543 unless the conduct that is the basis of such violation or of such failure occurs after such creditor receives notice effective under this section of the order for relief.".

(b) DEBTOR'S DUTIES—Section 521 of title 11, United States Code, as amended by sections 106, 225, and 305, is amended—

(1) in subsection (a), as so designated by section 106, by amending paragraph (1) to read as follows:

"(1) file—

"(A) a list of creditors; and

"(B) unless the court orders otherwise—

"(i) a schedule of assets and liabilities;

"(ii) a schedule of current income and current expenditures;

"(iii) a statement of the debtor's financial affairs and, if section 342(b) applies, a certificate—

"(I) of an attorney whose name is indicated on the petition as the attorney for the debtor, or a bankruptcy petition preparer signing the petition under section 110(b)(1), indicating that such attorney or the bankruptcy petition preparer delivered to the debtor the notice required by section 342(b); or

"(II) if no attorney is so indicated, and no bankruptcy petition preparer signed the petition, of the debtor that such notice was received and read by the debtor;

"(iv) copies of all payment advices or other evidence of payment received within 60 days before the date of the filing of the petition, by the debtor from any employer of the debtor;

"(v) a statement of the amount of monthly net income, itemized to show how the amount is calculated; and

"(vi) a statement disclosing any reasonably anticipated increase in income or expenditures over the 12-month period following the date of the filing of the petition;"; and

(2) by adding at the end the following:

"(e)(1) If the debtor in a case under chapter 7 or 13 is an individual and if a creditor files with the court at any time a request to receive a copy of the petition, schedules, and statement of financial affairs filed by the debtor, then the court shall make such petition, such schedules, and such statement available to such creditor.

"(2)(A) The debtor shall provide—

"(i) not later than 7 days before the date first set for the first meeting of creditors, to the trustee a copy of the Federal income tax return required under applicable law (or at the election of the debtor, a transcript of such return) for the most recent tax year ending immediately before the commencement of the case and for which a Federal income tax return was filed; and

"(ii) at the same time the debtor complies with clause (i), a copy of such return (or if elected under clause (i), such transcript) to any creditor that timely requests such copy.

"(B) If the debtor fails to comply with clause (i) or (ii) of subparagraph (A), the court shall dismiss the case unless the debtor demonstrates that the failure to so comply is due to circumstances beyond the control of the debtor.

"(C) If a creditor requests a copy of such tax return or such transcript and if the debtor fails to provide a copy of such tax return or such transcript to such creditor at the time the debtor provides such tax return or such transcript to the trustee, then the court shall dismiss the case unless the debtor demonstrates that the failure to provide a copy of such tax return or such transcript is due to circumstances beyond the control of the debtor.

"(3) If a creditor in a case under chapter 13 files with the court at any time a request to receive a copy of the plan filed by the debtor, then the court shall make available to such creditor a copy of the plan—

"(A) at a reasonable cost; and

"(B) not later than 5 days after such request is filed.

"(f) At the request of the court, the United States trustee, or any party in interest in a case under chapter 7, 11, or 13, a debtor who is an individual shall file with the court—

"(1) at the same time filed with the taxing authority, a copy of each Federal income tax return required under applicable law (or at the election of the debtor, a transcript of such tax return) with respect to each tax year of the debtor ending while the case is pending under such chapter;

"(2) at the same time filed with the taxing authority, each Federal income tax return required under applicable law (or at the election of the debtor, a transcript of such tax return) that had not been filed with such authority as of the date of the commencement of the case and that was subsequently filed for any tax year of the debtor ending in the 3-year period ending on the date of the commencement of the case;

"(3) a copy of each amendment to any Federal income tax return or transcript filed with the court under paragraph (1) or (2); and

"(4) in a case under chapter 13—

"(A) on the date that is either 90 days after the end of such tax year or 1 year after the date of the commencement of the case, whichever is later, if a plan is not confirmed before such later date; and

"(B) annually after the plan is confirmed and until the case is closed, not later than the date that is 45 days before the anniversary of the confirmation of the plan;

a statement, under penalty of perjury, of the income and expenditures of the debtor during the tax year of the debtor most recently concluded before such statement is filed under this paragraph, and of the monthly income of the debtor, that shows how income, expenditures, and monthly income are calculated.

"(g)(1) A statement referred to in subsection (f)(4) shall disclose—

"(A) the amount and sources of the income of the debtor;

"(B) the identity of any person responsible with the debtor for the support of any dependent of the debtor; and

"(C) the identity of any person who contributed, and the amount contributed, to the household in which the debtor resides.

"(2) The tax returns, amendments, and statement of income and expenditures described in subsections (e)(2)(A) and (f) shall be available to the United States trustee (or the bankruptcy administrator, if any), the trustee, and any party in interest for inspection and copying, subject to the requirements of section 315(c) of the Bankruptcy Abuse Prevention and Consumer Protection Act of 2005.

"(h) If requested by the United States trustee or by the trustee, the debtor shall provide—

"(1) a document that establishes the identity of the debtor, including a driver's license, passport, or other document that contains a photograph of the debtor; or

"(2) such other personal identifying information relating to the debtor that establishes the identity of the debtor.".

(c)(1) Not later than 180 days after the date of the enactment of this Act, the Director of the Administrative Office of the United States Courts shall establish procedures for safeguarding the confidentiality of any tax information required to be provided under this section.

(2) The procedures under paragraph (1) shall include restrictions on creditor access to tax information that is required to be provided under this section.

(3) Not later than 540 days after the date of enactment of this Act, the Director of the Administrative Office of the United States Courts shall prepare and submit to the President pro tempore of the Senate and the Speaker of the House of Representatives a report that—

(A) assesses the effectiveness of the procedures established under paragraph (1); and

(B) if appropriate, includes proposed legislation to—

(i) further protect the confidentiality of tax information; and

(ii) provide penalties for the improper use by any person of the tax information required to be provided under this section.

Sec. 316 DISMISSAL FOR FAILURE TO TIMELY FILE SCHEDULES OR PROVIDE REQUIRED INFORMATION.

Section 521 of title 11, United States Code, as amended by sections 106, 225, 305, and 315, is amended by adding at the end the following:

"(i)(1) Subject to paragraphs (2) and (4) and notwithstanding section 707(a), if an individual debtor in a voluntary case under chapter 7 or 13 fails to file all of the information required under subsection (a)(1) within 45 days after the date of the filing of the petition, the case shall be automatically dismissed effective on the 46th day after the date of the filing of the petition.

"(2) Subject to paragraph (4) and with respect to a case described in paragraph (1), any party in interest may request the court to enter an order dismissing the case. If requested, the court shall enter an order of dismissal not later than 5 days after such request.

"(3) Subject to paragraph (4) and upon request of the debtor made within 45 days after the date of the filing of the petition described in paragraph (1), the court may allow the debtor an additional period of not to exceed 45 days to file the information required under subsection (a)(1) if the court finds justification for extending the period for the filing.

"(4) Notwithstanding any other provision of this subsection, on the motion of the trustee filed before the expiration of the applicable period of time specified in paragraph (1), (2), or (3), and after notice and a hearing, the court may decline to dismiss the case if the court finds that the debtor attempted in good faith to file all the information required by subsection (a)(1)(B)(iv) and that the best interests of creditors would be served by administration of the case.".

Sec. 317 ADEQUATE TIME TO PREPARE FOR HEARING ON CONFIRMATION OF THE PLAN.

Section 1324 of title 11, United States Code, is amended—

(1) by striking "After" and inserting the following:

"(a) Except as provided in subsection (b) and after"; and

(2) by adding at the end the following:

"(b) The hearing on confirmation of the plan may be held not earlier than 20 days and not later than 45 days after the date of the meeting of creditors under section 341(a), unless the court determines that it would be in the best interests of the creditors and the estate to hold such hearing at an earlier date and there is no objection to such earlier date.".

Sec. 318 CHAPTER 13 PLANS TO HAVE A 5-YEAR DURATION IN CERTAIN CASES.

Title 11, United States Code, is amended—

(1) by amending section 1322(d) to read as follows:

"(d)(1) If the current monthly income of the debtor and the debtor's spouse combined, when multiplied by 12, is not less than—

"(A) in the case of a debtor in a household of 1 person, the median family income of the applicable State for 1 earner;

"(B) in the case of a debtor in a household of 2, 3, or 4 individuals, the highest median family income of the applicable State for a family of the same number or fewer individuals; or

"(C) in the case of a debtor in a household exceeding 4 individuals, the highest median family income of the applicable State for a family of 4 or fewer individuals, plus $525 per month for each individual in excess of 4,

the plan may not provide for payments over a period that is longer than 5 years.

"(2) If the current monthly income of the debtor and the debtor's spouse combined, when multiplied by 12, is less than—

"(A) in the case of a debtor in a household of 1 person, the median family income of the applicable State for 1 earner;

"(B) in the case of a debtor in a household of 2, 3, or 4 individuals, the highest median family income of the applicable State for a family of the same number or fewer individuals; or

"(C) in the case of a debtor in a household exceeding 4 individuals, the highest median family income of the applicable State for a family of 4 or fewer individuals, plus $525 per month for each individual in excess of 4,

the plan may not provide for payments over a period that is longer than 3 years, unless the court, for cause, approves a longer period, but the court may not approve a period that is longer than 5 years.";

(2) in section 1325(b)(1)(B), by striking "three-year period" and inserting "applicable commitment period"; and

(3) in section 1325(b), as amended by section 102, by adding at the end the following:

"(4) For purposes of this subsection, the 'applicable commitment period'—

"(A) subject to subparagraph (B), shall be—

"(i) 3 years; or

"(ii) not less than 5 years, if the current monthly income of the debtor and the debtor's spouse combined, when multiplied by 12, is not less than—

"(I) in the case of a debtor in a household of 1 person, the median family income of the applicable State for 1 earner;

"(II) in the case of a debtor in a household of 2, 3, or 4 individuals, the highest median family income of the applicable State for a family of the same number or fewer individuals; or

"(III) in the case of a debtor in a household exceeding 4 individuals, the highest median family income of the applicable State for a family of 4 or fewer individuals, plus $525 per month for each individual in excess of 4; and

"(B) may be less than 3 or 5 years, whichever is applicable under subparagraph (A), but only if the plan provides for payment in full of all allowed unsecured claims over a shorter period."; and

(4) in section 1329(c), by striking "three years" and inserting "the applicable commitment period under section 1325(b)(1)(B)".

Sec. 319 SENSE OF CONGRESS REGARDING EXPANSION OF RULE 9011 OF THE FEDERAL RULES OF BANKRUPTCY PROCEDURE.

It is the sense of Congress that rule 9011 of the Federal Rules of Bankruptcy Procedure (11 U.S.C. App.) should be modified to include a requirement that all documents (including schedules), signed and unsigned, submitted to the court or to a trustee by debtors who represent themselves and debtors who are represented by attorneys be submitted only after the debtors or the debtors' attorneys have made reasonable inquiry to verify that the information contained in such documents is—

(1) well grounded in fact; and

(2) warranted by existing law or a good faith argument for the extension, modification, or reversal of existing law.

Sec. 320 PROMPT RELIEF FROM STAY IN INDIVIDUAL CASES.

Section 362(e) of title 11, United States Code, is amended—

(1) by inserting "(1)" after "(e)"; and

(2) by adding at the end the following:

"(2) Notwithstanding paragraph (1), in a case under chapter 7, 11, or 13 in which the debtor is an individual, the stay under subsection (a) shall terminate on the date that is 60 days after a request is made by a party in interest under subsection (d), unless—

"(A) a final decision is rendered by the court during the 60-day period beginning on the date of the request; or

"(B) such 60-day period is extended—

"(i) by agreement of all parties in interest; or

"(ii) by the court for such specific period of time as the court finds is required for good cause, as described in findings made by the court.".

Sec. 321 CHAPTER 11 CASES FILED BY INDIVIDUALS.

(a) PROPERTY OF THE ESTATE—

(1) IN GENERAL—Subchapter I of chapter 11 of title 11, United States Code, is amended by adding at the end the following:

"§ 1115. Property of the estate

"(a) In a case in which the debtor is an individual, property of the estate includes, in addition to the property specified in section 541—

"(1) all property of the kind specified in section 541 that the debtor acquires after the commencement of the case but before the case is closed, dismissed, or converted to a case under chapter 7, 12, or 13, whichever occurs first; and

"(2) earnings from services performed by the debtor after the commencement of the case but before the case is closed, dismissed, or converted to a case under chapter 7, 12, or 13, whichever occurs first.

"(b) Except as provided in section 1104 or a confirmed plan or order confirming a plan, the debtor shall remain in possession of all property of the estate.".

(2) CLERICAL AMENDMENT—The table of sections for subchapter I of chapter 11 of title 11, United States Code, is amended by adding at the end the following:

"1115. Property of the estate.".

(b) CONTENTS OF PLAN—Section 1123(a) of title 11, United States Code, is amended—

(1) in paragraph (6), by striking "and" at the end;

(2) in paragraph (7), by striking the period and inserting "; and"; and

(3) by adding at the end the following:

"(8) in a case in which the debtor is an individual, provide for the payment to creditors under the plan of all or such portion of earnings from personal services performed by the debtor after the commencement of the case or other future income of the debtor as is necessary for the execution of the plan.".

(c) CONFIRMATION OF PLAN—

(1) REQUIREMENTS RELATING TO VALUE OF PROPERTY—Section 1129(a) of title 11, United States Code, as amended by section 213, is amended by adding at the end the following:

"(15) In a case in which the debtor is an individual and in which the holder of an allowed unsecured claim objects to the confirmation of the plan—

"(A) the value, as of the effective date of the plan, of the property to be distributed under the plan on account of such claim is not less than the amount of such claim; or

"(B) the value of the property to be distributed under the plan is not less than the projected disposable income of the debtor (as defined in section 1325(b)(2)) to be received during the 5-year period beginning on the date that the first payment is due under the plan, or during the period for which the plan provides payments, whichever is longer.".

(2) REQUIREMENT RELATING TO INTERESTS IN PROPERTY—Section 1129(b)(2)(B)(ii) of title 11, United States Code, is amended by inserting before the period at the end the following: ", except that in a case in which the debtor is an individual, the debtor may retain property included in the estate under section 1115, subject to the requirements of subsection (a)(14) of this section".

(d) EFFECT OF CONFIRMATION—Section 1141(d) of title 11, United States Code, is amended—

(1) in paragraph (2), by striking "The confirmation of a plan does not discharge an individual debtor" and inserting "A discharge under this chapter does not discharge a debtor who is an individual"; and

(2) by adding at the end the following:

"(5) In a case in which the debtor is an individual—

"(A) unless after notice and a hearing the court orders otherwise for cause, confirmation of the plan does not discharge any debt provided for in the plan until the court grants a discharge on completion of all payments under the plan;

"(B) at any time after the confirmation of the plan, and after notice and a hearing, the court may grant a discharge to the debtor who has not completed payments under the plan if—

"(i) the value, as of the effective date of the plan, of property actually distributed under the plan on account of each allowed unsecured claim is not less than the amount that would have been paid on such claim if the estate of the debtor had been liquidated under chapter 7 on such date; and

"(ii) modification of the plan under section 1127 is not practicable; and".

(e) MODIFICATION OF PLAN—Section 1127 of title 11, United States Code, is amended by adding at the end the following:

"(e) If the debtor is an individual, the plan may be modified at any time after confirmation of the plan but before the completion of payments under the plan, whether or not the plan has been substantially consummated, upon request of the debtor, the trustee, the United States trustee, or the holder of an allowed unsecured claim, to—

"(1) increase or reduce the amount of payments on claims of a particular class provided for by the plan;

"(2) extend or reduce the time period for such payments; or

"(3) alter the amount of the distribution to a creditor whose claim is provided for by the plan to the extent necessary to take account of any payment of such claim made other than under the plan.

"(f)(1) Sections 1121 through 1128 and the requirements of section 1129 apply to any modification under subsection (a).

"(2) The plan, as modified, shall become the plan only after there has been disclosure under section 1125 as the court may direct, notice and a hearing, and such modification is approved.".

Sec. 322 LIMITATIONS ON HOMESTEAD EXEMPTION.

(a) EXEMPTIONS—Section 522 of title 11, United States Code, as amended by sections 224 and 308, is amended by adding at the end the following:

"(p)(1) Except as provided in paragraph (2) of this subsection and sections 544 and 548, as a result of electing under subsection (b)(3)(A) to exempt property under State or local law, a debtor may not exempt any amount of interest that was acquired by the debtor during the 1215-day period preceding the date of the filing of the petition that exceeds in the aggregate $125,000 in value in—

"(A) real or personal property that the debtor or a dependent of the debtor uses as a residence;

"(B) a cooperative that owns property that the debtor or a dependent of the debtor uses as a residence;

"(C) a burial plot for the debtor or a dependent of the debtor; or

"(D) real or personal property that the debtor or dependent of the debtor claims as a homestead.

"(2)(A) The limitation under paragraph (1) shall not apply to an exemption claimed under subsection (b)(3)(A) by a family farmer for the principal residence of such farmer.

"(B) For purposes of paragraph (1), any amount of such interest does not include any interest transferred from a debtor's previous principal residence (which was acquired prior to the beginning of such 1215-day period) into the debtor's current principal residence, if the debtor's previous and current residences are located in the same State.

"(q)(1) As a result of electing under subsection (b)(3)(A) to exempt property under State or local law, a debtor may not exempt any amount of an interest in property described in subparagraphs (A), (B), (C), and (D) of subsection (p)(1) which exceeds in the aggregate $125,000 if—

"(A) the court determines, after notice and a hearing, that the debtor has been convicted of a felony (as defined in section 3156 of title 18), which under the circumstances, demonstrates that the filing of the case was an abuse of the provisions of this title; or

"(B) the debtor owes a debt arising from—

"(i) any violation of the Federal securities laws (as defined in section 3(a)(47) of the Securities Exchange Act of 1934), any State securities laws, or any regulation or order issued under Federal securities laws or State securities laws;

"(ii) fraud, deceit, or manipulation in a fiduciary capacity or in connection with the purchase or sale of any security registered under section 12 or 15(d) of the Securities Exchange Act of 1934 or under section 6 of the Securities Act of 1933;

"(iii) any civil remedy under section 1964 of title 18; or

"(iv) any criminal act, intentional tort, or willful or reckless misconduct that caused serious physical injury or death to another individual in the preceding 5 years.

"(2) Paragraph (1) shall not apply to the extent the amount of an interest in property described in subparagraphs (A), (B), (C), and (D) of subsection (p)(1) is reasonably necessary for the support of the debtor and any dependent of the debtor.".

(b) ADJUSTMENT OF DOLLAR AMOUNTS—Paragraphs (1) and (2) of section 104(b) of title 11, United States Code, as amended by section 224, are amended by inserting "522(p), 522(q)," after "522(n),".

Sec. 323 EXCLUDING EMPLOYEE BENEFIT PLAN PARTICIPANT CONTRIBUTIONS AND OTHER PROPERTY FROM THE ESTATE.

Section 541(b) of title 11, United States Code, as amended by section 225, is amended by adding after paragraph (6), as added by section 225(a)(1)(C), the following:

"(7) any amount—

"(A) withheld by an employer from the wages of employees for payment as contributions—

"(i) to—

"(I) an employee benefit plan that is subject to title I of the Employee Retirement Income Security Act of 1974 or under an employee benefit plan which is a governmental plan under section 414(d) of the Internal Revenue Code of 1986;

"(II) a deferred compensation plan under section 457 of the Internal Revenue Code of 1986; or

"(III) a tax-deferred annuity under section 403(b) of the Internal Revenue Code of 1986;

except that such amount under this subparagraph shall not constitute disposable income as defined in section 1325(b)(2); or

"(ii) to a health insurance plan regulated by State law whether or not subject to such title; or

"(B) received by an employer from employees for payment as contributions—

"(i) to—

"(I) an employee benefit plan that is subject to title I of the Employee Retirement Income Security Act of 1974 or under an employee benefit plan which is a governmental plan under section 414(d) of the Internal Revenue Code of 1986;

"(II) a deferred compensation plan under section 457 of the Internal Revenue Code of 1986; or

"(III) a tax-deferred annuity under section 403(b) of the Internal Revenue Code of 1986;

except that such amount under this subparagraph shall not constitute disposable income, as defined in section 1325(b)(2); or

"(ii) to a health insurance plan regulated by State law whether or not subject to such title;".

Sec. 324 EXCLUSIVE JURISDICTION IN MATTERS INVOLVING BANKRUPTCY PROFESSIONALS.

(a) IN GENERAL—Section 1334 of title 28, United States Code, is amended—

(1) in subsection (b), by striking "Notwithstanding" and inserting "Except as provided in subsection (e)(2), and notwithstanding"; and

(2) by striking subsection (e) and inserting the following:

"(e) The district court in which a case under title 11 is commenced or is pending shall have exclusive jurisdiction—

"(1) of all the property, wherever located, of the debtor as of the commencement of such case, and of property of the estate; and

"(2) over all claims or causes of action that involve construction of section 327 of title 11, United States Code, or rules relating to disclosure requirements under section 327.".

(b) APPLICABILITY—This section shall only apply to cases filed after the date of enactment of this Act.

Sec. 325 UNITED STATES TRUSTEE PROGRAM FILING FEE INCREASE.

(a) ACTIONS UNDER CHAPTER 7, 11, OR 13 OF TITLE 11, UNITED STATES CODE—Section 1930(a) of title 28, United States Code, is amended—

(1) by striking paragraph (1) and inserting the following:

"(1) For a case commenced under—

"(A) chapter 7 of title 11, $200; and

"(B) chapter 13 of title 11, $150."; and

(2) in paragraph (3), by striking "$800" and inserting "$1000".

(b) UNITED STATES TRUSTEE SYSTEM FUND—Section 589a(b) of title 28, United States Code, is amended—

(1) by striking paragraph (1) and inserting the following:

"(1)(A) 40.63 percent of the fees collected under section 1930(a)(1)(A) of this title; and

"(B) 70.00 percent of the fees collected under section 1930(a)(1)(B);";

(2) in paragraph (2), by striking "one-half" and inserting "75 percent"; and

(3) in paragraph (4), by striking "one-half" and inserting "100 percent".

(c) COLLECTION AND DEPOSIT OF MISCELLANEOUS BANKRUPTCY FEES—Section 406(b) of the Judiciary Appropriations Act, 1990 (28 U.S.C. 1931 note) is amended by striking "pursuant to 28 U.S.C. section 1930(b)" and all that follows through "28 U.S.C. section 1931" and inserting "under section 1930(b) of title 28, United States Code, 31.25 of the fees collected under section 1930(a)(1)(A) of that title, 30.00 percent of the fees collected under section 1930(a)(1)(B) of that title, and 25 percent of the fees collected under section 1930(a)(3) of that title shall be deposited as offsetting receipts to the fund established under section 1931 of that title".

(d) SUNSET DATE—The amendments made by subsections (b) and (c) shall be effective during the 2-year period beginning on the date of enactment of this Act.

(e) USE OF INCREASED RECEIPTS—

(1) JUDGES' SALARIES AND BENEFITS—The amount of fees collected under paragraphs (1) and (3) of section 1930(a) of title 28, United States Code, during the 5-year period beginning on the date of enactment of this Act, that is greater than the amount that would have been collected if the amendments made by subsection (a) had not taken effect shall be used, to the extent necessary, to pay the salaries and benefits of the judges appointed pursuant to section 1223 of this Act.

(2) REMAINDER—Any amount described in paragraph (1), which is not used for the purpose described in paragraph (1), shall be deposited into the Treasury of the United States to the extent necessary to offset the decrease in governmental receipts resulting from the amendments made by subsections (b) and (c).

Sec. 326 SHARING OF COMPENSATION.

Section 504 of title 11, United States Code, is amended by adding at the end the following:

"(c) This section shall not apply with respect to sharing, or agreeing to share, compensation with a bona fide public service attorney referral program that operates in accordance with non-Federal law regulating attorney referral services and with rules of professional responsibility applicable to attorney acceptance of referrals.".

Sec. 327 FAIR VALUATION OF COLLATERAL.

Section 506(a) of title 11, United States Code, is amended by—

(1) inserting "(1)" after "(a)"; and

(2) by adding at the end the following:

"(2) If the debtor is an individual in a case under chapter 7 or 13, such value with respect to personal property securing an allowed claim shall be determined based on the replacement value of such property as of the date of the filing of the petition without deduction for costs of sale or marketing. With respect to property acquired for personal, family, or household purposes, replacement value shall mean the price a retail merchant would charge for property of that kind considering the age and condition of the property at the time value is determined.".

Sec. 328 DEFAULTS BASED ON NONMONETARY OBLIGATIONS.

(a) EXECUTORY CONTRACTS AND UNEXPIRED LEASES—Section 365 of title 11, United States Code, is amended—

(1) in subsection (b)—

(A) in paragraph (1)(A), by striking the semicolon at the end and inserting the following: "other than a default that is a breach of a provision relating to the satisfaction of any provision (other than a penalty rate or penalty provision) relating to a default arising from any failure to perform nonmonetary obligations under an unexpired lease of real property, if it is impossible for the trustee to cure such default by performing nonmonetary acts at and after the time of assumption, except that if such default arises from a failure to operate in accordance with a nonresidential real property lease, then such default shall be cured by performance at and after the time of assumption in accordance with such lease, and pecuniary losses resulting from such default shall be compensated in accordance with the provisions of this paragraph;"; and

(B) in paragraph (2)(D), by striking "penalty rate or provision" and inserting "penalty rate or penalty provision";

(2) in subsection (c)—

(A) in paragraph (2), by inserting "or" at the end;

(B) in paragraph (3), by striking "; or" at the end and inserting a period; and

(C) by striking paragraph (4);

(3) in subsection (d)—

(A) by striking paragraphs (5) through (9); and

(B) by redesignating paragraph (10) as paragraph (5); and

(4) in subsection (f)(1) by striking "; except that" and all that follows through the end of the paragraph and inserting a period.

(b) IMPAIRMENT OF CLAIMS OR INTERESTS—Section 1124(2) of title 11, United States Code, is amended—

(1) in subparagraph (A), by inserting "or of a kind that section 365(b)(2) expressly does not require to be cured" before the semicolon at the end;

(2) in subparagraph (C), by striking "and" at the end;

(3) by redesignating subparagraph (D) as subparagraph (E); and

(4) by inserting after subparagraph (C) the following:

"(D) if such claim or such interest arises from any failure to perform a nonmonetary obligation, other than a default arising from failure to operate a nonresidential real property lease subject to section 365(b)(1)(A), compensates the holder of such claim or such interest (other than the debtor or an insider) for any actual pecuniary loss incurred by such holder as a result of such failure; and".

Sec. 329 CLARIFICATION OF POSTPETITION WAGES AND BENEFITS.

Section 503(b)(1)(A) of title 11, United States Code, is amended to read as follows:

"(A) the actual, necessary costs and expenses of preserving the estate including—

"(i) wages, salaries, and commissions for services rendered after the commencement of the case; and

"(ii) wages and benefits awarded pursuant to a judicial proceeding or a proceeding of the National Labor Relations Board as back pay attributable to any period of time occurring after commencement of the case under this title, as a result of a violation of Federal or State law by the debtor, without regard to the time of the occurrence of unlawful conduct on which such award is based or to whether any services were rendered, if the court determines that payment of wages and benefits by reason of the operation of this clause will not substantially increase the probability of layoff or termination of current employees, or of nonpayment of domestic support obligations, during the case under this title;".

Sec. 330 DELAY OF DISCHARGE DURING PENDENCY OF CERTAIN PROCEEDINGS.

(a) CHAPTER 7—Section 727(a) of title 11, United States Code, as amended by section 106, is amended—

(1) in paragraph (10), by striking "or" at the end;

(2) in paragraph (11) by striking the period at the end and inserting "; or"; and

(3) by inserting after paragraph (11) the following:

"(12) the court after notice and a hearing held not more than 10 days before the date of the entry of the order granting the discharge finds that there is reasonable cause to believe that—

"(A) section 522(q)(1) may be applicable to the debtor; and

"(B) there is pending any proceeding in which the debtor may be found guilty of a felony of the kind described in section 522(q)(1)(A) or liable for a debt of the kind described in section 522(q)(1)(B).".

(b) CHAPTER 11—Section 1141(d) of title 11, United States Code, as amended by section 321, is amended by adding at the end the following:

"(C) unless after notice and a hearing held not more than 10 days before the date of the entry of the order granting the discharge, the court finds that there is no reasonable cause to believe that—

"(i) section 522(q)(1) may be applicable to the debtor; and

"(ii) there is pending any proceeding in which the debtor may be found guilty of a felony of the kind described in section 522(q)(1)(A) or liable for a debt of the kind described in section 522(q)(1)(B).".

(c) CHAPTER 12—Section 1228 of title 11, United States Code, is amended—

(1) in subsection (a) by striking "As" and inserting "Subject to subsection (d), as",

(2) in subsection (b) by striking "At" and inserting "Subject to subsection (d), at", and

(3) by adding at the end the following:

"(f) The court may not grant a discharge under this chapter unless the court after notice and a hearing held not more than 10 days before the date of the entry of the order granting the discharge finds that there is no reasonable cause to believe that—

"(1) section 522(q)(1) may be applicable to the debtor; and

"(2) there is pending any proceeding in which the debtor may be found guilty of a felony of the kind described in section 522(q)(1)(A) or liable for a debt of the kind described in section 522(q)(1)(B).".

(d) CHAPTER 13—Section 1328 of title 11, United States Code, as amended by section 106, is amended—

(1) in subsection (a) by striking "As" and inserting "Subject to subsection (d), as",

(2) in subsection (b) by striking "At" and inserting "Subject to subsection (d), at", and

(3) by adding at the end the following:

"(h) The court may not grant a discharge under this chapter unless the court after notice and a hearing held not more than 10 days before the date of the entry of the order granting the discharge finds that there is no reasonable cause to believe that—

"(1) section 522(q)(1) may be applicable to the debtor; and

"(2) there is pending any proceeding in which the debtor may be found guilty of a felony of the kind described in section 522(q)(1)(A) or liable for a debt of the kind described in section 522(q)(1)(B).".

Sec. 331 Limitation on Retention Bonuses, Severance Pay, and Certain Other Payments.

Section 503 of title 11, United States Code, is amended by adding at the end the following:

"(c) Notwithstanding subsection (b), there shall neither be allowed, nor paid—

"(1) a transfer made to, or an obligation incurred for the benefit of, an insider of the debtor for the purpose of inducing such person to remain with the debtor's business, absent a finding by the court based on evidence in the record that—

"(A) the transfer or obligation is essential to retention of the person because the individual has a bona fide job offer from another business at the same or greater rate of compensation;

"(B) the services provided by the person are essential to the survival of the business; and

"(C) either—

"(i) the amount of the transfer made to, or obligation incurred for the benefit of, the person is not greater than an amount equal to 10 times the amount of the mean transfer or obligation of a similar kind given to nonmanagement employees for any purpose during the calendar year in which the transfer is made or the obligation is incurred; or

"(ii) if no such similar transfers were made to, or obligations were incurred for the benefit of, such nonmanagement employees during such calendar year, the amount of the transfer or obligation is not greater than an amount equal to 25 percent of the amount of any similar transfer or obligation made to or incurred for the benefit of such insider for any purpose during the calendar year before the year in which such transfer is made or obligation is incurred;

"(2) a severance payment to an insider of the debtor, unless—

"(A) the payment is part of a program that is generally applicable to all full-time employees; and

"(B) the amount of the payment is not greater than 10 times the amount of the mean severance pay given to nonmanagement employees during the calendar year in which the payment is made; or

"(3) other transfers or obligations that are outside the ordinary course of business and not justified by the facts and circumstances of the case, including transfers made to, or obligations incurred for the benefit of, officers, managers, or consultants hired after the date of the filing of the petition.".

Sec. 332 Fraudulent Involuntary Bankruptcy.

(a) Short Title—This section may be cited as the "Involuntary Bankruptcy Improvement Act of 2005".

(b) INVOLUNTARY CASES—Section 303 of title 11, United States Code, is amended by adding at the end the following:

"(*l*)(1) If—

"(A) the petition under this section is false or contains any materially false, fictitious, or fraudulent statement;

"(B) the debtor is an individual; and

"(C) the court dismisses such petition,

the court, upon the motion of the debtor, shall seal all the records of the court relating to such petition, and all references to such petition.

"(2) If the debtor is an individual and the court dismisses a petition under this section, the court may enter an order prohibiting all consumer reporting agencies (as defined in section 603(f) of the Fair Credit Reporting Act (15 U.S.C. 1681a(f))) from making any consumer report (as defined in section 603(d) of that Act) that contains any information relating to such petition or to the case commenced by the filing of such petition.

"(3) Upon the expiration of the statute of limitations described in section 3282 of title 18, for a violation of section 152 or 157 of such title, the court, upon the motion of the debtor and for good cause, may expunge any records relating to a petition filed under this section.".

(c) BANKRUPTCY FRAUD—Section 157 of title 18, United States Code, is amended by inserting ", including a fraudulent involuntary bankruptcy petition under section 303 of such title" after "title 11".

TITLE IV

GENERAL AND SMALL BUSINESS BANKRUPTCY PROVISIONS

Subtitle A General Business Bankruptcy Provisions

Sec. 401 ADEQUATE PROTECTION FOR INVESTORS.

(a) DEFINITION—Section 101 of title 11, United States Code, is amended by inserting after paragraph (48) the following:

"(48A) 'securities self regulatory organization' means either a securities association registered with the Securities and Exchange Commission under section 15A of the Securities Exchange Act of 1934 or a national securities exchange registered with the Securities and Exchange Commission under section 6 of the Securities Exchange Act of 1934;".

(b) AUTOMATIC STAY—Section 362(b) of title 11, United States Code, as amended by sections 224, 303, and 311, is amended by inserting after paragraph (24) the following:

"(25) under subsection (a), of—

"(A) the commencement or continuation of an investigation or action by a securities self regulatory organization to enforce such organization's regulatory power;

"(B) the enforcement of an order or decision, other than for monetary sanctions, obtained in an action by such securities self regulatory organization to enforce such organization's regulatory power; or

"(C) any act taken by such securities self regulatory organization to delist, delete, or refuse to permit quotation of any stock that does not meet applicable regulatory requirements;".

Sec. 402 MEETINGS OF CREDITORS AND EQUITY SECURITY HOLDERS.

Section 341 of title 11, United States Code, is amended by adding at the end the following:

"(e) Notwithstanding subsections (a) and (b), the court, on the request of a party in interest and after notice and a hearing, for cause may order that the United States trustee not convene a meeting of creditors or equity security holders if the debtor has filed a plan as to which the debtor solicited acceptances prior to the commencement of the case.".

Sec. 403 PROTECTION OF REFINANCE OF SECURITY INTEREST.

Subparagraphs (A), (B), and (C) of section 547(e)(2) of title 11, United States Code, are each amended by striking "10" each place it appears and inserting "30".

Sec. 404 EXECUTORY CONTRACTS AND UNEXPIRED LEASES.

(a) IN GENERAL—Section 365(d)(4) of title 11, United States Code, is amended to read as follows:

"(4)(A) Subject to subparagraph (B), an unexpired lease of nonresidential real property under which the debtor is the lessee shall be deemed rejected, and the trustee shall immediately surrender that nonresidential real property to the lessor, if the trustee does not assume or reject the unexpired lease by the earlier of—

"(i) the date that is 120 days after the date of the order for relief; or

"(ii) the date of the entry of an order confirming a plan.

"(B)(i) The court may extend the period determined under subparagraph (A), prior to the expiration of the 120-day period, for 90 days on the motion of the trustee or lessor for cause.

"(ii) If the court grants an extension under clause (i), the court may grant a subsequent extension only upon prior written consent of the lessor in each instance.".

(b) EXCEPTION—Section 365(f)(1) of title 11, United States Code, is amended by striking "subsection" the first place it appears and inserting "subsections (b) and".

Sec. 405 CREDITORS AND EQUITY SECURITY HOLDERS COMMITTEES.

(a) APPOINTMENT—Section 1102(a) of title 11, United States Code, is amended by adding at the end the following:

"(4) On request of a party in interest and after notice and a hearing, the court may order the United States trustee to change the membership of a committee appointed under this subsection, if the court determines that the change is necessary to ensure adequate representation of creditors or equity security holders. The court may order the United States trustee to increase the number of members of a committee to include a creditor that is a small business concern (as described in section 3(a)(1) of the Small Business Act), if the court determines that the creditor holds claims (of the kind represented by the committee) the aggregate amount of which, in comparison to the annual gross revenue of that creditor, is disproportionately large.".

(b) INFORMATION—Section 1102(b) of title 11, United States Code, is amended by adding at the end the following:

"(3) A committee appointed under subsection (a) shall—

"(A) provide access to information for creditors who—

"(i) hold claims of the kind represented by that committee; and

"(ii) are not appointed to the committee;

"(B) solicit and receive comments from the creditors described in subparagraph (A); and

"(C) be subject to a court order that compels any additional report or disclosure to be made to the creditors described in subparagraph (A).".

Sec. 406 AMENDMENT TO SECTION 546 OF TITLE 11, UNITED STATES CODE.

Section 546 of title 11, United States Code, is amended—

(1) by redesignating the second subsection (g) (as added by section 222(a) of Public Law 103-394) as subsection (h);

(2) in subsection (h), as so redesignated, by inserting "and subject to the prior rights of holders of security interests in such goods or the proceeds of such goods" after "consent of a creditor"; and

(3) by adding at the end the following:

"(i)(1) Notwithstanding paragraphs (2) and (3) of section 545, the trustee may not avoid a warehouseman's lien for storage, transportation, or other costs incidental to the storage and handling of goods.

"(2) The prohibition under paragraph (1) shall be applied in a manner consistent with any State statute applicable to such lien that is similar to section 7-209 of the Uniform Commercial Code, as in effect on the date of enactment of the Bankruptcy Abuse Prevention and Consumer Protection Act of 2005, or any successor to such section 7-209.".

Sec. 407 AMENDMENTS TO SECTION 330(a) OF TITLE 11, UNITED STATES CODE.

Section 330(a) of title 11, United States Code, is amended—

(1) in paragraph (3)—

(A) by striking "(A) In" and inserting "In"; and

(B) by inserting "to an examiner, trustee under chapter 11, or professional person" after "awarded"; and

(2) by adding at the end the following:

"(7) In determining the amount of reasonable compensation to be awarded to a trustee, the court shall treat such compensation as a commission, based on section 326.".

Sec. 408 POSTPETITION DISCLOSURE AND SOLICITATION.

Section 1125 of title 11, United States Code, is amended by adding at the end the following:

"(g) Notwithstanding subsection (b), an acceptance or rejection of the plan may be solicited from a holder of a claim or interest if such solicitation complies with applicable nonbankruptcy law and if such holder was solicited before the commencement of the case in a manner complying with applicable nonbankruptcy law.".

Sec. 409 PREFERENCES.

Section 547(c) of title 11, United States Code, is amended—

(1) by striking paragraph (2) and inserting the following:

"(2) to the extent that such transfer was in payment of a debt incurred by the debtor in the ordinary course of business or financial affairs of the debtor and the transferee, and such transfer was—

"(A) made in the ordinary course of business or financial affairs of the debtor and the transferee; or

"(B) made according to ordinary business terms;";

(2) in paragraph (8), by striking the period at the end and inserting "; or"; and

(3) by adding at the end the following:

"(9) if, in a case filed by a debtor whose debts are not primarily consumer debts, the aggregate value of all property that constitutes or is affected by such transfer is less than $5,000.".

Sec. 410 VENUE OF CERTAIN PROCEEDINGS.

Section 1409(b) of title 28, United States Code, is amended by inserting ", or a debt (excluding a consumer debt) against a noninsider of less than $10,000," after "$5,000". Section 1409(b) of title 28, United States Code, is further amended by striking "$5,000" and inserting "$15,000".

Sec. 411 PERIOD FOR FILING PLAN UNDER CHAPTER 11.

Section 1121(d) of title 11, United States Code, is amended—

(1) by striking "On" and inserting "(1) Subject to paragraph (2), on"; and

(2) by adding at the end the following:

"(2)(A) The 120-day period specified in paragraph (1) may not be extended beyond a date that is 18 months after the date of the order for relief under this chapter.

"(B) The 180-day period specified in paragraph (1) may not be extended beyond a date that is 20 months after the date of the order for relief under this chapter.".

Sec. 412 FEES ARISING FROM CERTAIN OWNERSHIP INTERESTS.

Section 523(a)(16) of title 11, United States Code, is amended—

(1) by striking "dwelling" the first place it appears;

(2) by striking "ownership or" and inserting "ownership,";

(3) by striking "housing" the first place it appears; and

(4) by striking "but only" and all that follows through "such period," and inserting "or a lot in a homeowners association, for as long as the debtor or the trustee has a legal, equitable, or possessory ownership interest in such unit, such corporation, or such lot,".

Sec. 413 CREDITOR REPRESENTATION AT FIRST MEETING OF CREDITORS.

Section 341(c) of title 11, United States Code, is amended by inserting at the end the following: "Notwithstanding any local court rule, provision of a State constitution, any otherwise applicable nonbankruptcy law, or any other requirement that representation at the meeting of creditors under subsection (a) be by an attorney, a creditor holding a consumer debt or any representative of the creditor (which may include an entity or an employee of an entity and may be a representative for more than 1 creditor) shall be permitted to appear at and participate in the meeting of creditors in a case under chapter 7 or 13, either alone or in conjunction with an attorney for the creditor. Nothing in this subsection shall be construed to require any creditor to be represented by an attorney at any meeting of creditors.".

Sec. 414 DEFINITION OF DISINTERESTED PERSON.

Section 101(14) of title 11, United States Code, is amended to read as follows:

"(14) 'disinterested person' means a person that—

"(A) is not a creditor, an equity security holder, or an insider;

"(B) is not and was not, within 2 years before the date of the filing of the petition, a director, officer, or employee of the debtor; and

"(C) does not have an interest materially adverse to the interest of the estate or of any class of creditors or equity security holders, by reason of any direct or indirect relationship to, connection with, or interest in, the debtor, or for any other reason;".

Sec. 415 FACTORS FOR COMPENSATION OF PROFESSIONAL PERSONS.

Section 330(a)(3) of title 11, United States Code, is amended—

(1) in subparagraph (D), by striking "and" at the end;

(2) by redesignating subparagraph (E) as subparagraph (F); and

(3) by inserting after subparagraph (D) the following:

"(E) with respect to a professional person, whether the person is board certified or otherwise has demonstrated skill and experience in the bankruptcy field; and".

Sec. 416 APPOINTMENT OF ELECTED TRUSTEE.

Section 1104(b) of title 11, United States Code, is amended—

(1) by inserting "(1)" after "(b)"; and

(2) by adding at the end the following:

"(2)(A) If an eligible, disinterested trustee is elected at a meeting of creditors under paragraph (1), the United States trustee shall file a report certifying that election.

"(B) Upon the filing of a report under subparagraph (A)—

"(i) the trustee elected under paragraph (1) shall be considered to have been selected and appointed for purposes of this section; and

"(ii) the service of any trustee appointed under subsection (d) shall terminate.

"(C) The court shall resolve any dispute arising out of an election described in subparagraph (A).".

Sec. 417 UTILITY SERVICE.

Section 366 of title 11, United States Code, is amended—

(1) in subsection (a), by striking "subsection (b)" and inserting "subsections (b) and (c)"; and

(2) by adding at the end the following:

"(c)(1)(A) For purposes of this subsection, the term 'assurance of payment' means—

"(i) a cash deposit;

"(ii) a letter of credit;

"(iii) a certificate of deposit;

"(iv) a surety bond;

"(v) a prepayment of utility consumption; or

"(vi) another form of security that is mutually agreed on between the utility and the debtor or the trustee.

"(B) For purposes of this subsection an administrative expense priority shall not constitute an assurance of payment.

"(2) Subject to paragraphs (3) and (4), with respect to a case filed under chapter 11, a utility referred to in subsection (a) may alter, refuse, or discontinue utility service, if during the 30-day period beginning on the date of the filing of the petition, the utility does not receive from the debtor or the trustee adequate assurance of payment for utility service that is satisfactory to the utility.

"(3)(A) On request of a party in interest and after notice and a hearing, the court may order modification of the amount of an assurance of payment under paragraph (2).

"(B) In making a determination under this paragraph whether an assurance of payment is adequate, the court may not consider—

"(i) the absence of security before the date of the filing of the petition;

"(ii) the payment by the debtor of charges for utility service in a timely manner before the date of the filing of the petition; or

"(iii) the availability of an administrative expense priority.

"(4) Notwithstanding any other provision of law, with respect to a case subject to this subsection, a utility may recover or set off against a security deposit provided to the utility by the debtor before the date of the filing of the petition without notice or order of the court.".

Sec. 418 BANKRUPTCY FEES.

Section 1930 of title 28, United States Code, is amended—

(1) in subsection (a), by striking "Notwithstanding section 1915 of this title, the" and inserting "The"; and

(2) by adding at the end the following:

"(f)(1) Under the procedures prescribed by the Judicial Conference of the United States, the district court or the bankruptcy court may waive the filing fee in a case under chapter 7 of title 11 for an individual if the court determines that such individual has income less than 150 percent of the income official poverty line (as defined by the Office of Management and Budget, and revised annually in accordance with section 673(2) of the Omnibus Budget Reconciliation Act of 1981) applicable to a family of the size involved and is unable to pay that fee in installments. For purposes of this paragraph, the term "filing fee" means the filing fee required by subsection (a), or any other fee prescribed by the Judicial Conference under subsections (b) and (c) that is payable to the clerk upon the commencement of a case under chapter 7.

"(2) The district court or the bankruptcy court may waive for such debtors other fees prescribed under subsections (b) and (c).

"(3) This subsection does not restrict the district court or the bankruptcy court from waiving, in accordance with Judicial Conference policy, fees prescribed under this section for other debtors and creditors.".

Sec. 419 MORE COMPLETE INFORMATION REGARDING ASSETS OF THE ESTATE.

(a) IN GENERAL—

(1) DISCLOSURE—The Judicial Conference of the United States, in accordance with section 2075 of title 28 of the United States Code and after consideration of the views of the Director of the Executive Office for United States Trustees, shall propose amended Federal Rules of Bankruptcy Procedure and in accordance with rule 9009 of the Federal Rules of Bankruptcy Procedure shall prescribe official bankruptcy forms directing debtors under chapter 11 of title 11 of United States Code, to disclose the information described in paragraph (2) by filing and serving periodic financial and other reports designed to provide such information.

(2) INFORMATION—The information referred to in paragraph (1) is the value, operations, and profitability of any closely held corporation, partnership, or of any other entity in which the debtor holds a substantial or controlling interest.

(b) PURPOSE—The purpose of the rules and reports under subsection (a) shall be to assist parties in interest taking steps to ensure that the debtor's interest in any entity referred to in subsection (a)(2) is used for the payment of allowed claims against debtor.

Subtitle B Small Business Bankruptcy Provisions

Sec. 431 FLEXIBLE RULES FOR DISCLOSURE STATEMENT AND PLAN.

Section 1125 of title 11, United States Code, is amended—

(1) in subsection (a)(1), by inserting before the semicolon "and in determining whether a disclosure statement provides adequate information, the court shall consider the complexity of the case, the benefit of additional information to creditors and other parties in interest, and the cost of providing additional information"; and

(2) by striking subsection (f), and inserting the following:

"(f) Notwithstanding subsection (b), in a small business case—

"(1) the court may determine that the plan itself provides adequate information and that a separate disclosure statement is not necessary;

"(2) the court may approve a disclosure statement submitted on standard forms approved by the court or adopted under section 2075 of title 28; and

"(3)(A) the court may conditionally approve a disclosure statement subject to final approval after notice and a hearing;

"(B) acceptances and rejections of a plan may be solicited based on a conditionally approved disclosure statement if the debtor provides adequate information to each holder of a claim or interest that is solicited, but a conditionally approved disclosure statement shall be mailed not later than 25 days before the date of the hearing on confirmation of the plan; and

"(C) the hearing on the disclosure statement may be combined with the hearing on confirmation of a plan.".

Sec. 432 DEFINITIONS.

(a) DEFINITIONS—Section 101 of title 11, United States Code, is amended by striking paragraph (51C) and inserting the following:

"(51C) 'small business case' means a case filed under chapter 11 of this title in which the debtor is a small business debtor;

"(51D) 'small business debtor'—

"(A) subject to subparagraph (B), means a person engaged in commercial or business activities (including any affiliate of such person that is also a debtor under this title and excluding a person whose primary activity is the business of owning or operating real property or activities incidental thereto) that has aggregate noncontingent liquidated secured and unsecured debts as of the date of the petition or the date of the order for relief in an amount not more than $2,000,000 (excluding debts owed to 1 or more affiliates or insiders) for a case in which the United States trustee has not appointed under section 1102(a)(1) a committee of unsecured creditors or where the court has determined that the committee of unsecured creditors is not sufficiently active and representative to provide effective oversight of the debtor; and

"(B) does not include any member of a group of affiliated debtors that has aggregate noncontingent liquidated secured and unsecured debts in an amount greater than $2,000,000 (excluding debt owed to 1 or more affiliates or insiders);".

(b) CONFORMING AMENDMENT—Section 1102(a)(3) of title 11, United States Code, is amended by inserting "debtor" after "small business".

(c) ADJUSTMENT OF DOLLAR AMOUNTS—Section 104(b) of title 11, United States Code, as amended by section 226, is amended by inserting "101(51D)," after "101(3)," each place it appears.

Sec. 433 STANDARD FORM DISCLOSURE STATEMENT AND PLAN.

Within a reasonable period of time after the date of enactment of this Act, the Judicial Conference of the United States shall prescribe in accordance with rule 9009 of the Federal Rules of Bankruptcy Procedure official standard form disclosure statements and plans of reorganization for small business debtors (as defined in section 101 of title 11, United States Code, as amended by this Act), designed to achieve a practical balance between—

(1) the reasonable needs of the courts, the United States trustee, creditors, and other parties in interest for reasonably complete information; and

(2) economy and simplicity for debtors.

Sec. 434 UNIFORM NATIONAL REPORTING REQUIREMENTS.

(a) REPORTING REQUIRED—

(1) IN GENERAL—Chapter 3 of title 11, United States Code, is amended by inserting after section 307 the following:

"§ 308. Debtor reporting requirements

"(a) For purposes of this section, the term 'profitability' means, with respect to a debtor, the amount of money that the debtor has earned or lost during current and recent fiscal periods.

"(b) A small business debtor shall file periodic financial and other reports containing information including—

"(1) the debtor's profitability;

"(2) reasonable approximations of the debtor's projected cash receipts and cash disbursements over a reasonable period;

"(3) comparisons of actual cash receipts and disbursements with projections in prior reports;

"(4)(A) whether the debtor is—

"(i) in compliance in all material respects with postpetition require-ments imposed by this title and the Federal Rules of Bankruptcy Procedure; and

"(ii) timely filing tax returns and other required government filings and paying taxes and other administrative expenses when due;

"(B) if the debtor is not in compliance with the requirements referred to in subparagraph (A)(i) or filing tax returns and other required govern-ment filings and making the payments referred to in subparagraph (A)(ii), what the failures are and how, at what cost, and when the debtor intends to remedy such failures; and

"(C) such other matters as are in the best interests of the debtor and creditors, and in the public interest in fair and efficient procedures under chapter 11 of this title.".

(2) CLERICAL AMENDMENT—The table of sections for chapter 3 of title 11, United States Code, is amended by inserting after the item relating to section 307 the following:

"308. Debtor reporting requirements.".

(b) EFFECTIVE DATE—The amendments made by subsection (a) shall take effect 60 days after the date on which rules are prescribed under section 2075 of title 28, United States Code, to establish forms to be used to comply with section 308 of title 11, United States Code, as added by subsection (a).

Sec. 435 UNIFORM REPORTING RULES AND FORMS FOR SMALL BUSINESS CASES.

(a) PROPOSAL OF RULES AND FORMS—The Judicial Conference of the United States shall propose in accordance with section 2073 of title 28 of the United States Code amended Federal Rules of Bankruptcy Procedure, and shall prescribe in accordance with rule 9009 of the Federal Rules of Bankruptcy Procedure official bankruptcy forms, directing small business debtors to file periodic financial and other reports containing information, including information relating to—

(1) the debtor's profitability;

(2) the debtor's cash receipts and disbursements; and

(3) whether the debtor is timely filing tax returns and paying taxes and other administrative expenses when due.

(b) PURPOSE—The rules and forms proposed under subsection (a) shall be designed to achieve a practical balance among—

(1) the reasonable needs of the bankruptcy court, the United States trustee, creditors, and other parties in interest for reasonably complete information;

(2) a small business debtor's interest that required reports be easy and inexpensive to complete; and

(3) the interest of all parties that the required reports help such debtor to understand such debtor's financial condition and plan the such debtor's future.

Sec. 436 DUTIES IN SMALL BUSINESS CASES.

(a) DUTIES IN CHAPTER 11 CASES—Subchapter I of chapter 11 of title 11, United States Code, as amended by section 321, is amended by adding at the end the following:

"§ 1116. Duties of trustee or debtor in possession in small business cases

"In a small business case, a trustee or the debtor in possession, in addition to the duties provided in this title and as otherwise required by law, shall—

"(1) append to the voluntary petition or, in an involuntary case, file not later than 7 days after the date of the order for relief—

"(A) its most recent balance sheet, statement of operations, cash-flow statement, and Federal income tax return; or

"(B) a statement made under penalty of perjury that no balance sheet, statement of operations, or cash-flow statement has been prepared and no Federal tax return has been filed;

"(2) attend, through its senior management personnel and counsel, meetings scheduled by the court or the United States trustee, including initial debtor interviews, scheduling conferences, and meetings of creditors convened under section 341 unless the court, after notice and a hearing, waives that requirement upon a finding of extraordinary and compelling circumstances;

"(3) timely file all schedules and statements of financial affairs, unless the court, after notice and a hearing, grants an extension, which shall not extend such time period to a date later than 30 days after the date of the order for relief, absent extraordinary and compelling circumstances;

"(4) file all postpetition financial and other reports required by the Federal Rules of Bankruptcy Procedure or by local rule of the district court;

"(5) subject to section 363(c)(2), maintain insurance customary and appropriate to the industry;

"(6)(A) timely file tax returns and other required government filings; and

"(B) subject to section 363(c)(2), timely pay all taxes entitled to administrative expense priority except those being contested by appropriate proceedings being diligently prosecuted; and

"(7) allow the United States trustee, or a designated representative of the United States trustee, to inspect the debtor's business premises, books, and records at reasonable times, after reasonable prior written notice, unless notice is waived by the debtor.".

(b) CLERICAL AMENDMENT—The table of sections for chapter 11 of title 11, United States Code, as amended by section 321, is amended by inserting after the item relating to section 1115 the following:

"1116. Duties of trustee or debtor in possession in small business cases.".

Sec. 437 PLAN FILING AND CONFIRMATION DEADLINES.

Section 1121 of title 11, United States Code, is amended by striking subsection (e) and inserting the following:

"(e) In a small business case—

"(1) only the debtor may file a plan until after 180 days after the date of the order for relief, unless that period is—

"(A) extended as provided by this subsection, after notice and a hearing; or

"(B) the court, for cause, orders otherwise;

"(2) the plan and a disclosure statement (if any) shall be filed not later than 300 days after the date of the order for relief; and

"(3) the time periods specified in paragraphs (1) and (2), and the time fixed in section 1129(e) within which the plan shall be confirmed, may be extended only if—

"(A) the debtor, after providing notice to parties in interest (including the United States trustee), demonstrates by a preponderance of the evidence that it is more likely than not that the court will confirm a plan within a reasonable period of time;

"(B) a new deadline is imposed at the time the extension is granted; and

"(C) the order extending time is signed before the existing deadline has expired.".

Sec. 438 PLAN CONFIRMATION DEADLINE.

Section 1129 of title 11, United States Code, is amended by adding at the end the following:

"(e) In a small business case, the court shall confirm a plan that complies with the applicable provisions of this title and that is filed in accordance with section 1121(e) not later than 45 days after the plan is filed unless the time for confirmation is extended in accordance with section 1121(e)(3).".

Sec. 439 DUTIES OF THE UNITED STATES TRUSTEE.

Section 586(a) of title 28, United States Code, is amended—

(1) in paragraph (3)—

(A) in subparagraph (G), by striking "and" at the end;

(B) by redesignating subparagraph (H) as subparagraph (I); and

(C) by inserting after subparagraph (G) the following:

"(H) in small business cases (as defined in section 101 of title 11), performing the additional duties specified in title 11 pertaining to such cases; and';

(2) in paragraph (5), by striking "and" at the end;

(3) in paragraph (6), by striking the period at the end and inserting a semicolon; and

(4) by adding at the end the following:

"(7) in each of such small business cases—

"(A) conduct an initial debtor interview as soon as practicable after the date of the order for relief but before the first meeting scheduled under section 341(a) of title 11, at which time the United States trustee shall—

"(i) begin to investigate the debtor's viability;

"(ii) inquire about the debtor's business plan;

"(iii) explain the debtor's obligations to file monthly operating reports and other required reports;

"(iv) attempt to develop an agreed scheduling order; and

"(v) inform the debtor of other obligations;

"(B) if determined to be appropriate and advisable, visit the appropriate business premises of the debtor, ascertain the state of the debtor's books and records, and verify that the debtor has filed its tax returns; and

"(C) review and monitor diligently the debtor's activities, to identify as promptly as possible whether the debtor will be unable to confirm a plan; and

"(8) in any case in which the United States trustee finds material grounds for any relief under section 1112 of title 11, the United States trustee shall apply promptly after making that finding to the court for relief.".

Sec. 440 SCHEDULING CONFERENCES.

Section 105(d) of title 11, United States Code, is amended—

(1) in the matter preceding paragraph (1), by striking ", may"; and

(2) by striking paragraph (1) and inserting the following:

"(1) shall hold such status conferences as are necessary to further the expeditious and economical resolution of the case; and".

Sec. 441 SERIAL FILER PROVISIONS.

Section 362 of title 11, United States Code, as amended by sections 106, 305, and 311, is amended—

(1) in subsection (k), as so redesignated by section 305—

(A) by striking "An" and inserting "(1) Except as provided in paragraph (2), an"; and

(B) by adding at the end the following:

"(2) If such violation is based on an action taken by an entity in the good faith belief that subsection (h) applies to the debtor, the recovery under paragraph (1) of this subsection against such entity shall be limited to actual damages."; and

(2) by adding at the end the following:

"(n)(1) Except as provided in paragraph (2), subsection (a) does not apply in a case in which the debtor—

"(A) is a debtor in a small business case pending at the time the petition is filed;

"(B) was a debtor in a small business case that was dismissed for any reason by an order that became final in the 2-year period ending on the date of the order for relief entered with respect to the petition;

"(C) was a debtor in a small business case in which a plan was confirmed in the 2-year period ending on the date of the order for relief entered with respect to the petition; or

"(D) is an entity that has acquired substantially all of the assets or business of a small business debtor described in subparagraph (A), (B), or (C), unless such entity establishes by a preponderance of the evidence that such entity acquired substantially all of the assets or business of such small business debtor in good faith and not for the purpose of evading this paragraph.

"(2) Paragraph (1) does not apply—

"(A) to an involuntary case involving no collusion by the debtor with creditors; or

"(B) to the filing of a petition if—

"(i) the debtor proves by a preponderance of the evidence that the filing of the petition resulted from circumstances beyond the control of the debtor not foreseeable at the time the case then pending was filed; and

"(ii) it is more likely than not that the court will confirm a feasible plan, but not a liquidating plan, within a reasonable period of time.".

Sec. 442 EXPANDED GROUNDS FOR DISMISSAL OR CONVERSION AND APPOINTMENT OF TRUSTEE.

(a) EXPANDED GROUNDS FOR DISMISSAL OR CONVERSION—Section 1112 of title 11, United States Code, is amended by striking subsection (b) and inserting the following:

"(b)(1) Except as provided in paragraph (2) of this subsection, subsection (c) of this section, and section 1104(a)(3), on request of a party in interest, and after notice and a hearing, absent unusual circumstances specifically identified by the court that establish that the requested conversion or dismissal is not in the best interests of creditors and the estate, the court shall convert a case under this chapter to a case under chapter 7 or dismiss a case under this chapter, whichever is in the best interests of creditors and the estate, if the movant establishes cause.

"(2) The relief provided in paragraph (1) shall not be granted absent unusual circumstances specifically identified by the court that establish that such relief is not in the best interests of creditors and the estate, if the debtor or another party in interest objects and establishes that—

"(A) there is a reasonable likelihood that a plan will be confirmed within the timeframes established in sections 1121(e) and 1129(e) of this title, or if such sections do not apply, within a reasonable period of time; and

"(B) the grounds for granting such relief include an act or omission of the debtor other than under paragraph (4)(A)—

"(i) for which there exists a reasonable justification for the act or omission; and

"(ii) that will be cured within a reasonable period of time fixed by the court.

"(3) The court shall commence the hearing on a motion under this subsection not later than 30 days after filing of the motion, and shall decide the motion not later than 15 days after commencement of such hearing, unless the movant expressly consents to a continuance for a specific period of time or compelling circumstances prevent the court from meeting the time limits established by this paragraph.

"(4) For purposes of this subsection, the term 'cause' includes—

"(A) substantial or continuing loss to or diminution of the estate and the absence of a reasonable likelihood of rehabilitation;

"(B) gross mismanagement of the estate;

"(C) failure to maintain appropriate insurance that poses a risk to the estate or to the public;

"(D) unauthorized use of cash collateral substantially harmful to 1 or more creditors;

"(E) failure to comply with an order of the court;

155

"(F) unexcused failure to satisfy timely any filing or reporting requirement established by this title or by any rule applicable to a case under this chapter;

"(G) failure to attend the meeting of creditors convened under section 341(a) or an examination ordered under rule 2004 of the Federal Rules of Bankruptcy Procedure without good cause shown by the debtor;

"(H) failure timely to provide information or attend meetings reasonably requested by the United States trustee (or the bankruptcy administrator, if any);

"(I) failure timely to pay taxes owed after the date of the order for relief or to file tax returns due after the date of the order for relief;

"(J) failure to file a disclosure statement, or to file or confirm a plan, within the time fixed by this title or by order of the court;

"(K) failure to pay any fees or charges required under chapter 123 of title 28;

"(L) revocation of an order of confirmation under section 1144;

"(M) inability to effectuate substantial consummation of a confirmed plan;

"(N) material default by the debtor with respect to a confirmed plan;

"(O) termination of a confirmed plan by reason of the occurrence of a condition specified in the plan; and

"(P) failure of the debtor to pay any domestic support obligation that first becomes payable after the date of the filing of the petition.".

(b) ADDITIONAL GROUNDS FOR APPOINTMENT OF TRUSTEE—Section 1104(a) of title 11, United States Code, is amended—

(1) in paragraph (1), by striking "or" at the end;

(2) in paragraph (2), by striking the period at the end and inserting "; or"; and

(3) by adding at the end the following:

"(3) if grounds exist to convert or dismiss the case under section 1112, but the court determines that the appointment of a trustee or an examiner is in the best interests of creditors and the estate.".

Sec. 443 STUDY OF OPERATION OF TITLE 11, UNITED STATES CODE, WITH RESPECT TO SMALL BUSINESSES.

Not later than 2 years after the date of enactment of this Act, the Administrator of the Small Business Administration, in consultation with the Attorney General, the Director of the Executive Office for United States Trustees, and the Director of the Administrative Office of the United States Courts, shall—

(1) conduct a study to determine—

(A) the internal and external factors that cause small businesses, especially sole proprietorships, to become debtors in cases under title

11, United States Code, and that cause certain small businesses to successfully complete cases under chapter 11 of such title; and

(B) how Federal laws relating to bankruptcy may be made more effective and efficient in assisting small businesses to remain viable; and

(2) submit to the President pro tempore of the Senate and the Speaker of the House of Representatives a report summarizing that study.

Sec. 444 PAYMENT OF INTEREST.

Section 362(d)(3) of title 11, United States Code, is amended—

(1) by inserting "or 30 days after the court determines that the debtor is subject to this paragraph, whichever is later" after "90-day period)"; and

(2) by striking subparagraph (B) and inserting the following:

"(B) the debtor has commenced monthly payments that—

"(i) may, in the debtor's sole discretion, notwithstanding section 363(c)(2), be made from rents or other income generated before, on, or after the date of the commencement of the case by or from the property to each creditor whose claim is secured by such real estate (other than a claim secured by a judgment lien or by an unmatured statutory lien); and

"(ii) are in an amount equal to interest at the then applicable nondefault contract rate of interest on the value of the creditor's interest in the real estate; or".

Sec. 445 PRIORITY FOR ADMINISTRATIVE EXPENSES.

Section 503(b) of title 11, United States Code, is amended—

(1) in paragraph (5), by striking "and" at the end;

(2) in paragraph (6), by striking the period at the end and inserting a semicolon; and

(3) by adding at the end the following:

"(7) with respect to a nonresidential real property lease previously assumed under section 365, and subsequently rejected, a sum equal to all monetary obligations due, excluding those arising from or relating to a failure to operate or a penalty provision, for the period of 2 years following the later of the rejection date or the date of actual turnover of the premises, without reduction or setoff for any reason whatsoever except for sums actually received or to be received from an entity other than the debtor, and the claim for remaining sums due for the balance of the term of the lease shall be a claim under section 502(b)(6);".

Sec. 446 Duties With Respect to a Debtor Who Is a Plan Administrator of an Employee Benefit Plan.

(a) In General—Section 521(a) of title 11, United States Code, as amended by sections 106 and 304, is amended—

(1) in paragraph (5), by striking "and" at the end;

(2) in paragraph (6), by striking the period at the end and inserting "; and"; and

(3) by adding after paragraph (6) the following:

"(7) unless a trustee is serving in the case, continue to perform the obligations required of the administrator (as defined in section 3 of the Employee Retirement Income Security Act of 1974) of an employee benefit plan if at the time of the commencement of the case the debtor (or any entity designated by the debtor) served as such administrator.".

(b) Duties of Trustees—Section 704(a) of title 11, United States Code, as amended by sections 102 and 219, is amended—

(1) in paragraph (10), by striking "and" at the end; and

(2) by adding at the end the following:

"(11) if, at the time of the commencement of the case, the debtor (or any entity designated by the debtor) served as the administrator (as defined in section 3 of the Employee Retirement Income Security Act of 1974) of an employee benefit plan, continue to perform the obligations required of the administrator; and".

(c) Conforming Amendment—Section 1106(a)(1) of title 11, United States Code, is amended to read as follows:

"(1) perform the duties of the trustee, as specified in paragraphs (2), (5), (7), (8), (9), (10), and (11) of section 704;".

Sec. 447 Appointment of Committee of Retired Employees.

Section 1114(d) of title 11, United States Code, is amended—

(1) by striking "appoint" and inserting "order the appointment of", and

(2) by adding at the end the following: "The United States trustee shall appoint any such committee.".

TITLE V

MUNICIPAL BANKRUPTCY PROVISIONS

Sec. 501 PETITION AND PROCEEDINGS RELATED TO PETITION.

(a) TECHNICAL AMENDMENT RELATING TO MUNICIPALITIES—Section 921(d) of title 11, United States Code, is amended by inserting "notwithstanding section 301(b)" before the period at the end.

(b) CONFORMING AMENDMENT—Section 301 of title 11, United States Code, is amended—

(1) by inserting "(a)" before "A voluntary"; and

(2) by striking the last sentence and inserting the following:

"(b) The commencement of a voluntary case under a chapter of this title constitutes an order for relief under such chapter.".

Sec. 502 APPLICABILITY OF OTHER SECTIONS TO CHAPTER 9.

Section 901(a) of title 11, United States Code, is amended—

(1) by inserting "555, 556," after "553,"; and

(2) by inserting "559, 560, 561, 562," after "557,".

TITLE VI

BANKRUPTCY DATA

Sec. 601 IMPROVED BANKRUPTCY STATISTICS.

(a) IN GENERAL—apter 6 of title 28, United States Code, is amended by adding at the end the following:

"§ 159. Bankruptcy statistics

"(a) The clerk of the district court, or the clerk of the bankruptcy court if one is certified pursuant to section 156(b) of this title, shall collect statistics regarding debtors who are individuals with primarily consumer debts seeking relief under chapters 7, 11, and 13 of title 11. Those statistics shall be in a standardized format prescribed by the Director of the Administrative Office of the United States Courts (referred to in this section as the 'Director').

"(b) The Director shall—

"(1) compile the statistics referred to in subsection (a);

"(2) make the statistics available to the public; and

"(3) not later than July 1, 2008, and annually thereafter, prepare, and submit to Congress a report concerning the information collected under subsection (a) that contains an analysis of the information.

"(c) The compilation required under subsection (b) shall—

"(1) be itemized, by chapter, with respect to title 11;

"(2) be presented in the aggregate and for each district; and

"(3) include information concerning—

"(A) the total assets and total liabilities of the debtors described in subsection (a), and in each category of assets and liabilities, as reported in the schedules prescribed pursuant to section 2075 of this title and filed by debtors;

"(B) the current monthly income, average income, and average expenses of debtors as reported on the schedules and statements that each such debtor files under sections 521 and 1322 of title 11;

"(C) the aggregate amount of debt discharged in cases filed during the reporting period, determined as the difference between the total amount of debt and obligations of a debtor reported on the schedules and the amount of such debt reported in categories which are predominantly nondischargeable;

"(D) the average period of time between the date of the filing of the petition and the closing of the case for cases closed during the reporting period;

"(E) for cases closed during the reporting period—

"(i) the number of cases in which a reaffirmation agreement was filed; and

"(ii)(I) the total number of reaffirmation agreements filed;

"(II) of those cases in which a reaffirmation agreement was filed, the number of cases in which the debtor was not represented by an attorney; and

"(III) of those cases in which a reaffirmation agreement was filed, the number of cases in which the reaffirmation agreement was approved by the court;

"(F) with respect to cases filed under chapter 13 of title 11, for the reporting period—

"(i)(I) the number of cases in which a final order was entered determining the value of property securing a claim in an amount less than the amount of the claim; and

"(II) the number of final orders entered determining the value of property securing a claim;

"(ii) the number of cases dismissed, the number of cases dismissed for failure to make payments under the plan, the number of cases refiled after dismissal, and the number of cases in which the plan was completed, separately itemized with respect to the number of modifications made before completion of the plan, if any; and

"(iii) the number of cases in which the debtor filed another case during the 6-year period preceding the filing;

"(G) the number of cases in which creditors were fined for misconduct and any amount of punitive damages awarded by the court for creditor misconduct; and

"(H) the number of cases in which sanctions under rule 9011 of the Federal Rules of Bankruptcy Procedure were imposed against debtor's attorney or damages awarded under such Rule.".

(b) CLERICAL AMENDMENT—The table of sections for chapter 6 of title 28, United States Code, is amended by adding at the end the following:

"159. Bankruptcy statistics.".

(c) EFFECTIVE DATE—The amendments made by this section shall take effect 18 months after the date of enactment of this Act.

Sec. 602 UNIFORM RULES FOR THE COLLECTION OF BANKRUPTCY DATA.

(a) AMENDMENT—Chapter 39 of title 28, United States Code, is amended by adding at the end the following:

"§ 589b. Bankruptcy data

"(a) RULES—The Attorney General shall, within a reasonable time after the effective date of this section, issue rules requiring uniform forms for (and from time to time thereafter to appropriately modify and approve)—

"(1) final reports by trustees in cases under chapters 7, 12, and 13 of title 11; and

"(2) periodic reports by debtors in possession or trustees in cases under chapter 11 of title 11.

"(b) REPORTS—Each report referred to in subsection (a) shall be designed (and the requirements as to place and manner of filing shall be established) so as to facilitate compilation of data and maximum possible access of the public, both by physical inspection at one or more central filing locations, and by electronic access through the Internet or other appropriate media.

"(c) REQUIRED INFORMATION—The information required to be filed in the reports referred to in subsection (b) shall be that which is in the best interests of debtors and creditors, and in the public interest in reasonable and adequate information to evaluate the efficiency and practicality of the Federal bankruptcy system. In issuing rules proposing the forms referred to in subsection (a), the Attorney General shall strike the best achievable practical balance between—

"(1) the reasonable needs of the public for information about the operational results of the Federal bankruptcy system;

"(2) economy, simplicity, and lack of undue burden on persons with a duty to file reports; and

"(3) appropriate privacy concerns and safeguards.

"(d) FINAL REPORTS—The uniform forms for final reports required under subsection (a) for use by trustees under chapters 7, 12, and 13 of title 11 shall, in addition to such other matters as are required by law or as the Attorney General in the discretion of the Attorney General shall propose, include with respect to a case under such title—

"(1) information about the length of time the case was pending;

"(2) assets abandoned;

"(3) assets exempted;

"(4) receipts and disbursements of the estate;

"(5) expenses of administration, including for use under section 707(b), actual costs of administering cases under chapter 13 of title 11;

"(6) claims asserted;

"(7) claims allowed; and

"(8) distributions to claimants and claims discharged without payment,

in each case by appropriate category and, in cases under chapters 12 and 13 of title 11, date of confirmation of the plan, each modification thereto, and defaults by the debtor in performance under the plan.

"(e) PERIODIC REPORTS—The uniform forms for periodic reports required under subsection (a) for use by trustees or debtors in possession under chapter 11 of title 11 shall, in addition to such other matters as are required by law or as the Attorney General in the discretion of the Attorney General shall propose, include—

"(1) information about the industry classification, published by the Department of Commerce, for the businesses conducted by the debtor;

"(2) length of time the case has been pending;

"(3) number of full-time employees as of the date of the order for relief and at the end of each reporting period since the case was filed;

"(4) cash receipts, cash disbursements and profitability of the debtor for the most recent period and cumulatively since the date of the order for relief;

"(5) compliance with title 11, whether or not tax returns and tax payments since the date of the order for relief have been timely filed and made;

"(6) all professional fees approved by the court in the case for the most recent period and cumulatively since the date of the order for relief (separately reported, for the professional fees incurred by or on behalf of the debtor, between those that would have been incurred absent a bankruptcy case and those not); and

"(7) plans of reorganization filed and confirmed and, with respect thereto, by class, the recoveries of the holders, expressed in aggregate dollar values and, in the case of claims, as a percentage of total claims of the class allowed.".

(b) CLERICAL AMENDMENT—The table of sections for chapter 39 of title 28, United States Code, is amended by adding at the end the following:

"589b. Bankruptcy data.".

Sec. 603 AUDIT PROCEDURES.

(a) IN GENERAL—

(1) ESTABLISHMENT OF PROCEDURES—The Attorney General (in judicial districts served by United States trustees) and the Judicial Conference of the United States (in judicial districts served by bankruptcy administrators) shall establish procedures to determine the accuracy, veracity, and completeness of petitions, schedules, and other information that the debtor is required to provide under sections 521 and 1322 of title 11, United States Code, and, if applicable, section 111 of such title, in cases filed under chapter 7 or 13 of such title in which the debtor is an individual. Such audits shall be in accordance with generally accepted auditing standards and performed by independent certified public accountants or independent licensed public accountants, provided that the Attorney General and the Judicial Conference, as appropriate, may develop alternative auditing standards not later than 2 years after the date of enactment of this Act.

(2) PROCEDURES—Those procedures required by paragraph (1) shall—

(A) establish a method of selecting appropriate qualified persons to contract to perform those audits;

(B) establish a method of randomly selecting cases to be audited, except that not less than 1 out of every 250 cases in each Federal judicial district shall be selected for audit;

(C) require audits of schedules of income and expenses that reflect greater than average variances from the statistical norm of the district in which the schedules were filed if those variances occur by reason of higher income or higher expenses than the statistical norm of the district in which the schedules were filed; and

(D) establish procedures for providing, not less frequently than annually, public information concerning the aggregate results of such audits including the percentage of cases, by district, in which a material misstatement of income or expenditures is reported.

(b) AMENDMENTS—Section 586 of title 28, United States Code, is amended—

(1) in subsection (a), by striking paragraph (6) and inserting the following:

"(6) make such reports as the Attorney General directs, including the results of audits performed under section 603(a) of the Bankruptcy Abuse Prevention and Consumer Protection Act of 2005;"; and

(2) by adding at the end the following:

"(f)(1) The United States trustee for each district is authorized to contract with auditors to perform audits in cases designated by the United States trustee, in accordance with the procedures established under section 603(a) of the Bankruptcy Abuse Prevention and Consumer Protection Act of 2005.

"(2)(A) The report of each audit referred to in paragraph (1) shall be filed with the court and transmitted to the United States trustee. Each report shall clearly and conspicuously specify any material misstatement of income or expenditures or of assets identified by the person performing the audit. In any case in which a material misstatement of income or expenditures or of assets has been reported, the clerk of the district court (or the clerk of the bankruptcy court if one is certified under section 156(b) of this title) shall give notice of the misstatement to the creditors in the case.

"(B) If a material misstatement of income or expenditures or of assets is reported, the United States trustee shall—

"(i) report the material misstatement, if appropriate, to the United States Attorney pursuant to section 3057 of title 18; and

"(ii) if advisable, take appropriate action, including but not limited to commencing an adversary proceeding to revoke the debtor's discharge pursuant to section 727(d) of title 11.".

(c) AMENDMENTS TO SECTION 521 OF TITLE 11, U.S.C—Section 521(a) of title 11, United States Code, as so designated by section 106, is amended in each of paragraphs (3) and (4) by inserting "or an auditor serving under section 586(f) of title 28" after "serving in the case".

(d) AMENDMENTS TO SECTION 727 OF TITLE 11, U.S.C—Section 727(d) of title 11, United States Code, is amended—

(1) in paragraph (2), by striking "or" at the end;

(2) in paragraph (3), by striking the period at the end and inserting "; or"; and

(3) by adding at the end the following:

"(4) the debtor has failed to explain satisfactorily—

"(A) a material misstatement in an audit referred to in section 586(f) of title 28; or

"(B) a failure to make available for inspection all necessary accounts, papers, documents, financial records, files, and all other papers, things, or property belonging to the debtor that are requested for an audit referred to in section 586(f) of title 28.".

(e) EFFECTIVE DATE—The amendments made by this section shall take effect 18 months after the date of enactment of this Act.

Sec. 604 SENSE OF CONGRESS REGARDING AVAILABILITY OF BANKRUPTCY DATA.

It is the sense of Congress that—

(1) the national policy of the United States should be that all data held by bankruptcy clerks in electronic form, to the extent such data reflects only public records (as defined in section 107 of title 11, United States Code), should be released in a usable electronic form in bulk to the public, subject to such appropriate privacy concerns and safeguards as Congress and the Judicial Conference of the United States may determine; and

(2) there should be established a bankruptcy data system in which—

(A) a single set of data definitions and forms are used to collect data nationwide; and

(B) data for any particular bankruptcy case are aggregated in the same electronic record.

TITLE VII

BANKRUPTCY TAX PROVISIONS

Sec. 701 TREATMENT OF CERTAIN LIENS.

(a) TREATMENT OF CERTAIN LIENS—Section 724 of title 11, United States Code, is amended—

(1) in subsection (b), in the matter preceding paragraph (1), by inserting "(other than to the extent that there is a properly perfected unavoidable tax lien arising in connection with an ad valorem tax on real or personal property of the estate)" after "under this title";

(2) in subsection (b)(2), by inserting "(except that such expenses, other than claims for wages, salaries, or commissions that arise after the date of the filing of the petition, shall be limited to expenses incurred under chapter 7 of this title and shall not include expenses incurred under chapter 11 of this title)" after "507(a)(1)"; and

(3) by adding at the end the following:

"(e) Before subordinating a tax lien on real or personal property of the estate, the trustee shall—

"(1) exhaust the unencumbered assets of the estate; and

"(2) in a manner consistent with section 506(c), recover from property securing an allowed secured claim the reasonable, necessary costs and expenses of preserving or disposing of such property.

"(f) Notwithstanding the exclusion of ad valorem tax liens under this section and subject to the requirements of subsection (e), the following may be paid from property of the estate which secures a tax lien, or the proceeds of such property:

"(1) Claims for wages, salaries, and commissions that are entitled to priority under section 507(a)(4).

"(2) Claims for contributions to an employee benefit plan entitled to priority under section 507(a)(5).".

(b) DETERMINATION OF TAX LIABILITY—Section 505(a)(2) of title 11, United States Code, is amended—

(1) in subparagraph (A), by striking "or" at the end;

(2) in subparagraph (B), by striking the period at the end and inserting "; or"; and

(3) by adding at the end the following:

"(C) the amount or legality of any amount arising in connection with an ad valorem tax on real or personal property of the estate, if the applicable period for contesting or redetermining that amount under any law (other than a bankruptcy law) has expired.".

Sec. 702 Treatment of Fuel Tax Claims.

Section 501 of title 11, United States Code, is amended by adding at the end the following:

"(e) A claim arising from the liability of a debtor for fuel use tax assessed consistent with the requirements of section 31705 of title 49 may be filed by the base jurisdiction designated pursuant to the International Fuel Tax Agreement (as defined in section 31701 of title 49) and, if so filed, shall be allowed as a single claim.".

Sec. 703 Notice of Request for a Determination of Taxes.

Section 505(b) of title 11, United States Code, is amended—

(1) in the first sentence, by inserting "at the address and in the manner designated in paragraph (1)" after "determination of such tax";

(2) by striking "(1) upon payment" and inserting "(A) upon payment";

(3) by striking "(A) such governmental unit" and inserting "(i) such governmental unit";

(4) by striking "(B) such governmental unit" and inserting "(ii) such governmental unit";

(5) by striking "(2) upon payment" and inserting "(B) upon payment";

(6) by striking "(3) upon payment" and inserting "(C) upon payment";

(7) by striking "(b)" and inserting "(2)"; and

(8) by inserting before paragraph (2), as so designated, the following:

"(b)(1)(A) The clerk shall maintain a list under which a Federal, State, or local governmental unit responsible for the collection of taxes within the district may—

"(i) designate an address for service of requests under this subsection; and

"(ii) describe where further information concerning additional requirements for filing such requests may be found.

"(B) If such governmental unit does not designate an address and provide such address to the clerk under subparagraph (A), any request made under this subsection may be served at the address for the filing of a tax return or protest with the appropriate taxing authority of such governmental unit.".

Sec. 704 Rate of Interest on Tax Claims.

(a) In General—Subchapter I of chapter 5 of title 11, United States Code, is amended by adding at the end the following:

"§ 511. Rate of interest on tax claims

"(a) If any provision of this title requires the payment of interest on a tax claim or on an administrative expense tax, or the payment of interest to enable a creditor to receive the present value of the allowed amount of a tax claim, the rate of interest shall be the rate determined under applicable nonbankruptcy law.

"(b) In the case of taxes paid under a confirmed plan under this title, the rate of interest shall be determined as of the calendar month in which the plan is confirmed.".

(b) CLERICAL AMENDMENT—The table of sections for subchapter I of chapter 5 of title 11, United States Code, is amended by adding at the end the following:

"511. Rate of interest on tax claims.".

Sec. 705 PRIORITY OF TAX CLAIMS.

Section 507(a)(8) of title 11, United States Code, is amended—

(1) in subparagraph (A)—

(A) in the matter preceding clause (i), by inserting "for a taxable year ending on or before the date of the filing of the petition" after "gross receipts";

(B) in clause (i), by striking "for a taxable year ending on or before the date of the filing of the petition"; and

(C) by striking clause (ii) and inserting the following:

"(ii) assessed within 240 days before the date of the filing of the petition, exclusive of—

"(I) any time during which an offer in compromise with respect to that tax was pending or in effect during that 240-day period, plus 30 days; and

"(II) any time during which a stay of proceedings against collections was in effect in a prior case under this title during that 240-day period, plus 90 days."; and

(2) by adding at the end the following:

"An otherwise applicable time period specified in this paragraph shall be suspended for any period during which a governmental unit is prohibited under applicable nonbankruptcy law from collecting a tax as a result of a request by the debtor for a hearing and an appeal of any collection action taken or proposed against the debtor, plus 90 days; plus any time during which the stay of proceedings was in effect in a prior case under this title or during which collection was precluded by the existence of 1 or more confirmed plans under this title, plus 90 days.".

Sec. 706 PRIORITY PROPERTY TAXES INCURRED.

Section 507(a)(8)(B) of title 11, United States Code, is amended by striking "assessed" and inserting "incurred".

Sec. 707 No Discharge of Fraudulent Taxes in Chapter 13.

Section 1328(a)(2) of title 11, United States Code, as amended by section 314, is amended by striking "paragraph" and inserting "section 507(a)(8)(C) or in paragraph (1)(B), (1)(C),".

Sec. 708 No Discharge of Fraudulent Taxes in Chapter 11.

Section 1141(d) of title 11, United States Code, as amended by sections 321 and 330, is amended by adding at the end the following:

"(6) Notwithstanding paragraph (1), the confirmation of a plan does not discharge a debtor that is a corporation from any debt—

"(A) of a kind specified in paragraph (2)(A) or (2)(B) of section 523(a) that is owed to a domestic governmental unit, or owed to a person as the result of an action filed under subchapter III of chapter 37 of title 31 or any similar State statute; or

"(B) for a tax or customs duty with respect to which the debtor—

"(i) made a fraudulent return; or

"(ii) willfully attempted in any manner to evade or to defeat such tax or such customs duty.".

Sec. 709 Stay of Tax Proceedings Limited to Prepetition Taxes.

Section 362(a)(8) of title 11, United States Code, is amended by striking "the debtor" and inserting "a corporate debtor's tax liability for a taxable period the bankruptcy court may determine or concerning the tax liability of a debtor who is an individual for a taxable period ending before the date of the order for relief under this title".

Sec. 710 Periodic Payment of Taxes in Chapter 11 Cases.

Section 1129(a)(9) of title 11, United States Code, is amended—

(1) in subparagraph (B), by striking "and" at the end;

(2) in subparagraph (C), by striking "deferred cash payments," and all that follows through the end of the subparagraph, and inserting "regular installment payments in cash—

"(i) of a total value, as of the effective date of the plan, equal to the allowed amount of such claim;

"(ii) over a period ending not later than 5 years after the date of the order for relief under section 301, 302, or 303; and

"(iii) in a manner not less favorable than the most favored nonpriority unsecured claim provided for by the plan (other than cash payments made to a class of creditors under section 1122(b)); and"; and

(3) by adding at the end the following:

"(D) with respect to a secured claim which would otherwise meet the description of an unsecured claim of a governmental unit under section 507(a)(8), but for the secured status of that claim, the holder of that claim will receive on account of that claim, cash payments, in the same manner and over the same period, as prescribed in subparagraph (C).".

Sec. 711 AVOIDANCE OF STATUTORY TAX LIENS PROHIBITED.

Section 545(2) of title 11, United States Code, is amended by inserting before the semicolon at the end the following: ", except in any case in which a purchaser is a purchaser described in section 6323 of the Internal Revenue Code of 1986, or in any other similar provision of State or local law".

Sec. 712 PAYMENT OF TAXES IN THE CONDUCT OF BUSINESS.

(a) PAYMENT OF TAXES REQUIRED—Section 960 of title 28, United States Code, is amended—

(1) by inserting "(a)" before "Any"; and

(2) by adding at the end the following:

"(b) A tax under subsection (a) shall be paid on or before the due date of the tax under applicable nonbankruptcy law, unless—

"(1) the tax is a property tax secured by a lien against property that is abandoned under section 554 of title 11, within a reasonable period of time after the lien attaches, by the trustee in a case under title 11; or

"(2) payment of the tax is excused under a specific provision of title 11.

"(c) In a case pending under chapter 7 of title 11, payment of a tax may be deferred until final distribution is made under section 726 of title 11, if—

"(1) the tax was not incurred by a trustee duly appointed or elected under chapter 7 of title 11; or

"(2) before the due date of the tax, an order of the court makes a finding of probable insufficiency of funds of the estate to pay in full the administrative expenses allowed under section 503(b) of title 11 that have the same priority in distribution under section 726(b) of title 11 as the priority of that tax.".

(b) PAYMENT OF AD VALOREM TAXES REQUIRED—Section 503(b)(1)(B)(i) of title 11, United States Code, is amended by inserting "whether secured or unsecured, including property taxes for which liability is in rem, in personam, or both," before "except".

(c) REQUEST FOR PAYMENT OF ADMINISTRATIVE EXPENSE TAXES ELIMINAT-ED—Section 503(b)(1) of title 11, United States Code, is amended—

(1) in subparagraph (B), by striking "and" at the end;

(2) in subparagraph (C), by adding "and" at the end; and

(3) by adding at the end the following:

"(D) notwithstanding the requirements of subsection (a), a governmental unit shall not be required to file a request for the payment of an expense described in subparagraph (B) or (C), as a condition of its being an allowed administrative expense;".

(d) PAYMENT OF TAXES AND FEES AS SECURED CLAIMS—Section 506 of title 11, United States Code, is amended—

(1) in subsection (b), by inserting "or State statute" after "agreement"; and

(2) in subsection (c), by inserting ", including the payment of all ad valorem property taxes with respect to the property" before the period at the end.

Sec. 713 TARDILY FILED PRIORITY TAX CLAIMS.

Section 726(a)(1) of title 11, United States Code, is amended by striking "before the date on which the trustee commences distribution under this section;" and inserting the following: "on or before the earlier of—

"(A) the date that is 10 days after the mailing to creditors of the summary of the trustee's final report; or

"(B) the date on which the trustee commences final distribution under this section;".

Sec. 714 INCOME TAX RETURNS PREPARED BY TAX AUTHORITIES.

Section 523(a) of title 11, United States Code, as amended by sections 215 and 224, is amended—

(1) in paragraph (1)(B)—

(A) in the matter preceding clause (i), by inserting "or equivalent report or notice," after "a return,";

(B) in clause (i), by inserting "or given" after "filed"; and

(C) in clause (ii)—

(i) by inserting "or given" after "filed"; and

(ii) by inserting ", report, or notice" after "return"; and

(2) by adding at the end the following:

"For purposes of this subsection, the term "return" means a return that satisfies the requirements of applicable nonbankruptcy law (including applicable filing requirements). Such term includes a return prepared pursuant to section 6020(a) of the Internal Revenue Code of 1986, or similar State or local law, or a written stipulation to a judgment or a final order entered by a nonbankruptcy tribunal, but does not include a return made pursuant to section 6020(b) of the Internal Revenue Code of 1986, or a similar State or local law.".

Sec. 715 DISCHARGE OF THE ESTATE'S LIABILITY FOR UNPAID TAXES.

Section 505(b)(2) of title 11, United States Code, as amended by section 703, is amended by inserting "the estate," after "misrepresentation,".

Sec. 716 REQUIREMENT TO FILE TAX RETURNS TO CONFIRM CHAPTER 13 PLANS.

(a) FILING OF PREPETITION TAX RETURNS REQUIRED FOR PLAN CONFIRMATION—Section 1325(a) of title 11, United States Code, as amended by sections 102, 213, and 306, is amended by inserting after paragraph (8) the following:

"(9) the debtor has filed all applicable Federal, State, and local tax returns as required by section 1308.".

(b) ADDITIONAL TIME PERMITTED FOR FILING TAX RETURNS—

(1) IN GENERAL—Subchapter I of chapter 13 of title 11, United States Code, is amended by adding at the end the following:

"§ 1308. Filing of prepetition tax returns

"(a) Not later than the day before the date on which the meeting of the creditors is first scheduled to be held under section 341(a), if the debtor was required to file a tax return under applicable nonbankruptcy law, the debtor shall file with appropriate tax authorities all tax returns for all taxable periods ending during the 4-year period ending on the date of the filing of the petition.

"(b)(1) Subject to paragraph (2), if the tax returns required by subsection (a) have not been filed by the date on which the meeting of creditors is first scheduled to be held under section 341(a), the trustee may hold open that meeting for a reasonable period of time to allow the debtor an additional period of time to file any unfiled returns, but such additional period of time shall not extend beyond—

"(A) for any return that is past due as of the date of the filing of the petition, the date that is 120 days after the date of that meeting; or

"(B) for any return that is not past due as of the date of the filing of the petition, the later of—

"(i) the date that is 120 days after the date of that meeting; or

"(ii) the date on which the return is due under the last automatic extension of time for filing that return to which the debtor is entitled, and for which request is timely made, in accordance with applicable nonbankruptcy law.

172

"(2) After notice and a hearing, and order entered before the tolling of any applicable filing period determined under this subsection, if the debtor demonstrates by a preponderance of the evidence that the failure to file a return as required under this subsection is attributable to circumstances beyond the control of the debtor, the court may extend the filing period established by the trustee under this subsection for—

"(A) a period of not more than 30 days for returns described in paragraph (1); and

"(B) a period not to extend after the applicable extended due date for a return described in paragraph (2).

"(c) For purposes of this section, the term 'return' includes a return prepared pursuant to subsection (a) or (b) of section 6020 of the Internal Revenue Code of 1986, or a similar State or local law, or a written stipulation to a judgment or a final order entered by a nonbankruptcy tribunal.".

(2) CONFORMING AMENDMENT—The table of sections for subchapter I of chapter 13 of title 11, United States Code, is amended by adding at the end the following:

"1308. Filing of prepetition tax returns.".

(c) DISMISSAL OR CONVERSION ON FAILURE TO COMPLY—Section 1307 of title 11, United States Code, is amended—

(1) by redesignating subsections (e) and (f) as subsections (f) and (g), respectively; and

(2) by inserting after subsection (d) the following:

"(e) Upon the failure of the debtor to file a tax return under section 1308, on request of a party in interest or the United States trustee and after notice and a hearing, the court shall dismiss a case or convert a case under this chapter to a case under chapter 7 of this title, whichever is in the best interest of the creditors and the estate.".

(d) TIMELY FILED CLAIMS—Section 502(b)(9) of title 11, United States Code, is amended by inserting before the period at the end the following: ", and except that in a case under chapter 13, a claim of a governmental unit for a tax with respect to a return filed under section 1308 shall be timely if the claim is filed on or before the date that is 60 days after the date on which such return was filed as required".

(e) RULES FOR OBJECTIONS TO CLAIMS AND TO CONFIRMATION—It is the sense of Congress that the Judicial Conference of the United States should, as soon as practicable after the date of enactment of this Act, propose amended Federal Rules of Bankruptcy Procedure that provide—

(1) notwithstanding the provisions of Rule 3015(f), in cases under chapter 13 of title 11, United States Code, that an objection to the confirmation of a plan filed by a governmental unit on or before the date that is 60 days after the date on which the debtor files all tax returns required under sections 1308 and 1325(a)(7) of title 11, United States

Code, shall be treated for all purposes as if such objection had been timely filed before such confirmation; and

(2) in addition to the provisions of Rule 3007, in a case under chapter 13 of title 11, United States Code, that no objection to a claim for a tax with respect to which a return is required to be filed under section 1308 of title 11, United States Code, shall be filed until such return has been filed as required.

Sec. 717 STANDARDS FOR TAX DISCLOSURE.

Section 1125(a)(1) of title 11, United States Code, is amended—

(1) by inserting "including a discussion of the potential material Federal tax consequences of the plan to the debtor, any successor to the debtor, and a hypothetical investor typical of the holders of claims or interests in the case," after "records,"; and

(2) by striking "a hypothetical reasonable investor typical of holders of claims or interests" and inserting "such a hypothetical investor".

Sec. 718 SETOFF OF TAX REFUNDS.

Section 362(b) of title 11, United States Code, as amended by sections 224, 303, 311, and 401, is amended by inserting after paragraph (25) the following:

"(26) under subsection (a), of the setoff under applicable nonbankruptcy law of an income tax refund, by a governmental unit, with respect to a taxable period that ended before the date of the order for relief against an income tax liability for a taxable period that also ended before the date of the order for relief, except that in any case in which the setoff of an income tax refund is not permitted under applicable nonbankruptcy law because of a pending action to determine the amount or legality of a tax liability, the governmental unit may hold the refund pending the resolution of the action, unless the court, on the motion of the trustee and after notice and a hearing, grants the taxing authority adequate protection (within the meaning of section 361) for the secured claim of such authority in the setoff under section 506(a);".

Sec. 719 SPECIAL PROVISIONS RELATED TO THE TREATMENT OF STATE AND LOCAL TAXES.

(a) IN GENERAL—

(1) SPECIAL PROVISIONS—Section 346 of title 11, United States Code, is amended to read as follows:

"§ 346. Special provisions related to the treatment of State and local taxes

"(a) Whenever the Internal Revenue Code of 1986 provides that a separate taxable estate or entity is created in a case concerning a debtor under this title, and the income, gain, loss, deductions, and credits of such estate shall be taxed to or claimed by the estate, a separate taxable estate is also created for purposes of any State and local law imposing a tax on or measured by income and such income, gain, loss, deductions, and credits shall be taxed to or claimed by the estate and may not be taxed to or claimed by the debtor. The preceding sentence shall not apply if the case is dismissed. The trustee shall make tax returns of income required under any such State or local law.

"(b) Whenever the Internal Revenue Code of 1986 provides that no separate taxable estate shall be created in a case concerning a debtor under this title, and the income, gain, loss, deductions, and credits of an estate shall be taxed to or claimed by the debtor, such income, gain, loss, deductions, and credits shall be taxed to or claimed by the debtor under a State or local law imposing a tax on or measured by income and may not be taxed to or claimed by the estate. The trustee shall make such tax returns of income of corporations and of partnerships as are required under any State or local law, but with respect to partnerships, shall make such returns only to the extent such returns are also required to be made under such Code. The estate shall be liable for any tax imposed on such corporation or partnership, but not for any tax imposed on partners or members.

"(c) With respect to a partnership or any entity treated as a partnership under a State or local law imposing a tax on or measured by income that is a debtor in a case under this title, any gain or loss resulting from a distribution of property from such partnership, or any distributive share of any income, gain, loss, deduction, or credit of a partner or member that is distributed, or considered distributed, from such partnership, after the commencement of the case, is gain, loss, income, deduction, or credit, as the case may be, of the partner or member, and if such partner or member is a debtor in a case under this title, shall be subject to tax in accordance with subsection (a) or (b).

"(d) For purposes of any State or local law imposing a tax on or measured by income, the taxable period of a debtor in a case under this title shall terminate only if and to the extent that the taxable period of such debtor terminates under the Internal Revenue Code of 1986.

"(e) The estate in any case described in subsection (a) shall use the same accounting method as the debtor used immediately before the commencement of the case, if such method of accounting complies with applicable nonbankruptcy tax law.

"(f) For purposes of any State or local law imposing a tax on or measured by income, a transfer of property from the debtor to the estate or from the estate to the debtor shall not be treated as a disposition for purposes of any provision assigning tax consequences to a disposition, except to the extent that such transfer is treated as a disposition under the Internal Revenue Code of 1986.

"(g) Whenever a tax is imposed pursuant to a State or local law imposing a tax on or measured by income pursuant to subsection (a) or (b), such tax shall be imposed at rates generally applicable to the same types of entities under such State or local law.

175

"(h) The trustee shall withhold from any payment of claims for wages, salaries, commissions, dividends, interest, or other payments, or collect, any amount required to be withheld or collected under applicable State or local tax law, and shall pay such withheld or collected amount to the appropriate governmental unit at the time and in the manner required by such tax law, and with the same priority as the claim from which such amount was withheld or collected was paid.

"(i)(1) To the extent that any State or local law imposing a tax on or measured by income provides for the carryover of any tax attribute from one taxable period to a subsequent taxable period, the estate shall succeed to such tax attribute in any case in which such estate is subject to tax under subsection (a).

"(2) After such a case is closed or dismissed, the debtor shall succeed to any tax attribute to which the estate succeeded under paragraph (1) to the extent consistent with the Internal Revenue Code of 1986.

"(3) The estate may carry back any loss or tax attribute to a taxable period of the debtor that ended before the date of the order for relief under this title to the extent that—

"(A) applicable State or local tax law provides for a carryback in the case of the debtor; and

"(B) the same or a similar tax attribute may be carried back by the estate to such a taxable period of the debtor under the Internal Revenue Code of 1986.

"(j)(1) For purposes of any State or local law imposing a tax on or measured by income, income is not realized by the estate, the debtor, or a successor to the debtor by reason of discharge of indebtedness in a case under this title, except to the extent, if any, that such income is subject to tax under the Internal Revenue Code of 1986.

"(2) Whenever the Internal Revenue Code of 1986 provides that the amount excluded from gross income in respect of the discharge of indebtedness in a case under this title shall be applied to reduce the tax attributes of the debtor or the estate, a similar reduction shall be made under any State or local law imposing a tax on or measured by income to the extent such State or local law recognizes such attributes. Such State or local law may also provide for the reduction of other attributes to the extent that the full amount of income from the discharge of indebtedness has not been applied.

"(k)(1) Except as provided in this section and section 505, the time and manner of filing tax returns and the items of income, gain, loss, deduction, and credit of any taxpayer shall be determined under applicable nonbankruptcy law.

"(2) For Federal tax purposes, the provisions of this section are subject to the Internal Revenue Code of 1986 and other applicable Federal nonbankruptcy law.".

(2) CLERICAL AMENDMENT—The table of sections for chapter 3 of title 11, United States Code, is amended by striking the item relating to section 346 and inserting the following:

"346. Special provisions related to the treatment of State and local taxes.".

(b) CONFORMING AMENDMENTS—Title 11 of the United States Code is amended—

(1) by striking section 728;

(2) in the table of sections for chapter 7 by striking the item relating to section 728;

(3) in section 1146—

(A) by striking subsections (a) and (b); and

(B) by redesignating subsections (c) and (d) as subsections (a) and (b), respectively; and

(4) in section 1231—

(A) by striking subsections (a) and (b); and

(B) by redesignating subsections (c) and (d) as subsections (a) and (b), respectively.

Sec. 720 DISMISSAL FOR FAILURE TO TIMELY FILE TAX RETURNS.

Section 521 of title 11, United States Code, as amended by sections 106, 225, 305, 315, and 316, is amended by adding at the end the following:

"(j)(1) Notwithstanding any other provision of this title, if the debtor fails to file a tax return that becomes due after the commencement of the case or to properly obtain an extension of the due date for filing such return, the taxing authority may request that the court enter an order converting or dismissing the case.

"(2) If the debtor does not file the required return or obtain the extension referred to in paragraph (1) within 90 days after a request is filed by the taxing authority under that paragraph, the court shall convert or dismiss the case, whichever is in the best interests of creditors and the estate.".

TITLE VIII

ANCILLARY AND OTHER CROSS-BORDER CASES

Sec. 801 AMENDMENT TO ADD CHAPTER 15 TO TITLE 11, UNITED STATES CODE.

(a) IN GENERAL—Title 11, United States Code, is amended by inserting after chapter 13 the following:

"**CHAPTER 15—ANCILLARY AND OTHER CROSS-BORDER CASES**

"Sec.

"**§ 1501. Purpose and scope of application**

"(a) The purpose of this chapter is to incorporate the Model Law on Cross-Border Insolvency so as to provide effective mechanisms for dealing with cases of cross-border insolvency with the objectives of—

"(1) cooperation between—

"(A) courts of the United States, United States trustees, trustees, examiners, debtors, and debtors in possession; and

"(B) the courts and other competent authorities of foreign countries involved in cross-border insolvency cases;

"(2) greater legal certainty for trade and investment;

"(3) fair and efficient administration of cross-border insolvencies that protects the interests of all creditors, and other interested entities, including the debtor;

"(4) protection and maximization of the value of the debtor's assets; and

"(5) facilitation of the rescue of financially troubled businesses, thereby protecting investment and preserving employment.

"(b) This chapter applies where—

"(1) assistance is sought in the United States by a foreign court or a foreign representative in connection with a foreign proceeding;

"(2) assistance is sought in a foreign country in connection with a case under this title;

"(3) a foreign proceeding and a case under this title with respect to the same debtor are pending concurrently; or

"(4) creditors or other interested persons in a foreign country have an interest in requesting the commencement of, or participating in, a case or proceeding under this title.

"(c) This chapter does not apply to—

"(1) a proceeding concerning an entity, other than a foreign insurance company, identified by exclusion in section 109(b);

"(2) an individual, or to an individual and such individual's spouse, who have debts within the limits specified in section 109(e) and who are citizens of the United States or aliens lawfully admitted for permanent residence in the United States; or

"(3) an entity subject to a proceeding under the Securities Investor Protection Act of 1970, a stockbroker subject to subchapter III of chapter 7 of this title, or a commodity broker subject to subchapter IV of chapter 7 of this title.

"(d) The court may not grant relief under this chapter with respect to any deposit, escrow, trust fund, or other security required or permitted under any applicable State insurance law or regulation for the benefit of claim holders in the United States.

"SUBCHAPTER I—GENERAL PROVISIONS

"§ 1502. Definitions

"For the purposes of this chapter, the term—

"(1) 'debtor' means an entity that is the subject of a foreign proceeding;

"(2) 'establishment' means any place of operations where the debtor carries out a nontransitory economic activity;

"(3) 'foreign court' means a judicial or other authority competent to control or supervise a foreign proceeding;

"(4) 'foreign main proceeding' means a foreign proceeding pending in the country where the debtor has the center of its main interests;

"(5) 'foreign nonmain proceeding' means a foreign proceeding, other than a foreign main proceeding, pending in a country where the debtor has an establishment;

"(6) 'trustee' includes a trustee, a debtor in possession in a case under any chapter of this title, or a debtor under chapter 9 of this title;

"(7) 'recognition' means the entry of an order granting recognition of a foreign main proceeding or foreign nonmain proceeding under this chapter; and

"(8) 'within the territorial jurisdiction of the United States', when used with reference to property of a debtor, refers to tangible property located within the territory of the United States and intangible property deemed under applicable nonbankruptcy law to be located within that territory, including any property subject to attachment or garnishment that may properly be seized or garnished by an action in a Federal or State court in the United States.

"§ 1503. International obligations of the United States

"To the extent that this chapter conflicts with an obligation of the United States arising out of any treaty or other form of agreement to which it is a party with one or more other countries, the requirements of the treaty or agreement prevail.

"§ 1504. Commencement of ancillary case

"A case under this chapter is commenced by the filing of a petition for recognition of a foreign proceeding under section 1515.

"§ 1505. Authorization to act in a foreign country

"A trustee or another entity (including an examiner) may be authorized by the court to act in a foreign country on behalf of an estate created under section 541. An entity authorized to act under this section may act in any way permitted by the applicable foreign law.

"§ 1506. Public policy exception

"Nothing in this chapter prevents the court from refusing to take an action governed by this chapter if the action would be manifestly contrary to the public policy of the United States.

"§ 1507. Additional assistance

"(a) Subject to the specific limitations stated elsewhere in this chapter the court, if recognition is granted, may provide additional assistance to a foreign representative under this title or under other laws of the United States.

"(b) In determining whether to provide additional assistance under this title or under other laws of the United States, the court shall consider whether such additional assistance, consistent with the principles of comity, will reasonably assure—

"(1) just treatment of all holders of claims against or interests in the debtor's property;

"(2) protection of claim holders in the United States against prejudice and inconvenience in the processing of claims in such foreign proceeding;

"(3) prevention of preferential or fraudulent dispositions of property of the debtor;

"(4) distribution of proceeds of the debtor's property substantially in accordance with the order prescribed by this title; and

"(5) if appropriate, the provision of an opportunity for a fresh start for the individual that such foreign proceeding concerns.

"§ 1508. Interpretation

"In interpreting this chapter, the court shall consider its international origin, and the need to promote an application of this chapter that is consistent with the application of similar statutes adopted by foreign jurisdictions.

"SUBCHAPTER II—ACCESS OF FOREIGN REPRESENTATIVES AND CREDITORS TO THE COURT

"§ 1509. Right of direct access

"(a) A foreign representative may commence a case under section 1504 by filing directly with the court a petition for recognition of a foreign proceeding under section 1515.

"(b) If the court grants recognition under section 1517, and subject to any limitations that the court may impose consistent with the policy of this chapter—

"(1) the foreign representative has the capacity to sue and be sued in a court in the United States;

"(2) the foreign representative may apply directly to a court in the United States for appropriate relief in that court; and

"(3) a court in the United States shall grant comity or cooperation to the foreign representative.

"(c) A request for comity or cooperation by a foreign representative in a court in the United States other than the court which granted recognition shall be accompanied by a certified copy of an order granting recognition under section 1517.

"(d) If the court denies recognition under this chapter, the court may issue any appropriate order necessary to prevent the foreign representative from obtaining comity or cooperation from courts in the United States.

"(e) Whether or not the court grants recognition, and subject to sections 306 and 1510, a foreign representative is subject to applicable nonbankruptcy law.

"(f) Notwithstanding any other provision of this section, the failure of a foreign representative to commence a case or to obtain recognition under this chapter does not affect any right the foreign representative may have to sue in a court in the United States to collect or recover a claim which is the property of the debtor.

"§ 1510. Limited jurisdiction

"The sole fact that a foreign representative files a petition under section 1515 does not subject the foreign representative to the jurisdiction of any court in the United States for any other purpose.

"§ 1511. Commencement of case under section 301 or 303

"(a) Upon recognition, a foreign representative may commence—

"(1) an involuntary case under section 303; or

"(2) a voluntary case under section 301 or 302, if the foreign proceeding is a foreign main proceeding.

"(b) The petition commencing a case under subsection (a) must be accompanied by a certified copy of an order granting recognition. The court where the petition for recognition has been filed must be advised of the foreign representative's intent to commence a case under subsection (a) prior to such commencement.

"§ 1512. Participation of a foreign representative in a case under this title

"Upon recognition of a foreign proceeding, the foreign representative in the recognized proceeding is entitled to participate as a party in interest in a case regarding the debtor under this title.

"§ 1513. Access of foreign creditors to a case under this title

"(a) Foreign creditors have the same rights regarding the commencement of, and participation in, a case under this title as domestic creditors.

"(b)(1) Subsection (a) does not change or codify present law as to the priority of claims under section 507 or 726, except that the claim of a foreign creditor under those sections shall not be given a lower priority than that of general unsecured claims without priority solely because the holder of such claim is a foreign creditor.

"(2)(A) Subsection (a) and paragraph (1) do not change or codify present law as to the allowability of foreign revenue claims or other foreign public law claims in a proceeding under this title.

"(B) Allowance and priority as to a foreign tax claim or other foreign public law claim shall be governed by any applicable tax treaty of the United States, under the conditions and circumstances specified therein.

"§ 1514. Notification to foreign creditors concerning a case under this title

"(a) Whenever in a case under this title notice is to be given to creditors generally or to any class or category of creditors, such notice shall also be given to the known creditors generally, or to creditors in the notified class or category, that do not have addresses in the United States. The court may order that appropriate steps be taken with a view to notifying any creditor whose address is not yet known.

"(b) Such notification to creditors with foreign addresses described in subsection (a) shall be given individually, unless the court considers that, under the circumstances, some other form of notification would be more appropriate. No letter or other formality is required.

"(c) When a notification of commencement of a case is to be given to foreign creditors, such notification shall—

"(1) indicate the time period for filing proofs of claim and specify the place for filing such proofs of claim;

"(2) indicate whether secured creditors need to file proofs of claim; and

"(3) contain any other information required to be included in such notification to creditors under this title and the orders of the court.

"(d) Any rule of procedure or order of the court as to notice or the filing of a proof of claim shall provide such additional time to creditors with foreign addresses as is reasonable under the circumstances.

"SUBCHAPTER III—RECOGNITION OF A FOREIGN PROCEEDING AND RELIEF

"§ 1515. Application for recognition

"(a) A foreign representative applies to the court for recognition of a foreign proceeding in which the foreign representative has been appointed by filing a petition for recognition.

"(b) A petition for recognition shall be accompanied by—

"(1) a certified copy of the decision commencing such foreign proceeding and appointing the foreign representative;

"(2) a certificate from the foreign court affirming the existence of such foreign proceeding and of the appointment of the foreign representative; or

"(3) in the absence of evidence referred to in paragraphs (1) and (2), any other evidence acceptable to the court of the existence of such foreign proceeding and of the appointment of the foreign representative.

"(c) A petition for recognition shall also be accompanied by a statement identifying all foreign proceedings with respect to the debtor that are known to the foreign representative.

"(d) The documents referred to in paragraphs (1) and (2) of subsection (b) shall be translated into English. The court may require a translation into English of additional documents.

"§ 1516. Presumptions concerning recognition

"(a) If the decision or certificate referred to in section 1515(b) indicates that the foreign proceeding is a foreign proceeding and that the person or body is a foreign representative, the court is entitled to so presume.

"(b) The court is entitled to presume that documents submitted in support of the petition for recognition are authentic, whether or not they have been legalized.

"(c) In the absence of evidence to the contrary, the debtor's registered office, or habitual residence in the case of an individual, is presumed to be the center of the debtor's main interests.

"§ 1517. Order granting recognition

"(a) Subject to section 1506, after notice and a hearing, an order recognizing a foreign proceeding shall be entered if—

"(1) such foreign proceeding for which recognition is sought is a foreign main proceeding or foreign nonmain proceeding within the meaning of section 1502;

"(2) the foreign representative applying for recognition is a person or body; and

"(3) the petition meets the requirements of section 1515.

"(b) Such foreign proceeding shall be recognized—

"(1) as a foreign main proceeding if it is pending in the country where the debtor has the center of its main interests; or

"(2) as a foreign nonmain proceeding if the debtor has an establishment within the meaning of section 1502 in the foreign country where the proceeding is pending.

"(c) A petition for recognition of a foreign proceeding shall be decided upon at the earliest possible time. Entry of an order recognizing a foreign proceeding constitutes recognition under this chapter.

"(d) The provisions of this subchapter do not prevent modification or termination of recognition if it is shown that the grounds for granting it were fully or partially lacking or have ceased to exist, but in considering such action the court shall give due weight to possible prejudice to parties that have relied upon the order granting recognition. A case under this chapter may be closed in the manner prescribed under section 350.

"§ 1518. Subsequent information

"From the time of filing the petition for recognition of a foreign proceeding, the foreign representative shall file with the court promptly a notice of change of status concerning—

"(1) any substantial change in the status of such foreign proceeding or the status of the foreign representative's appointment; and

"(2) any other foreign proceeding regarding the debtor that becomes known to the foreign representative.

"§ 1519. Relief that may be granted upon filing petition for recognition

"(a) From the time of filing a petition for recognition until the court rules on the petition, the court may, at the request of the foreign representative, where relief is urgently needed to protect the assets of the debtor or the interests of the creditors, grant relief of a provisional nature, including—

"(1) staying execution against the debtor's assets;

"(2) entrusting the administration or realization of all or part of the debtor's assets located in the United States to the foreign representative or another person authorized by the court, including an examiner, in order to protect and preserve the value of assets that, by their nature or because of other circumstances, are perishable, susceptible to devaluation or otherwise in jeopardy; and

"(3) any relief referred to in paragraph (3), (4), or (7) of section 1521(a).

"(b) Unless extended under section 1521(a)(6), the relief granted under this section terminates when the petition for recognition is granted.

"(c) It is a ground for denial of relief under this section that such relief would interfere with the administration of a foreign main proceeding.

"(d) The court may not enjoin a police or regulatory act of a governmental unit, including a criminal action or proceeding, under this section.

"(e) The standards, procedures, and limitations applicable to an injunction shall apply to relief under this section.

"(f) The exercise of rights not subject to the stay arising under section 362(a) pursuant to paragraph (6), (7), (17), or (27) of section 362(b) or pursuant to section 362(n) shall not be stayed by any order of a court or administrative agency in any proceeding under this chapter.

"§ 1520. Effects of recognition of a foreign main proceeding

"(a) Upon recognition of a foreign proceeding that is a foreign main proceeding—

"(1) sections 361 and 362 apply with respect to the debtor and the property of the debtor that is within the territorial jurisdiction of the United States;

"(2) sections 363, 549, and 552 apply to a transfer of an interest of the debtor in property that is within the territorial jurisdiction of the United States to the same extent that the sections would apply to property of an estate;

"(3) unless the court orders otherwise, the foreign representative may operate the debtor's business and may exercise the rights and powers of a trustee under and to the extent provided by sections 363 and 552; and

"(4) section 552 applies to property of the debtor that is within the territorial jurisdiction of the United States.

"(b) Subsection (a) does not affect the right to commence an individual action or proceeding in a foreign country to the extent necessary to preserve a claim against the debtor.

"(c) Subsection (a) does not affect the right of a foreign representative or an entity to file a petition commencing a case under this title or the right of any party to file claims or take other proper actions in such a case.

"§ 1521. Relief that may be granted upon recognition

"(a) Upon recognition of a foreign proceeding, whether main or nonmain, where necessary to effectuate the purpose of this chapter and to protect the assets of the debtor or the interests of the creditors, the court may, at the request of the foreign representative, grant any appropriate relief, including—

"(1) staying the commencement or continuation of an individual action or proceeding concerning the debtor's assets, rights, obligations or liabilities to the extent they have not been stayed under section 1520(a);

"(2) staying execution against the debtor's assets to the extent it has not been stayed under section 1520(a);

"(3) suspending the right to transfer, encumber or otherwise dispose of any assets of the debtor to the extent this right has not been suspended under section 1520(a);

"(4) providing for the examination of witnesses, the taking of evidence or the delivery of information concerning the debtor's assets, affairs, rights, obligations or liabilities;

"(5) entrusting the administration or realization of all or part of the debtor's assets within the territorial jurisdiction of the United States to the foreign representative or another person, including an examiner, authorized by the court;

"(6) extending relief granted under section 1519(a); and

"(7) granting any additional relief that may be available to a trustee, except for relief available under sections 522, 544, 545, 547, 548, 550, and 724(a).

"(b) Upon recognition of a foreign proceeding, whether main or nonmain, the court may, at the request of the foreign representative, entrust the distribution of all or part of the debtor's assets located in the United States to the foreign representative or another person, including an examiner, authorized by the court, provided that the court is satisfied that the interests of creditors in the United States are sufficiently protected.

"(c) In granting relief under this section to a representative of a foreign nonmain proceeding, the court must be satisfied that the relief relates to assets that, under the law of the United States, should be administered in the foreign nonmain proceeding or concerns information required in that proceeding.

"(d) The court may not enjoin a police or regulatory act of a governmental unit, including a criminal action or proceeding, under this section.

"(e) The standards, procedures, and limitations applicable to an injunction shall apply to relief under paragraphs (1), (2), (3), and (6) of subsection (a).

"(f) The exercise of rights not subject to the stay arising under section 362(a) pursuant to paragraph (6), (7), (17), or (27) of section 362(b) or pursuant to section 362(n) shall not be stayed by any order of a court or administrative agency in any proceeding under this chapter.

"§ 1522. Protection of creditors and other interested persons

"(a) The court may grant relief under section 1519 or 1521, or may modify or terminate relief under subsection (c), only if the interests of the creditors and other interested entities, including the debtor, are sufficiently protected.

"(b) The court may subject relief granted under section 1519 or 1521, or the operation of the debtor's business under section 1520(a)(3), to conditions it considers appropriate, including the giving of security or the filing of a bond.

"(c) The court may, at the request of the foreign representative or an entity affected by relief granted under section 1519 or 1521, or at its own motion, modify or terminate such relief.

"(d) Section 1104(d) shall apply to the appointment of an examiner under this chapter. Any examiner shall comply with the qualification requirements imposed on a trustee by section 322.

"§ 1523. Actions to avoid acts detrimental to creditors

"(a) Upon recognition of a foreign proceeding, the foreign representative has standing in a case concerning the debtor pending under another chapter of this title to initiate actions under sections 522, 544, 545, 547, 548, 550, 553, and 724(a).

"(b) When a foreign proceeding is a foreign nonmain proceeding, the court must be satisfied that an action under subsection (a) relates to assets that, under United States law, should be administered in the foreign nonmain proceeding.

"§ 1524. Intervention by a foreign representative

"Upon recognition of a foreign proceeding, the foreign representative may intervene in any proceedings in a State or Federal court in the United States in which the debtor is a party.

"SUBCHAPTER IV—COOPERATION WITH FOREIGN COURTS AND FOREIGN REPRESENTATIVES

"§ 1525. Cooperation and direct communication between the court and foreign courts or foreign representatives

"(a) Consistent with section 1501, the court shall cooperate to the maximum extent possible with a foreign court or a foreign representative, either directly or through the trustee.

"(b) The court is entitled to communicate directly with, or to request information or assistance directly from, a foreign court or a foreign representative, subject to the rights of a party in interest to notice and participation.

"§ 1526. Cooperation and direct communication between the trustee and foreign courts or foreign representatives

"(a) Consistent with section 1501, the trustee or other person, including an examiner, authorized by the court, shall, subject to the supervision of the court, cooperate to the maximum extent possible with a foreign court or a foreign representative.

"(b) The trustee or other person, including an examiner, authorized by the court is entitled, subject to the supervision of the court, to communicate directly with a foreign court or a foreign representative.

"§ 1527. Forms of cooperation

"Cooperation referred to in sections 1525 and 1526 may be implemented by any appropriate means, including—

"(1) appointment of a person or body, including an examiner, to act at the direction of the court;

"(2) communication of information by any means considered appropriate by the court;

"(3) coordination of the administration and supervision of the debtor's assets and affairs;

"(4) approval or implementation of agreements concerning the coordination of proceedings; and

"(5) coordination of concurrent proceedings regarding the same debtor.

"SUBCHAPTER V—CONCURRENT PROCEEDINGS

"§ 1528. Commencement of a case under this title after recognition of a foreign main proceeding

"After recognition of a foreign main proceeding, a case under another chapter of this title may be commenced only if the debtor has assets in the United States. The effects of such case shall be restricted to the assets of the debtor that are within the territorial jurisdiction of the United States and, to the extent necessary to implement cooperation and coordination under sections 1525, 1526, and 1527, to other assets of the debtor that are within the jurisdiction of the court under sections 541(a) of this title, and 1334(e) of title 28, to the extent that such other assets are not subject to the jurisdiction and control of a foreign proceeding that has been recognized under this chapter.

"§ 1529. Coordination of a case under this title and a foreign proceeding

"If a foreign proceeding and a case under another chapter of this title are pending concurrently regarding the same debtor, the court shall seek cooperation and coordination under sections 1525, 1526, and 1527, and the following shall apply:

"(1) If the case in the United States pending at the time the petition for recognition of such foreign proceeding is filed—

"(A) any relief granted under section 1519 or 1521 must be consistent with the relief granted in the case in the United States; and

"(B) section 1520 does not apply even if such foreign proceeding is recognized as a foreign main proceeding.

"(2) If a case in the United States under this title commences after recognition, or after the date of the filing of the petition for recognition, of such foreign proceeding—

"(A) any relief in effect under section 1519 or 1521 shall be reviewed by the court and shall be modified or terminated if inconsistent with the case in the United States; and

"(B) if such foreign proceeding is a foreign main proceeding, the stay and suspension referred to in section 1520(a) shall be modified or terminated if inconsistent with the relief granted in the case in the United States.

"(3) In granting, extending, or modifying relief granted to a representative of a foreign nonmain proceeding, the court must be satisfied that the relief relates to assets that, under the laws of the United States, should be administered in the foreign nonmain proceeding or concerns information required in that proceeding.

"(4) In achieving cooperation and coordination under sections 1528 and 1529, the court may grant any of the relief authorized under section 305.

"§ 1530. Coordination of more than 1 foreign proceeding

"In matters referred to in section 1501, with respect to more than 1 foreign proceeding regarding the debtor, the court shall seek cooperation and coordination under sections 1525, 1526, and 1527, and the following shall apply:

"(1) Any relief granted under section 1519 or 1521 to a representative of a foreign nonmain proceeding after recognition of a foreign main proceeding must be consistent with the foreign main proceeding.

"(2) If a foreign main proceeding is recognized after recognition, or after the filing of a petition for recognition, of a foreign nonmain proceeding, any relief in effect under section 1519 or 1521 shall be reviewed by the court and shall be modified or terminated if inconsistent with the foreign main proceeding.

"(3) If, after recognition of a foreign nonmain proceeding, another foreign nonmain proceeding is recognized, the court shall grant, modify, or terminate relief for the purpose of facilitating coordination of the proceedings.

"§ 1531. Presumption of insolvency based on recognition of a foreign main proceeding

"In the absence of evidence to the contrary, recognition of a foreign main proceeding is, for the purpose of commencing a proceeding under section 303, proof that the debtor is generally not paying its debts as such debts become due.

"§ 1532. Rule of payment in concurrent proceedings

"Without prejudice to secured claims or rights in rem, a creditor who has received payment with respect to its claim in a foreign proceeding pursuant to a law relating to insolvency may not receive a payment for the same claim in a case under any other chapter of this title regarding the debtor, so long as the payment to other creditors of the same class is proportionately less than the payment the creditor has already received.".

(b) CLERICAL AMENDMENT—The table of chapters for title 11, United States Code, is amended by inserting after the item relating to chapter 13 the following:

"**15. Ancillary and Other Cross-Border Cases** . . . . **1501**".

Sec. 802 Other Amendments to Titles 11 and 28, United States Code.

(a) Applicability of Chapters—Section 103 of title 11, United States Code, is amended—

(1) in subsection (a), by inserting before the period the following: ", and this chapter, sections 307, 362(n), 555 through 557, and 559 through 562 apply in a case under chapter 15"; and

(2) by adding at the end the following:

"(k) Chapter 15 applies only in a case under such chapter, except that—

"(1) sections 1505, 1513, and 1514 apply in all cases under this title; and

"(2) section 1509 applies whether or not a case under this title is pending.".

(b) Definitions—Section 101 of title 11, United States Code, is amended by striking paragraphs (23) and (24) and inserting the following:

"(23) 'foreign proceeding' means a collective judicial or administrative proceeding in a foreign country, including an interim proceeding, under a law relating to insolvency or adjustment of debt in which proceeding the assets and affairs of the debtor are subject to control or supervision by a foreign court, for the purpose of reorganization or liquidation;

"(24) 'foreign representative' means a person or body, including a person or body appointed on an interim basis, authorized in a foreign proceeding to administer the reorganization or the liquidation of the debtor's assets or affairs or to act as a representative of such foreign proceeding;".

(c) Amendments to Title 28, United States Code—

(1) Procedures—Section 157(b)(2) of title 28, United States Code, is amended—

(A) in subparagraph (N), by striking "and" at the end;

(B) in subparagraph (O), by striking the period at the end and inserting "; and"; and

(C) by adding at the end the following:

"(P) recognition of foreign proceedings and other matters under chapter 15 of title 11.".

(2) Bankruptcy Cases and Proceedings—Section 1334(c) of title 28, United States Code, is amended by striking "Nothing in" and inserting "Except with respect to a case under chapter 15 of title 11, nothing in".

(3) Duties of Trustees—Section 586(a)(3) of title 28, United States Code, is amended by striking "or 13" and inserting "13, or 15".

(4) Venue of Cases Ancillary to Foreign Proceedings—Section 1410 of title 28, United States Code, is amended to read as follows:

"§ 1410. Venue of cases ancillary to foreign proceedings

"A case under chapter 15 of title 11 may be commenced in the district court of the United States for the district—

"(1) in which the debtor has its principal place of business or principal assets in the United States;

"(2) if the debtor does not have a place of business or assets in the United States, in which there is pending against the debtor an action or proceeding in a Federal or State court; or

"(3) in a case other than those specified in paragraph (1) or (2), in which venue will be consistent with the interests of justice and the convenience of the parties, having regard to the relief sought by the foreign representative.".

(d) OTHER SECTIONS OF TITLE 11—Title 11 of the United States Code is amended—

(1) in section 109(b), by striking paragraph (3) and inserting the following:

"(3)(A) a foreign insurance company, engaged in such business in the United States; or

"(B) a foreign bank, savings bank, cooperative bank, savings and loan association, building and loan association, or credit union, that has a branch or agency (as defined in section 1(b) of the International Banking Act of 1978 in the United States.";

(2) in section 303, by striking subsection (k);

(3) by striking section 304;

(4) in the table of sections for chapter 3 by striking the item relating to section 304;

(5) in section 306 by striking ", 304," each place it appears;

(6) in section 305(a) by striking paragraph (2) and inserting the following:

"(2)(A) a petition under section 1515 for recognition of a foreign proceeding has been granted; and

"(B) the purposes of chapter 15 of this title would be best served by such dismissal or suspension."; and

(7) in section 508—

(A) by striking subsection (a); and

(B) in subsection (b), by striking "(b)".

TITLE IX

FINANCIAL CONTRACT PROVISIONS

Sec. 901 TREATMENT OF CERTAIN AGREEMENTS BY CONSERVATORS OR RECEIVERS OF INSURED DEPOSITORY INSTITUTIONS.

(a) DEFINITION OF QUALIFIED FINANCIAL CONTRACT—

(1) FDIC-INSURED DEPOSITORY INSTITUTIONS—Section 11(e)(8)(D) of the Federal Deposit Insurance Act (12 U.S.C. 1821(e)(8)(D)) is amended—

(A) by striking "subsection—" and inserting "subsection, the following definitions shall apply:"; and

(B) in clause (i), by inserting ", resolution, or order" after "any similar agreement that the Corporation determines by regulation".

(2) INSURED CREDIT UNIONS—Section 207(c)(8)(D) of the Federal Credit Union Act (12 U.S.C. 1787(c)(8)(D)) is amended—

(A) by striking "subsection—" and inserting "subsection, the following definitions shall apply:"; and

(B) in clause (i), by inserting ", resolution, or order" after "any similar agreement that the Board determines by regulation".

(b) DEFINITION OF SECURITIES CONTRACT—

(1) FDIC-INSURED DEPOSITORY INSTITUTIONS—Section 11(e)(8)(D)(ii) of the Federal Deposit Insurance Act (12 U.S.C. 1821(e)(8)(D)(ii)) is amended to read as follows:

"(ii) SECURITIES CONTRACT—The term 'securities contract'—

"(I) means a contract for the purchase, sale, or loan of a security, a certificate of deposit, a mortgage loan, or any interest in a mortgage loan, a group or index of securities, certificates of deposit, or mortgage loans or interests therein (including any interest therein or based on the value thereof) or any option on any of the foregoing, including any option to purchase or sell any such security, certificate of deposit, mortgage loan, interest, group or index, or option, and including any repurchase or reverse repurchase transaction on any such security, certificate of deposit, mortgage loan, interest, group or index, or option;

"(II) does not include any purchase, sale, or repurchase obligation under a participation in a commercial mortgage loan unless the Corporation determines by regulation, resolution, or order to include any such agreement within the meaning of such term;

"(III) means any option entered into on a national securities exchange relating to foreign currencies;

"(IV) means the guarantee by or to any securities clearing agency of any settlement of cash, securities, certificates of deposit, mortgage loans or interests therein, group or index of securities, certificates of deposit, or mortgage loans or interests therein (including any interest therein or based on the value thereof) or option on any of the foregoing, including any option to purchase or sell any such security, certificate of deposit, mortgage loan, interest, group or index, or option;

"(V) means any margin loan;

"(VI) means any other agreement or transaction that is similar to any agreement or transaction referred to in this clause;

"(VII) means any combination of the agreements or transactions referred to in this clause;

"(VIII) means any option to enter into any agreement or transaction referred to in this clause;

"(IX) means a master agreement that provides for an agreement or transaction referred to in subclause (I), (III), (IV), (V), (VI), (VII), or (VIII), together with all supplements to any such master agreement, without regard to whether the master agreement provides for an agreement or transaction that is not a securities contract under this clause, except that the master agreement shall be considered to be a securities contract under this clause only with respect to each agreement or transaction under the master agreement that is referred to in subclause (I), (III), (IV), (V), (VI), (VII), or (VIII); and

"(X) means any security agreement or arrangement or other credit enhancement related to any agreement or transaction referred to in this clause, including any guarantee or reimbursement obligation in connection with any agreement or transaction referred to in this clause.".

(2) INSURED CREDIT UNIONS—Section 207(c)(8)(D)(ii) of the Federal Credit Union Act (12 U.S.C. 1787(c)(8)(D)(ii)) is amended to read as follows:

"(ii) SECURITIES CONTRACT—The term 'securities contract'—

"(I) means a contract for the purchase, sale, or loan of a security, a certificate of deposit, a mortgage loan, or any interest in a mortgage loan, a group or index of securities, certificates of deposit, or mortgage loans or interests therein (including any interest therein or based on the value thereof) or any option on any of the foregoing, including any option to purchase or sell any such security, certificate of deposit, mortgage loan, interest, group or index, or option, and including any repurchase or reverse repurchase transaction on any such security, certificate of deposit, mortgage loan, interest, group or index, or option;

"(II) does not include any purchase, sale, or repurchase obligation under a participation in a commercial mortgage loan unless the Board determines by regulation, resolution, or order to include any such agreement within the meaning of such term;

"(III) means any option entered into on a national securities exchange relating to foreign currencies;

"(IV) means the guarantee by or to any securities clearing agency of any settlement of cash, securities, certificates of deposit, mortgage loans or interests therein, group or index of securities, certificates of deposit, or mortgage loans or interests therein (including any interest therein or based on the value thereof) or option on any of the foregoing, including any option to purchase or sell any such security, certificate of deposit, mortgage loan, interest, group or index, or option;

"(V) means any margin loan;

"(VI) means any other agreement or transaction that is similar to any agreement or transaction referred to in this clause;

"(VII) means any combination of the agreements or transactions referred to in this clause;

"(VIII) means any option to enter into any agreement or transaction referred to in this clause;

"(IX) means a master agreement that provides for an agreement or transaction referred to in subclause (I), (III), (IV), (V), (VI), (VII), or (VIII), together with all supplements to any such master agreement, without regard to whether the master agreement provides for an agreement or transaction that is not a securities contract under this clause, except that the master agreement shall be considered to be a securities contract under this clause only with respect to each agreement or transaction under the master agreement that is referred to in subclause (I), (III), (IV), (V), (VI), (VII), or (VIII); and

"(X) means any security agreement or arrangement or other credit enhancement related to any agreement or transaction referred to in this clause, including any guarantee or reimbursement obligation in connection with any agreement or transaction referred to in this clause.".

(c) DEFINITION OF COMMODITY CONTRACT—

(1) FDIC-INSURED DEPOSITORY INSTITUTIONS—Section 11(e)(8)(D)(iii) of the Federal Deposit Insurance Act (12 U.S.C. 1821(e)(8)(D)(iii)) is amended to read as follows:

"(iii) COMMODITY CONTRACT—The term 'commodity contract' means—

"(I) with respect to a futures commission merchant, a contract for the purchase or sale of a commodity for future delivery on, or subject to the rules of, a contract market or board of trade;

"(II) with respect to a foreign futures commission merchant, a foreign future;

"(III) with respect to a leverage transaction merchant, a leverage transaction;

"(IV) with respect to a clearing organization, a contract for the purchase or sale of a commodity for future delivery on, or subject to the rules of, a contract market or board of trade that is cleared by such clearing organization, or commodity option traded on, or subject to the rules of, a contract market or board of trade that is cleared by such clearing organization;

"(V) with respect to a commodity options dealer, a commodity option;

"(VI) any other agreement or transaction that is similar to any agreement or transaction referred to in this clause;

"(VII) any combination of the agreements or transactions referred to in this clause;

"(VIII) any option to enter into any agreement or transaction referred to in this clause;

"(IX) a master agreement that provides for an agreement or transaction referred to in subclause (I), (II), (III), (IV), (V), (VI), (VII), or (VIII), together with all supplements to any such master agreement, without regard to whether the master agreement provides for an agreement or transaction that is not a commodity contract under this clause, except that the master agreement shall be considered to be a commodity contract under this clause only with respect to each agreement or transaction under the master agreement that is referred to in subclause (I), (II), (III), (IV), (V), (VI), (VII), or (VIII); or

"(X) any security agreement or arrangement or other credit enhancement related to any agreement or transaction referred to in this clause, including any guarantee or reimbursement obligation in connection with any agreement or transaction referred to in this clause.".

(2) INSURED CREDIT UNIONS—Section 207(c)(8)(D)(iii) of the Federal Credit Union Act (12 U.S.C. 1787(c)(8)(D)(iii)) is amended to read as follows:

"(iii) COMMODITY CONTRACT—The term 'commodity contract' means—

"(I) with respect to a futures commission merchant, a contract for the purchase or sale of a commodity for future delivery on, or subject to the rules of, a contract market or board of trade;

"(II) with respect to a foreign futures commission merchant, a foreign future;

"(III) with respect to a leverage transaction merchant, a leverage transaction;

"(IV) with respect to a clearing organization, a contract for the purchase or sale of a commodity for future delivery on, or subject to the rules of, a contract market or board of trade that is cleared by such clearing organization, or commodity option traded on, or subject to the rules of, a contract market or board of trade that is cleared by such clearing organization;

"(V) with respect to a commodity options dealer, a commodity option;

"(VI) any other agreement or transaction that is similar to any agreement or transaction referred to in this clause;

"(VII) any combination of the agreements or transactions referred to in this clause;

"(VIII) any option to enter into any agreement or transaction referred to in this clause;

"(IX) a master agreement that provides for an agreement or transaction referred to in subclause (I), (II), (III), (IV), (V), (VI), (VII), or (VIII), together with all supplements to any such master agreement, without regard to whether the master agreement provides for an agreement or transaction that is not a commodity contract under this clause, except that the master agreement shall be considered to be a commodity contract under this clause only with respect to each agreement or transaction under the master agreement that is referred to in subclause (I), (II), (III), (IV), (V), (VI), (VII), or (VIII); or

"(X) any security agreement or arrangement or other credit enhancement related to any agreement or transaction referred to in this clause, including any guarantee or reimbursement obligation in connection with any agreement or transaction referred to in this clause.".

(d) DEFINITION OF FORWARD CONTRACT—

(1) FDIC-INSURED DEPOSITORY INSTITUTIONS—Section 11(e)(8)(D)(iv) of the Federal Deposit Insurance Act (12 U.S.C. 1821(e)(8)(D)(iv)) is amended to read as follows:

"(iv) FORWARD CONTRACT—The term 'forward contract' means—

"(I) a contract (other than a commodity contract) for the purchase, sale, or transfer of a commodity or any similar good, article, service, right, or interest which is presently or in the future becomes the subject of dealing in the forward contract trade, or product or byproduct thereof, with a maturity date more than 2 days after the date the contract is entered into, including, a repurchase transaction, reverse repurchase transaction, consignment, lease, swap, hedge transaction, deposit, loan, option, allocated transaction, unallocated transaction, or any other similar agreement;

"(II) any combination of agreements or transactions referred to in subclauses (I) and (III);

"(III) any option to enter into any agreement or transaction referred to in subclause (I) or (II);

"(IV) a master agreement that provides for an agreement or transaction referred to in subclauses (I), (II), or (III), together with all supplements to any such master agreement, without regard to whether the master agreement provides for an agreement or transaction that is not a forward contract under this clause, except that the master agreement shall be considered to be a forward contract under this clause only with respect to each agreement or transaction under the master agreement that is referred to in subclause (I), (II), or (III); or

"(V) any security agreement or arrangement or other credit enhancement related to any agreement or transaction referred to in subclause (I), (II), (III), or (IV), including any guarantee or reimbursement obligation in connection with any agreement or transaction referred to in any such subclause.".

(2) INSURED CREDIT UNIONS—Section 207(c)(8)(D)(iv) of the Federal Credit Union Act (12 U.S.C. 1787(c)(8)(D)(iv)) is amended to read as follows:

"(iv) FORWARD CONTRACT—The term 'forward contract' means—

"(I) a contract (other than a commodity contract) for the purchase, sale, or transfer of a commodity or any similar good, article, service, right, or interest which is presently or in the future becomes the subject of dealing in the forward contract trade, or product or byproduct thereof, with a maturity date more than 2 days after the date the contract is entered into, including, a repurchase transaction, reverse repurchase transaction, consignment, lease, swap, hedge transaction, deposit, loan, option, allocated transaction, unallocated transaction, or any other similar agreement;

"(II) any combination of agreements or transactions referred to in subclauses (I) and (III);

"(III) any option to enter into any agreement or transaction referred to in subclause (I) or (II);

"(IV) a master agreement that provides for an agreement or transaction referred to in subclauses (I), (II), or (III), together with all supplements to any such master agreement, without regard to whether the master agreement provides for an agreement or transaction that is not a forward contract under this clause, except that the master agreement shall be considered to be a forward contract under this clause only with respect to each agreement or transaction under the master agreement that is referred to in subclause (I), (II), or (III); or

"(V) any security agreement or arrangement or other credit enhancement related to any agreement or transaction referred to in subclause (I), (II), (III), or (IV), including any guarantee or reimbursement obligation in connection with any agreement or transaction referred to in any such subclause.".

(e) DEFINITION OF REPURCHASE AGREEMENT—

(1) FDIC-INSURED DEPOSITORY INSTITUTIONS—Section 11(e)(8)(D)(v) of the Federal Deposit Insurance Act (12 U.S.C. 1821(e)(8)(D)(v)) is amended to read as follows:

"(v) REPURCHASE AGREEMENT—The term 'repurchase agreement' (which definition also applies to a reverse repurchase agreement)—

"(I) means an agreement, including related terms, which provides for the transfer of one or more certificates of deposit, mortgage-related securities (as such term is defined in the Securities Exchange Act of 1934), mortgage loans, interests in mortgage-related securities or mortgage loans, eligible bankers' acceptances, qualified foreign government securities or securities that are direct obligations of, or that are fully guaranteed by, the United States or any agency of the United States against the transfer of funds by the transferee of such certificates of deposit, eligible bankers' acceptances, securities, mortgage loans, or interests with a simultaneous agreement by such transferee to transfer to the transferor thereof certificates of deposit, eligible bankers' acceptances, securities, mortgage loans, or interests as described above, at a date certain not later than 1 year after such transfers or on demand, against the transfer of funds, or any other similar agreement;

"(II) does not include any repurchase obligation under a participation in a commercial mortgage loan unless the Corporation determines by regulation, resolution, or order to include any such participation within the meaning of such term;

"(III) means any combination of agreements or transactions referred to in subclauses (I) and (IV);

"(IV) means any option to enter into any agreement or transaction referred to in subclause (I) or (III);

"(V) means a master agreement that provides for an agreement or transaction referred to in subclause (I), (III), or (IV), together with all supplements to any such master agreement, without regard to whether the master agreement provides for an agreement or transaction that is not a repurchase agreement under this clause, except that the master agreement shall be considered to be a repurchase agreement under this subclause only with respect to each agreement or transaction under the master agreement that is referred to in subclause (I), (III), or (IV); and

"(VI) means any security agreement or arrangement or other credit enhancement related to any agreement or transaction referred to in subclause (I), (III), (IV), or (V), including any guarantee or reimbursement obligation in connection with any agreement or transaction referred to in any such subclause.

For purposes of this clause, the term 'qualified foreign government security' means a security that is a direct obligation of, or that is fully guaranteed by, the central government of a member of the Organization for Economic Cooperation and Development (as determined by regulation or order adopted by the appropriate Federal banking authority).".

(2) INSURED CREDIT UNIONS—Section 207(c)(8)(D)(v) of the Federal Credit Union Act (12 U.S.C. 1787(c)(8)(D)(v)) is amended to read as follows:

"(v) REPURCHASE AGREEMENT—The term 'repurchase agreement' (which definition also applies to a reverse repurchase agreement)—

"(I) means an agreement, including related terms, which provides for the transfer of one or more certificates of deposit, mortgage-related securities (as such term is defined in the Securities Exchange Act of 1934), mortgage loans, interests in mortgage-related securities or mortgage loans, eligible bankers' acceptances, qualified foreign government securities or securities that are direct obligations of, or that are fully guaranteed by, the United States or any agency of the United States against the transfer of funds by the transferee of such certificates of deposit, eligible bankers' acceptances, securities, mortgage loans, or interests with a simultaneous agreement by such transferee to transfer to the transferor thereof certificates of deposit, eligible bankers' acceptances, securities, mortgage loans, or interests as described above, at a date certain not later than 1 year after such transfers or on demand, against the transfer of funds, or any other similar agreement;

"(II) does not include any repurchase obligation under a participation in a commercial mortgage loan unless the Board determines by regulation, resolution, or order to include any such participation within the meaning of such term;

"(III) means any combination of agreements or transactions referred to in subclauses (I) and (IV);

"(IV) means any option to enter into any agreement or transaction referred to in subclause (I) or (III);

"(V) means a master agreement that provides for an agreement or transaction referred to in subclause (I), (III), or (IV), together with all supplements to any such master agreement, without regard to whether the master agreement provides for an agreement or transaction that is not a repurchase agreement under this clause, except that the master agreement shall be considered to be a repurchase agreement under this subclause only with respect to each agreement or transaction under the master agreement that is referred to in subclause (I), (III), or (IV); and

"(VI) means any security agreement or arrangement or other credit enhancement related to any agreement or transaction referred to in subclause (I), (III), (IV), or (V), including any guarantee or reimbursement obligation in connection with any agreement or transaction referred to in any such subclause.

For purposes of this clause, the term 'qualified foreign government security' means a security that is a direct obligation of, or that is fully guaranteed by, the central government of a member of the Organization for Economic Cooperation and Development (as determined by regulation or order adopted by the appropriate Federal banking authority).".

(f) DEFINITION OF SWAP AGREEMENT—

(1) FDIC-INSURED DEPOSITORY INSTITUTIONS—Section 11(e)(8)(D)(vi) of the Federal Deposit Insurance Act (12 U.S.C. 1821(e)(8)(D)(vi)) is amended to read as follows:

"(vi) SWAP AGREEMENT—The term 'swap agreement' means—

"(I) any agreement, including the terms and conditions incorporated by reference in any such agreement, which is an interest rate swap, option, future, or forward agreement, including a rate floor, rate cap, rate collar, cross-currency rate swap, and basis swap; a spot, same day-tomorrow, tomorrow-next, forward, or other foreign exchange or precious metals agreement; a currency swap, option, future, or forward agreement; an equity index or equity swap, option, future, or forward agreement; a debt index or debt swap, option, future, or forward agreement; a total return, credit spread or credit swap, option, future, or forward agreement; a commodity index or commodity swap, option, future, or forward agreement; or a weather swap, weather derivative, or weather option;

"(II) any agreement or transaction that is similar to any other agreement or transaction referred to in this clause and that is of a type that has been, is presently, or in the future becomes, the subject of recurrent dealings in the swap markets (including terms and conditions incorporated by reference in such agreement) and that is a forward, swap, future, or option on one or more rates, currencies, commodities, equity securities or other equity instruments, debt securities or other debt instruments, quantitative measures associated with an occurrence, extent of an occurrence, or contingency associated with a financial, commercial, or economic consequence, or economic or financial indices or measures of economic or financial risk or value;

"(III) any combination of agreements or transactions referred to in this clause;

"(IV) any option to enter into any agreement or transaction referred to in this clause;

"(V) a master agreement that provides for an agreement or transaction referred to in subclause (I), (II), (III), or (IV), together with all supplements to any such master agreement, without regard to whether the master agreement contains an agreement or transaction that is not a swap agreement under this clause, except that the master agreement shall be considered to be a swap agreement under this clause only with respect to each agreement or transaction under the master agreement that is referred to in subclause (I), (II), (III), or (IV); and

"(VI) any security agreement or arrangement or other credit enhancement related to any agreements or transactions referred to in subclause (I), (II), (III), (IV), or (V), including any guarantee or reimbursement obligation in connection with any agreement or transaction referred to in any such subclause.

Such term is applicable for purposes of this subsection only and shall not be construed or applied so as to challenge or affect the characterization, definition, or treatment of any swap agreement under any other statute, regulation, or rule, including the Securities Act of 1933, the Securities Exchange Act of 1934, the Public Utility Holding Company Act of 1935, the Trust Indenture Act of 1939, the Investment Company Act of 1940, the Investment Advisers Act of 1940, the Securities Investor Protection Act of 1970, the Commodity Exchange Act, the Gramm-Leach-Bliley Act, and the Legal Certainty for Bank Products Act of 2000.".

(2) INSURED CREDIT UNIONS—Section 207(c)(8)(D) of the Federal Credit Union Act (12 U.S.C. 1787(c)(8)(D)) is amended by adding at the end the following new clause:

"(vi) SWAP AGREEMENT—The term 'swap agreement' means—

"(I) any agreement, including the terms and conditions incorporated by reference in any such agreement, which is an interest rate swap, option, future, or forward agreement, including a rate floor, rate cap, rate collar, cross-currency rate swap, and basis swap; a spot, same day-tomorrow, tomorrow-next, forward, or other foreign exchange or precious metals agreement; a currency swap, option, future, or forward agreement; an equity index or equity swap, option, future, or forward agreement; a debt index or debt swap, option, future, or forward agreement; a total return, credit spread or credit swap, option, future, or forward agreement; a commodity index or commodity swap, option, future, or forward agreement; or a weather swap, weather derivative, or weather option;

"(II) any agreement or transaction that is similar to any other agreement or transaction referred to in this clause and that is of a type that has been, is presently, or in the future becomes, the subject of recurrent dealings in the swap markets (including terms and conditions incorporated by reference in such agreement) and that is a forward, swap, future, or option on one or more rates, currencies, commodities, equity securities or other equity instruments, debt securities or other debt instruments, quantitative measures associated with an occurrence, extent of an occurrence, or contingency associated with a financial, commercial, or economic consequence, or economic or financial indices or measures of economic or financial risk or value;

"(III) any combination of agreements or transactions referred to in this clause;

"(IV) any option to enter into any agreement or transaction referred to in this clause;

"(V) a master agreement that provides for an agreement or transaction referred to in subclause (I), (II), (III), or (IV), together with all supplements to any such master agreement, without regard to whether the master agreement contains an agreement or transaction that is not a swap agreement under this clause, except that the master agreement shall be considered to be a swap agreement under this clause only with respect to each agreement or transaction under the master agreement that is referred to in subclause (I), (II), (III), or (IV); and

"(VI) any security agreement or arrangement or other credit enhancement related to any agreements or transactions referred to in subclause (I), (II), (III), (IV), or (V), including any guarantee or reimbursement obligation in connection with any agreement or transaction referred to in any such subclause.

Such term is applicable for purposes of this subsection only and shall not be construed or applied so as to challenge or affect the characterization, definition, or treatment of any swap agreement under any other statute, regulation, or rule, including the Securities Act of 1933, the Securities Exchange Act of 1934, the Public Utility Holding Company Act of 1935, the Trust Indenture Act of 1939, the Investment Company Act of 1940, the Investment Advisers Act of 1940, the Securities Investor Protection Act of 1970, the Commodity Exchange Act, the Gramm-Leach-Bliley Act, and the Legal Certainty for Bank Products Act of 2000.".

(g) DEFINITION OF TRANSFER—

(1) FDIC-INSURED DEPOSITORY INSTITUTIONS—Section 11(e)(8)(D)(viii) of the Federal Deposit Insurance Act (12 U.S.C. 1821(e)(8)(D)(viii)) is amended to read as follows:

"(viii) TRANSFER—The term 'transfer' means every mode, direct or indirect, absolute or conditional, voluntary or involuntary, of disposing of or parting with property or with an interest in property, including retention of title as a security interest and foreclosure of the depository institution's equity of redemption.".

(2) INSURED CREDIT UNIONS—Section 207(c)(8)(D) of the Federal Credit Union Act (12 U.S.C. 1787(c)(8)(D)) (as amended by subsection (f) of this section) is amended by adding at the end the following new clause:

"(viii) TRANSFER—The term 'transfer' means every mode, direct or indirect, absolute or conditional, voluntary or involuntary, of disposing of or parting with property or with an interest in property, including retention of title as a security interest and foreclosure of the depository institution's equity of redemption.".

(h) TREATMENT OF QUALIFIED FINANCIAL CONTRACTS—

(1) FDIC-INSURED DEPOSITORY INSTITUTIONS—Section 11(e)(8) of the Federal Deposit Insurance Act (12 U.S.C. 1821(e)(8)) is amended—

(A) in subparagraph (A)—

(i) by striking "paragraph (10)" and inserting "paragraphs (9) and (10)";

(ii) in clause (i), by striking "to cause the termination or liquidation" and inserting "such person has to cause the termination, liquidation, or acceleration"; and

(iii) by striking clause (ii) and inserting the following new clause:

"(ii) any right under any security agreement or arrangement or other credit enhancement related to one or more qualified financial contracts described in clause (i);"; and

(B) in subparagraph (E), by striking clause (ii) and inserting the following:

"(ii) any right under any security agreement or arrangement or other credit enhancement related to one or more qualified financial contracts described in clause (i);".

(2) INSURED CREDIT UNIONS—Section 207(c)(8) of the Federal Credit Union Act (12 U.S.C. 1787(c)(8)) is amended—

(A) in subparagraph (A)—

(i) by striking "paragraph (12)" and inserting "paragraphs (9) and (10)";

(ii) in clause (i), by striking "to cause the termination or liquidation" and inserting "such person has to cause the termination, liquidation, or acceleration"; and

(iii) by striking clause (ii) and inserting the following new clause:

"(ii) any right under any security agreement or arrangement or other credit enhancement related to 1 or more qualified financial contracts described in clause (i);"; and

(B) in subparagraph (E), by striking clause (ii) and inserting the following new clause:

"(ii) any right under any security agreement or arrangement or other credit enhancement related to 1 or more qualified financial contracts described in clause (i);".

(i) AVOIDANCE OF TRANSFERS—

(1) FDIC-INSURED DEPOSITORY INSTITUTIONS—Section 11(e)(8)(C)(i) of the Federal Deposit Insurance Act (12 U.S.C. 1821(e)(8)(C)(i)) is amended by inserting "section 5242 of the Revised Statutes of the United States or any other Federal or State law relating to the avoidance of preferential or fraudulent transfers," before "the Corporation".

(2) INSURED CREDIT UNIONS—Section 207(c)(8)(C)(i) of the Federal Credit Union Act (12 U.S.C. 1787(c)(8)(C)(i)) is amended by inserting

"section 5242 of the Revised Statutes of the United States or any other Federal or State law relating to the avoidance of preferential or fraudulent transfers," before "the Board".

Sec. 902 AUTHORITY OF THE FDIC AND NCUAB WITH RESPECT TO FAILED AND FAILING INSTITUTIONS.

(a) FEDERAL DEPOSIT INSURANCE CORPORATION—

(1) IN GENERAL—Section 11(e)(8) of the Federal Deposit Insurance Act (12 U.S.C. 1821(e)(8)) is amended—

(A) in subparagraph (E), by striking "other than paragraph (12) of this subsection, subsection (d)(9)" and inserting "other than subsections (d)(9) and (e)(10)"; and

(B) by adding at the end the following new subparagraphs:

"(F) CLARIFICATION—No provision of law shall be construed as limiting the right or power of the Corporation, or authorizing any court or agency to limit or delay, in any manner, the right or power of the Corporation to transfer any qualified financial contract in accordance with paragraphs (9) and (10) of this subsection or to disaffirm or repudiate any such contract in accordance with subsection (e)(1) of this section.

"(G) WALKAWAY CLAUSES NOT EFFECTIVE—

"(i) IN GENERAL—Notwithstanding the provisions of subparagraphs (A) and (E), and sections 403 and 404 of the Federal Deposit Insurance Corporation Improvement Act of 1991, no walkaway clause shall be enforceable in a qualified financial contract of an insured depository institution in default.

"(ii) WALKAWAY CLAUSE DEFINED—For purposes of this subparagraph, the term 'walkaway clause' means a provision in a qualified financial contract that, after calculation of a value of a party's position or an amount due to or from 1 of the parties in accordance with its terms upon termination, liquidation, or acceleration of the qualified financial contract, either does not create a payment obligation of a party or extinguishes a payment obligation of a party in whole or in part solely because of such party's status as a nondefaulting party.".

(2) TECHNICAL AND CONFORMING AMENDMENT—Section 11(e)(12)(A) of the Federal Deposit Insurance Act (12 U.S.C. 1821(e)(12)(A)) is amended by inserting "or the exercise of rights or powers by" after "the appointment of".

(b) NATIONAL CREDIT UNION ADMINISTRATION BOARD—

(1) IN GENERAL—Section 207(c)(8) of the Federal Credit Union Act (12 U.S.C. 1787(c)(8)) is amended—

(A) in subparagraph (E) (as amended by section 901(h)), by striking "other than paragraph (12) of this subsection, subsection (b)(9)" and inserting "other than subsections (b)(9) and (c)(10)"; and

(B) by adding at the end the following new subparagraphs:

"(F) CLARIFICATION—No provision of law shall be construed as limiting the right or power of the Board, or authorizing any court or agency to limit or delay, in any manner, the right or power of the Board to transfer any qualified financial contract in accordance with paragraphs (9) and (10) of this subsection or to disaffirm or repudiate any such contract in accordance with subsection (c)(1) of this section.

"(G) WALKAWAY CLAUSES NOT EFFECTIVE—

"(i) IN GENERAL—Notwithstanding the provisions of subparagraphs (A) and (E), and sections 403 and 404 of the Federal Deposit Insurance Corporation Improvement Act of 1991, no walkaway clause shall be enforceable in a qualified financial contract of an insured credit union in default.

"(ii) WALKAWAY CLAUSE DEFINED—For purposes of this subparagraph, the term "walkaway clause" means a provision in a qualified financial contract that, after calculation of a value of a party's position or an amount due to or from 1 of the parties in accordance with its terms upon termination, liquidation, or acceleration of the qualified financial contract, either does not create a payment obligation of a party or extinguishes a payment obligation of a party in whole or in part solely because of such party's status as a nondefaulting party.".

(2) TECHNICAL AND CONFORMING AMENDMENT—Section 207(c)(12)(A) of the Federal Credit Union Act (12 U.S.C. 1787(c)(12)(A)) is amended by inserting "or the exercise of rights or powers by" after "the appointment of".

Sec. 903 AMENDMENTS RELATING TO TRANSFERS OF QUALIFIED FINANCIAL CONTRACTS.

(a) FDIC-INSURED DEPOSITORY INSTITUTIONS—

(1) TRANSFERS OF QUALIFIED FINANCIAL CONTRACTS TO FINANCIAL INSTITUTIONS—Section 11(e)(9) of the Federal Deposit Insurance Act (12 U.S.C. 1821(e)(9)) is amended to read as follows:

"(9) TRANSFER OF QUALIFIED FINANCIAL CONTRACTS—

"(A) IN GENERAL—In making any transfer of assets or liabilities of a depository institution in default which includes any qualified financial contract, the conservator or receiver for such depository institution shall either—

"(i) transfer to one financial institution, other than a financial institution for which a conservator, receiver, trustee in bankruptcy, or other legal custodian has been appointed or which is otherwise the subject of a bankruptcy or insolvency proceeding—

"(I) all qualified financial contracts between any person or any affiliate of such person and the depository institution in default;

"(II) all claims of such person or any affiliate of such person against such depository institution under any such contract (other than any claim which, under the terms of any such contract, is subordinated to the claims of general unsecured creditors of such institution);

"(III) all claims of such depository institution against such person or any affiliate of such person under any such contract; and

"(IV) all property securing or any other credit enhancement for any contract described in subclause (I) or any claim described in subclause (II) or (III) under any such contract; or

"(ii) transfer none of the qualified financial contracts, claims, property or other credit enhancement referred to in clause (i) (with respect to such person and any affiliate of such person).

"(B) TRANSFER TO FOREIGN BANK, FOREIGN FINANCIAL INSTITUTION, OR BRANCH OR AGENCY OF A FOREIGN BANK OR FINANCIAL INSTITUTION—In transferring any qualified financial contracts and related claims and property under subparagraph (A)(i), the conservator or receiver for the depository institution shall not make such transfer to a foreign bank, financial institution organized under the laws of a foreign country, or a branch or agency of a foreign bank or financial institution unless, under the law applicable to such bank, financial institution, branch or agency, to the qualified financial contracts, and to any netting contract, any security agreement or arrangement or other credit enhancement related to one or more qualified financial contracts, the contractual rights of the parties to such qualified financial contracts, netting contracts, security agreements or arrangements, or other credit enhancements are enforceable substantially to the same extent as permitted under this section.

"(C) TRANSFER OF CONTRACTS SUBJECT TO THE RULES OF A CLEARING ORGANIZATION—In the event that a conservator or receiver transfers any qualified financial contract and related claims, property, and credit enhancements pursuant to subparagraph (A)(i) and such contract is cleared by or subject to the rules of a clearing organization, the clearing organization shall not be required to accept the transferee as a member by virtue of the transfer.

"(D) DEFINITIONS—For purposes of this paragraph, the term 'financial institution' means a broker or dealer, a depository institution, a futures commission merchant, or any other institution, as determined by the Corporation by regulation to be a financial institution, and the term 'clearing organization' has the same meaning as in section 402 of the Federal Deposit Insurance Corporation Improvement Act of 1991.".

(2) NOTICE TO QUALIFIED FINANCIAL CONTRACT COUNTERPARTIES—Section 11(e)(10)(A) of the Federal Deposit Insurance Act (12 U.S.C. 1821(e)(10)(A)) is amended in the material immediately following clause

(ii) by striking "the conservator" and all that follows through the period and inserting the following: "the conservator or receiver shall notify any person who is a party to any such contract of such transfer by 5:00 p.m. (eastern time) on the business day following the date of the appointment of the receiver in the case of a receivership, or the business day following such transfer in the case of a conservatorship.".

(3) RIGHTS AGAINST RECEIVER AND CONSERVATOR AND TREATMENT OF BRIDGE BANKS—Section 11(e)(10) of the Federal Deposit Insurance Act (12 U.S.C. 1821(e)(10)) is amended—

(A) by redesignating subparagraph (B) as subparagraph (D); and

(B) by inserting after subparagraph (A) the following new subparagraphs:

"(B) CERTAIN RIGHTS NOT ENFORCEABLE—

"(i) RECEIVERSHIP—A person who is a party to a qualified financial contract with an insured depository institution may not exercise any right that such person has to terminate, liquidate, or net such contract under paragraph (8)(A) of this subsection or section 403 or 404 of the Federal Deposit Insurance Corporation Improvement Act of 1991, solely by reason of or incidental to the appointment of a receiver for the depository institution (or the insolvency or financial condition of the depository institution for which the receiver has been appointed)—

"(I) until 5:00 p.m. (eastern time) on the business day following the date of the appointment of the receiver; or

"(II) after the person has received notice that the contract has been transferred pursuant to paragraph (9)(A).

"(ii) CONSERVATORSHIP—A person who is a party to a qualified financial contract with an insured depository institution may not exercise any right that such person has to terminate, liquidate, or net such contract under paragraph (8)(E) of this subsection or section 403 or 404 of the Federal Deposit Insurance Corporation Improvement Act of 1991, solely by reason of or incidental to the appointment of a conservator for the depository institution (or the insolvency or financial condition of the depository institution for which the conservator has been appointed).

"(iii) NOTICE—For purposes of this paragraph, the Corporation as receiver or conservator of an insured depository institution shall be deemed to have notified a person who is a party to a qualified financial contract with such depository institution if the Corporation has taken steps reasonably calculated to provide notice to such person by the time specified in subparagraph (A).

"(C) TREATMENT OF BRIDGE BANKS—The following institutions shall not be considered to be a financial institution for which a conservator, receiver, trustee in bankruptcy, or other legal custodian has been appointed or which is otherwise the subject of a bankruptcy or insolvency proceeding for purposes of paragraph (9):

"(i) A bridge bank.

"(ii) A depository institution organized by the Corporation, for which a conservator is appointed either—

"(I) immediately upon the organization of the institution; or

"(II) at the time of a purchase and assumption transaction between the depository institution and the Corporation as receiver for a depository institution in default.".

(b) INSURED CREDIT UNIONS—

(1) TRANSFERS OF QUALIFIED FINANCIAL CONTRACTS TO FINANCIAL INSTITUTIONS—Section 207(c)(9) of the Federal Credit Union Act (12 U.S.C. 1787(c)(9)) is amended to read as follows:

"(9) TRANSFER OF QUALIFIED FINANCIAL CONTRACTS—

"(A) IN GENERAL—In making any transfer of assets or liabilities of a credit union in default which includes any qualified financial contract, the conservator or liquidating agent for such credit union shall either—

"(i) transfer to 1 financial institution, other than a financial institution for which a conservator, receiver, trustee in bankruptcy, or other legal custodian has been appointed or which is otherwise the subject of a bankruptcy or insolvency proceeding—

"(I) all qualified financial contracts between any person or any affiliate of such person and the credit union in default;

"(II) all claims of such person or any affiliate of such person against such credit union under any such contract (other than any claim which, under the terms of any such contract, is subordinated to the claims of general unsecured creditors of such credit union);

"(III) all claims of such credit union against such person or any affiliate of such person under any such contract; and

"(IV) all property securing or any other credit enhancement for any contract described in subclause (I) or any claim described in subclause (II) or (III) under any such contract; or

"(ii) transfer none of the qualified financial contracts, claims, property or other credit enhancement referred to in clause (i) (with respect to such person and any affiliate of such person).

"(B) TRANSFER TO FOREIGN BANK, FOREIGN FINANCIAL INSTITUTION, OR BRANCH OR AGENCY OF A FOREIGN BANK OR FINANCIAL INSTITUTION—In transferring any qualified financial contracts and related claims and property under subparagraph (A)(i), the conservator or liquidating agent for the credit union shall not make such transfer to a foreign bank, financial institution organized under the laws of a foreign country, or a branch or agency of a foreign bank or financial institution unless, under the law applicable to such bank, financial institution, branch or agency, to the qualified financial contracts, and to any netting contract, any security agreement or arrangement or other credit enhancement related to 1 or more qualified financial contracts, the contractual rights of the parties to such qualified financial contracts, netting contracts, security agreements or arrangements, or other credit enhancements are enforceable substantially to the same extent as permitted under this section.

"(C) TRANSFER OF CONTRACTS SUBJECT TO THE RULES OF A CLEARING ORGANIZATION—In the event that a conservator or liquidating agent transfers any qualified financial contract and related claims, property, and credit enhancements pursuant to subparagraph (A)(i) and such contract is cleared by or subject to the rules of a clearing organization, the clearing organization shall not be required to accept the transferee as a member by virtue of the transfer.

"(D) DEFINITIONS—For purposes of this paragraph—

"(i) the term 'financial institution' means a broker or dealer, a depository institution, a futures commission merchant, a credit union, or any other institution, as determined by the Board by regulation to be a financial institution; and

"(ii) the term 'clearing organization' has the same meaning as in section 402 of the Federal Deposit Insurance Corporation Improvement Act of 1991.".

(2) NOTICE TO QUALIFIED FINANCIAL CONTRACT COUNTERPARTIES—Section 207(c)(10)(A) of the Federal Credit Union Act (12 U.S.C. 1787(c)(10)(A)) is amended in the material immediately following clause (ii) by striking "the conservator" and all that follows through the period and inserting the following: "the conservator or liquidating agent shall notify any person who is a party to any such contract of such transfer by 5:00 p.m. (eastern time) on the business day following the date of the appointment of the liquidating agent in the case of a liquidation, or the business day following such transfer in the case of a conservatorship.".

(3) RIGHTS AGAINST LIQUIDATING AGENT AND CONSERVATOR AND TREATMENT OF BRIDGE BANKS—Section 207(c)(10) of the Federal Credit Union Act (12 U.S.C. 1787(c)(10)) is amended—

(A) by redesignating subparagraph (B) as subparagraph (D); and

(B) by inserting after subparagraph (A) the following new subparagraphs:

"(B) CERTAIN RIGHTS NOT ENFORCEABLE—

"(i) LIQUIDATION—A person who is a party to a qualified financial contract with an insured credit union may not exercise any right that such person has to terminate, liquidate, or net such contract under paragraph (8)(A) of this subsection or section 403 or 404 of the Federal Deposit Insurance Corporation Improvement Act of 1991, solely by reason of or incidental to the appointment of a liquidating agent for the credit union institution (or the insolvency or financial condition of the credit union for which the liquidating agent has been appointed)—

"(I) until 5:00 p.m. (eastern time) on the business day following the date of the appointment of the liquidating agent; or

"(II) after the person has received notice that the contract has been transferred pursuant to paragraph (9)(A).

"(ii) CONSERVATORSHIP—A person who is a party to a qualified financial contract with an insured credit union may not exercise any right that such person has to terminate, liquidate, or net such contract under paragraph (8)(E) of this subsection or section 403 or 404 of the Federal Deposit Insurance Corporation Improvement Act of 1991, solely by reason of or incidental to the appointment of a conservator for the credit union or the insolvency or financial condition of the credit union for which the conservator has been appointed).

"(iii) NOTICE—For purposes of this paragraph, the Board as conservator or liquidating agent of an insured credit union shall be deemed to have notified a person who is a party to a qualified financial contract with such credit union if the Board has taken steps reasonably calculated to provide notice to such person by the time specified in subparagraph (A).

"(C) TREATMENT OF BRIDGE BANKS—The following institutions shall not be considered to be a financial institution for which a conservator, receiver, trustee in bankruptcy, or other legal custodian has been appointed or which is otherwise the subject of a bankruptcy or insolvency proceeding for purposes of paragraph (9):

"(i) A bridge bank.

"(ii) A credit union organized by the Board, for which a conservator is appointed either—

"(I) immediately upon the organization of the credit union; or

"(II) at the time of a purchase and assumption transaction between the credit union and the Board as receiver for a credit union in default.".

Sec. 904 AMENDMENTS RELATING TO DISAFFIRMANCE OR REPUDIATION OF QUALIFIED FINANCIAL CONTRACTS.

(a) FDIC-INSURED DEPOSITORY INSTITUTIONS—Section 11(e) of the Federal Deposit Insurance Act (12 U.S.C. 1821(e)) is amended—

(1) by redesignating paragraphs (11) through (15) as paragraphs (12) through (16), respectively;

(2) by inserting after paragraph (10) the following new paragraph:

"(11) DISAFFIRMANCE OR REPUDIATION OF QUALIFIED FINANCIAL CONTRACTS—In exercising the rights of disaffirmance or repudiation of a conservator or receiver with respect to any qualified financial contract to which an insured depository institution is a party, the conservator or receiver for such institution shall either—

211

"(A) disaffirm or repudiate all qualified financial contracts between—

"(i) any person or any affiliate of such person; and

"(ii) the depository institution in default; or

"(B) disaffirm or repudiate none of the qualified financial contracts referred to in subparagraph (A) (with respect to such person or any affiliate of such person)."; and

(3) by adding at the end the following new paragraph:

"(17) SAVINGS CLAUSE—The meanings of terms used in this subsection are applicable for purposes of this subsection only, and shall not be construed or applied so as to challenge or affect the characterization, definition, or treatment of any similar terms under any other statute, regulation, or rule, including the Gramm-Leach-Bliley Act, the Legal Certainty for Bank Products Act of 2000, the securities laws (as that term is defined in section 3(a)(47) of the Securities Exchange Act of 1934), and the Commodity Exchange Act.".

(b) INSURED CREDIT UNIONS—Section 207(c) of the Federal Credit Union Act (12 U.S.C. 1787(c)) is amended—

(1) by redesignating paragraphs (11), (12), and (13) as paragraphs (12), (13), and (14), respectively;

(2) by inserting after paragraph (10) the following new paragraph:

"(11) DISAFFIRMANCE OR REPUDIATION OF QUALIFIED FINANCIAL CONTRACTS—In exercising the rights of disaffirmance or repudiation of a conservator or liquidating agent with respect to any qualified financial contract to which an insured credit union is a party, the conservator or liquidating agent for such credit union shall either—

"(A) disaffirm or repudiate all qualified financial contracts between—

"(i) any person or any affiliate of such person; and

"(ii) the credit union in default; or

"(B) disaffirm or repudiate none of the qualified financial contracts referred to in subparagraph (A) (with respect to such person or any affiliate of such person)."; and

(3) by adding at the end the following new paragraph:

"(15) SAVINGS CLAUSE—The meanings of terms used in this subsection are applicable for purposes of this subsection only, and shall not be construed or applied so as to challenge or affect the characterization, definition, or treatment of any similar terms under any other statute, regulation, or rule, including the Gramm-Leach-Bliley Act, the Legal Certainty for Bank Products Act of 2000, the securities laws (as that term is defined in section (a)(47) of the Securities Exchange Act of 1934), and the Commodity Exchange Act.".

Sec. 905 CLARIFYING AMENDMENT RELATING TO MASTER AGREEMENTS.

(a) FDIC-INSURED DEPOSITORY INSTITUTIONS—Section 11(e)(8)(D)(vii) of the Federal Deposit Insurance Act (12 U.S.C. 1821(e)(8)(D)(vii)) is amended to read as follows:

> "(vii) TREATMENT OF MASTER AGREEMENT AS ONE AGREEMENT— Any master agreement for any contract or agreement described in any preceding clause of this subparagraph (or any master agreement for such master agreement or agreements), together with all supplements to such master agreement, shall be treated as a single agreement and a single qualified financial contract. If a master agreement contains provisions relating to agreements or transactions that are not themselves qualified financial contracts, the master agreement shall be deemed to be a qualified financial contract only with respect to those transactions that are themselves qualified financial contracts.".

(b) INSURED CREDIT UNIONS—Section 207(c)(8)(D) of the Federal Credit Union Act (12 U.S.C. 1787(c)(8)(D)) is amended by inserting after clause (vi) (as added by section 901(f)) the following new clause:

> "(vii) TREATMENT OF MASTER AGREEMENT AS ONE AGREEMENT— Any master agreement for any contract or agreement described in any preceding clause of this subparagraph (or any master agreement for such master agreement or agreements), together with all supplements to such master agreement, shall be treated as a single agreement and a single qualified financial contract. If a master agreement contains provisions relating to agreements or transactions that are not themselves qualified financial contracts, the master agreement shall be deemed to be a qualified financial contract only with respect to those transactions that are themselves qualified financial contracts.".

Sec. 906 FEDERAL DEPOSIT INSURANCE CORPORATION IMPROVEMENT ACT OF 1991.

(a) DEFINITIONS—Section 402 of the Federal Deposit Insurance Corporation Improvement Act of 1991 (12 U.S.C. 4402) is amended—

(1) in paragraph (2)—

(A) in subparagraph (A)(ii), by inserting before the semicolon ", or is exempt from such registration by order of the Securities and Exchange Commission"; and

(B) in subparagraph (B), by inserting before the period ", that has been granted an exemption under section 4(c)(1) of the Commodity Exchange Act, or that is a multilateral clearing organization (as defined in section 408 of this Act)";

(2) in paragraph (6)—

(A) by redesignating subparagraphs (B) through (D) as subparagraphs (C) through (E), respectively;

(B) by inserting after subparagraph (A) the following new subparagraph:

"(B) an uninsured national bank or an uninsured State bank that is a member of the Federal Reserve System, if the national bank or State member bank is not eligible to make application to become an insured bank under section 5 of the Federal Deposit Insurance Act;"; and

(C) by amending subparagraph (C), so redesignated, to read as follows:

"(C) a branch or agency of a foreign bank, a foreign bank and any branch or agency of the foreign bank, or the foreign bank that established the branch or agency, as those terms are defined in section 1(b) of the International Banking Act of 1978;";

(3) in paragraph (11), by inserting before the period "and any other clearing organization with which such clearing organization has a netting contract";

(4) by amending paragraph (14)(A)(i) to read as follows:

"(i) means a contract or agreement between 2 or more financial institutions, clearing organizations, or members that provides for netting present or future payment obligations or payment entitlements (including liquidation or close out values relating to such obligations or entitlements) among the parties to the agreement; and'; and

(5) by adding at the end the following new paragraph:

"(15) PAYMENT—The term 'payment' means a payment of United States dollars, another currency, or a composite currency, and a noncash delivery, including a payment or delivery to liquidate an unmatured obligation.".

(b) ENFORCEABILITY OF BILATERAL NETTING CONTRACTS—Section 403 of the Federal Deposit Insurance Corporation Improvement Act of 1991 (12 U.S.C. 4403) is amended—

(1) by striking subsection (a) and inserting the following:

"(a) GENERAL RULE—Notwithstanding any other provision of State or Federal law (other than paragraphs (8)(E), (8)(F), and (10)(B) of section 11(e) of the Federal Deposit Insurance Act, paragraphs (8)(E), (8)(F), and (10)(B) of section 207(c) of the Federal Credit Union Act, or any order authorized under section 5(b)(2) of the Securities Investor Protection Act of 1970), the covered contractual payment obligations and the covered contractual payment entitlements between any 2 financial institutions shall be netted in accordance with, and subject to the conditions of, the terms of any applicable netting contract (except as provided in section 561(b)(2) of title 11, United States Code)."; and

(2) by adding at the end the following new subsection:

"(f) ENFORCEABILITY OF SECURITY AGREEMENTS—The provisions of any security agreement or arrangement or other credit enhancement related to one or more netting contracts between any 2 financial institutions shall be enforceable in accordance with their terms (except as provided in section 561(b)(2) of title 11, United States Code), and shall not be stayed, avoided, or otherwise limited by any State or Federal law (other than paragraphs (8)(E), (8)(F), and (10)(B) of section 11(e) of the Federal Deposit Insurance Act, paragraphs (8)(E), (8)(F), and (10)(B) of section 207(c) of the Federal Credit Union Act, and section 5(b)(2) of the Securities Investor Protection Act of 1970).".

(c) ENFORCEABILITY OF CLEARING ORGANIZATION NETTING CONTRACTS—Section 404 of the Federal Deposit Insurance Corporation Improvement Act of 1991 (12 U.S.C. 4404) is amended—

(1) by striking subsection (a) and inserting the following:

"(a) GENERAL RULE—Notwithstanding any other provision of State or Federal law (other than paragraphs (8)(E), (8)(F), and (10)(B) of section 11(e) of the Federal Deposit Insurance Act, paragraphs (8)(E), (8)(F), and (10)(B) of section 207(c) of the Federal Credit Union Act, and any order authorized under section 5(b)(2) of the Securities Investor Protection Act of 1970), the covered contractual payment obligations and the covered contractual payment entitlements of a member of a clearing organization to and from all other members of a clearing organization shall be netted in accordance with and subject to the conditions of any applicable netting contract (except as provided in section 561(b)(2) of title 11, United States Code)."; and

(2) by adding at the end the following new subsection:

"(h) ENFORCEABILITY OF SECURITY AGREEMENTS—The provisions of any security agreement or arrangement or other credit enhancement related to one or more netting contracts between any 2 members of a clearing organization shall be enforceable in accordance with their terms (except as provided in section 561(b)(2) of title 11, United States Code), and shall not be stayed, avoided, or otherwise limited by any State or Federal law (other than paragraphs (8)(E), (8)(F), and (10)(B) of section 11(e) of the Federal Deposit Insurance Act, paragraphs (8)(E), (8)(F), and (10)(B) of section 207(c) of the Federal Credit Union Act, and section 5(b)(2) of the Securities Investor Protection Act of 1970).".

(d) ENFORCEABILITY OF CONTRACTS WITH UNINSURED NATIONAL BANKS, UNINSURED FEDERAL BRANCHES AND AGENCIES, CERTAIN UNINSURED STATE MEMBER BANKS, AND EDGE ACT CORPORATIONS—The Federal Deposit Insurance Corporation Improvement Act of 1991 (12 U.S.C. 4401 et seq.) is amended—

(1) by redesignating section 407 as section 407A; and

(2) by inserting after section 406 the following new section:

"Sec. 407. Treatment of Contracts with Uninsured National Banks, Uninsured Federal Branches and Agencies, Certain Uninsured State Member Banks, and Edge Act Corporations.

"(a) IN GENERAL—Notwithstanding any other provision of law, paragraphs (8), (9), (10), and (11) of section 11(e) of the Federal Deposit Insurance Act shall apply to an uninsured national bank or uninsured Federal branch or Federal agency, a corporation chartered under section 25A of the Federal Reserve Act, or an uninsured State member bank which operates, or operates as, a multilateral clearing organization pursuant to section 409 of this Act, except that for such purpose—

"(1) any reference to the 'Corporation as receiver' or 'the receiver or the Corporation' shall refer to the receiver appointed by the Comptroller of the Currency in the case of an uninsured national bank or uninsured Federal branch or agency, or to the receiver appointed by the Board of Governors of the Federal Reserve System in the case of a corporation chartered under section 25A of the Federal Reserve Act or an uninsured State member bank;

"(2) any reference to the 'Corporation' (other than in section 11(e)(8)(D) of such Act), the 'Corporation, whether acting as such or as conservator or receiver', a "receiver', or a 'conservator' shall refer to the receiver or conservator appointed by the Comptroller of the Currency in the case of an uninsured national bank or uninsured Federal branch or agency, or to the receiver or conservator appointed by the Board of Governors of the Federal Reserve System in the case of a corporation chartered under section 25A of the Federal Reserve Act or an uninsured State member bank; and

"(3) any reference to an 'insured depository institution' or 'depository institution' shall refer to an uninsured national bank, an uninsured Federal branch or Federal agency, a corporation chartered under section 25A of the Federal Reserve Act, or an uninsured State member bank which operates, or operates as, a multilateral clearing organization pursuant to section 409 of this Act.

"(b) LIABILITY—The liability of a receiver or conservator of an uninsured national bank, uninsured Federal branch or agency, a corporation chartered under section 25A of the Federal Reserve Act, or an uninsured State member bank which operates, or operates as, a multilateral clearing organization pursuant to section 409 of this Act, shall be determined in the same manner and subject to the same limitations that apply to receivers and conservators of insured depository institutions under section 11(e) of the Federal Deposit Insurance Act.

"(c) REGULATORY AUTHORITY—

"(1) IN GENERAL—The Comptroller of the Currency in the case of an uninsured national bank or uninsured Federal branch or agency and the Board of Governors of the Federal Reserve System in the case of a corporation chartered under section 25A of the Federal Reserve Act, or an uninsured State member bank that operates, or operates as, a multilateral clearing organization pursuant to section 409 of this Act, in consultation with the Federal Deposit Insurance Corporation, may each promulgate regulations solely to implement this section.

"(2) SPECIFIC REQUIREMENT—In promulgating regulations, limited solely to implementing paragraphs (8), (9), (10), and (11) of section 11(e) of the Federal Deposit Insurance Act, the Comptroller of the Currency and the Board of Governors of the Federal Reserve System each shall ensure that the regulations generally are consistent with the regulations and policies of the Federal Deposit Insurance Corporation adopted pursuant to the Federal Deposit Insurance Act.

"(d) DEFINITIONS—For purposes of this section, the terms 'Federal branch', 'Federal agency', and 'foreign bank' have the same meanings as in section 1(b) of the International Banking Act of 1978.".

Sec. 907 BANKRUPTCY LAW AMENDMENTS.

(a) DEFINITIONS OF FORWARD CONTRACT, REPURCHASE AGREEMENT, SECURITIES CLEARING AGENCY, SWAP AGREEMENT, COMMODITY CONTRACT, AND SECURITIES CONTRACT—Title 11, United States Code, is amended—

(1) in section 101—

(A) in paragraph (25)—

(i) by striking "means a contract" and inserting "means—

"(A) a contract";

(ii) by striking ", or any combination thereof or option thereon;" and inserting ", or any other similar agreement;"; and

(iii) by adding at the end the following:

"(B) any combination of agreements or transactions referred to in subparagraphs (A) and (C);

"(C) any option to enter into an agreement or transaction referred to in subparagraph (A) or (B);

"(D) a master agreement that provides for an agreement or transaction referred to in subparagraph (A), (B), or (C), together with all supplements to any such master agreement, without regard to whether such master agreement provides for an agreement or transaction that is not a forward contract under this paragraph, except that such master agreement shall be considered to be a forward contract under this paragraph only with respect to each agreement or transaction under such master agreement that is referred to in subparagraph (A), (B), or (C); or

"(E) any security agreement or arrangement, or other credit enhancement related to any agreement or transaction referred to in subparagraph (A), (B), (C), or (D), including any guarantee or reimbursement obligation by or to a forward contract merchant or financial participant in connection with any agreement or transaction referred to in any such subparagraph, but not to exceed the damages in connection with any such agreement or transaction, measured in accordance with section 562;";

(B) in paragraph (46), by striking "on any day during the period beginning 90 days before the date of" and inserting "at any time before";

(C) by amending paragraph (47) to read as follows:

"(47) 'repurchase agreement' (which definition also applies to a reverse repurchase agreement)—

"(A) means—

"(i) an agreement, including related terms, which provides for the transfer of one or more certificates of deposit, mortgage related securities (as defined in section 3 of the Securities Exchange Act of 1934), mortgage loans, interests in mortgage related securities or mortgage loans, eligible bankers' acceptances, qualified foreign government securities (defined as a security that is a direct obligation of, or that is fully guaranteed by, the central government of a member of the Organization for Economic Cooperation and Development), or securities that are direct obligations of, or that are fully guaranteed by, the United States or any agency of the United States against the transfer of funds by the transferee of such certificates of deposit, eligible bankers' acceptances, securities, mortgage loans, or interests, with a simultaneous agreement by such transferee to transfer to the transferor thereof certificates of deposit, eligible bankers' acceptance, securities, mortgage loans, or interests of the kind described in this clause, at a date certain not later than 1 year after such transfer or on demand, against the transfer of funds;

"(ii) any combination of agreements or transactions referred to in clauses (i) and (iii);

"(iii) an option to enter into an agreement or transaction referred to in clause (i) or (ii);

"(iv) a master agreement that provides for an agreement or transaction referred to in clause (i), (ii), or (iii), together with all supplements to any such master agreement, without regard to whether such master agreement provides for an agreement or transaction that is not a repurchase agreement under this paragraph, except that such master agreement shall be considered to be a repurchase agreement under this paragraph only with respect to each agreement or transaction under the master agreement that is referred to in clause (i), (ii), or (iii); or

"(v) any security agreement or arrangement or other credit enhancement related to any agreement or transaction referred to in clause (i), (ii), (iii), or (iv), including any guarantee or reimbursement obligation by or to a repo participant or financial participant in connection with any agreement or transaction referred to in any such clause, but not to exceed the damages in connection with any such agreement or transaction, measured in accordance with section 562 of this title; and

"(B) does not include a repurchase obligation under a participation in a commercial mortgage loan;";

(D) in paragraph (48), by inserting ", or exempt from such registration under such section pursuant to an order of the Securities and Exchange Commission," after "1934"; and

(E) by amending paragraph (53B) to read as follows:

"(53B) 'swap agreement'—

"(A) means—

"(i) any agreement, including the terms and conditions incorporated by reference in such agreement, which is—

"(I) an interest rate swap, option, future, or forward agreement, including a rate floor, rate cap, rate collar, cross-currency rate swap, and basis swap;

"(II) a spot, same day-tomorrow, tomorrow-next, forward, or other foreign exchange or precious metals agreement;

"(III) a currency swap, option, future, or forward agreement;

"(IV) an equity index or equity swap, option, future, or forward agreement;

"(V) a debt index or debt swap, option, future, or forward agreement;

"(VI) a total return, credit spread or credit swap, option, future, or forward agreement;

"(VII) a commodity index or a commodity swap, option, future, or forward agreement; or

"(VIII) a weather swap, weather derivative, or weather option;

"(ii) any agreement or transaction that is similar to any other agreement or transaction referred to in this paragraph and that—

"(I) is of a type that has been, is presently, or in the future becomes, the subject of recurrent dealings in the swap markets (including terms and conditions incorporated by reference therein); and

"(II) is a forward, swap, future, or option on one or more rates, currencies, commodities, equity securities, or other equity instruments, debt securities or other debt instruments, quantitative measures associated with an occurrence, extent of an occurrence, or contingency associated with a financial, commercial, or economic consequence, or economic or financial indices or measures of economic or financial risk or value;

"(iii) any combination of agreements or transactions referred to in this subparagraph;

"(iv) any option to enter into an agreement or transaction referred to in this subparagraph;

"(v) a master agreement that provides for an agreement or transaction referred to in clause (i), (ii), (iii), or (iv), together with all supplements to any such master agreement, and without regard to whether the master agreement contains an agreement or transaction that is not a swap agreement under this paragraph, except that the master agreement shall be considered to be a swap agreement under this paragraph only with respect to each agreement or transaction under the master agreement that is referred to in clause (i), (ii), (iii), or (iv); or

"(vi) any security agreement or arrangement or other credit enhancement related to any agreements or transactions referred to in clause (i) through (v), including any guarantee or reimbursement obligation by or to a swap participant or financial participant in connection with any agreement or transaction referred to in any such clause, but not to exceed the damages in connection with any such agreement or transaction, measured in accordance with section 562; and

"(B) is applicable for purposes of this title only, and shall not be construed or applied so as to challenge or affect the characterization, definition, or treatment of any swap agreement under any other statute, regulation, or rule, including the Securities Act of 1933, the Securities Exchange Act of 1934, the Public Utility Holding Company Act of 1935, the Trust Indenture Act of 1939, the Investment Company Act of 1940, the Investment Advisers Act of 1940, the Securities Investor Protection Act of 1970, the Commodity Exchange Act, the Gramm-Leach-Bliley Act, and the Legal Certainty for Bank Products Act of 2000;";

(2) in section 741(7), by striking paragraph (7) and inserting the following:

"(7) 'securities contract'—

"(A) means—

"(i) a contract for the purchase, sale, or loan of a security, a certificate of deposit, a mortgage loan or any interest in a mortgage loan, a group or index of securities, certificates of deposit, or mortgage loans or interests therein (including an interest therein or based on the value thereof), or option on any of the foregoing, including an option to purchase or sell any such security, certificate of deposit, mortgage loan, interest, group or index, or option, and including any repurchase or reverse repurchase transaction on any such security, certificate of deposit, mortgage loan, interest, group or index, or option;

"(ii) any option entered into on a national securities exchange relating to foreign currencies;

"(iii) the guarantee by or to any securities clearing agency of a settlement of cash, securities, certificates of deposit, mortgage loans or interests therein, group or index of securities, or mortgage loans or interests therein (including any interest therein or based on the value thereof), or option on any of the foregoing, including an option to purchase or sell any such security, certificate of deposit, mortgage loan, interest, group or index, or option;

"(iv) any margin loan;

"(v) any other agreement or transaction that is similar to an agreement or transaction referred to in this subparagraph;

"(vi) any combination of the agreements or transactions referred to in this subparagraph;

"(vii) any option to enter into any agreement or transaction referred to in this subparagraph;

"(viii) a master agreement that provides for an agreement or transaction referred to in clause (i), (ii), (iii), (iv), (v), (vi), or (vii), together with all supplements to any such master agreement, without regard to whether the master agreement provides for an agreement or transaction that is not a securities contract under this subparagraph, except that such master agreement shall be considered to be a securities contract under this subparagraph only with respect to each agreement or transaction under such master agreement that is referred to in clause (i), (ii), (iii), (iv), (v), (vi), or (vii); or

"(ix) any security agreement or arrangement or other credit enhancement related to any agreement or transaction referred to in this subparagraph, including any guarantee or reimbursement obligation by or to a stockbroker, securities clearing agency, financial institution, or financial participant in connection with any agreement or transaction referred to in this subparagraph, but not to exceed the damages in connection with any such agreement or transaction, measured in accordance with section 562; and

"(B) does not include any purchase, sale, or repurchase obligation under a participation in a commercial mortgage loan;"; and

(3) in section 761(4)—

(A) by striking "or" at the end of subparagraph (D); and

(B) by adding at the end the following:

"(F) any other agreement or transaction that is similar to an agreement or transaction referred to in this paragraph;

"(G) any combination of the agreements or transactions referred to in this paragraph;

"(H) any option to enter into an agreement or transaction referred to in this paragraph;

"(I) a master agreement that provides for an agreement or transaction referred to in subparagraph (A), (B), (C), (D), (E), (F), (G), or (H), together with all supplements to such master agreement, without regard to whether the master agreement provides for an agreement or transaction that is not a commodity contract under this paragraph, except that the master agreement shall be considered to be a commodity contract under this paragraph only with respect to each agreement or transaction under the master agreement that is referred to in subparagraph (A), (B), (C), (D), (E), (F), (G), or (H); or

"(J) any security agreement or arrangement or other credit enhancement related to any agreement or transaction referred to in this paragraph, including any guarantee or reimbursement obligation by or to a commodity broker or financial participant in connection with any agreement or transaction referred to in this paragraph, but not to exceed the damages in connection with any such agreement or transaction, measured in accordance with section 562;".

(b) DEFINITIONS OF FINANCIAL INSTITUTION, FINANCIAL PARTICIPANT, AND FORWARD CONTRACT MERCHANT—Section 101 of title 11, United States Code, is amended—

(1) by striking paragraph (22) and inserting the following:

"(22) 'financial institution' means—

"(A) a Federal reserve bank, or an entity (domestic or foreign) that is a commercial or savings bank, industrial savings bank, savings and loan association, trust company, federally-insured credit union, or receiver, liquidating agent, or conservator for such entity and, when any such Federal reserve bank, receiver, liquidating agent, conservator or entity is acting as agent or custodian for a customer in connection with a securities contract (as defined in section 741) such customer; or

"(B) in connection with a securities contract (as defined in section 741) an investment company registered under the Investment Company Act of 1940;";

(2) by inserting after paragraph (22) the following:

"(22A) 'financial participant' means—

"(A) an entity that, at the time it enters into a securities contract, commodity contract, swap agreement, repurchase agreement, or forward contract, or at the time of the date of the filing of the petition, has one or more agreements or transactions described in paragraph (1), (2), (3), (4), (5), or (6) of section 561(a) with the debtor or any other entity (other than an affiliate) of a total gross dollar value of not less than $1,000,000,000 in notional or actual principal amount outstanding on any day during the previous 15-month period, or has gross mark-to-market positions of not less than $100,000,000 (aggregated across counterparties) in one or more such agreements or transactions with the debtor or any other entity (other than an affiliate) on any day during the previous 15-month period; or

"(B) a clearing organization (as defined in section 402 of the Federal Deposit Insurance Corporation Improvement Act of 1991);"; and

(3) by striking paragraph (26) and inserting the following:

"(26) 'forward contract merchant' means a Federal reserve bank, or an entity the business of which consists in whole or in part of entering into forward contracts as or with merchants in a commodity (as defined in section 761) or any similar good, article, service, right, or interest which is presently or in the future becomes the subject of dealing in the forward contract trade;".

(c) DEFINITION OF MASTER NETTING AGREEMENT AND MASTER NETTING AGREEMENT PARTICIPANT—Section 101 of title 11, United States Code, is amended by inserting after paragraph (38) the following new paragraphs:

"(38A) 'master netting agreement'—

"(A) means an agreement providing for the exercise of rights, including rights of netting, setoff, liquidation, termination, acceleration, or close out, under or in connection with one or more contracts that are described in any one or more of paragraphs (1) through (5) of section 561(a), or any security agreement or arrangement or other credit enhancement related to one or more of the foregoing, including any guarantee or reimbursement obligation related to 1 or more of the foregoing; and

"(B) if the agreement contains provisions relating to agreements or transactions that are not contracts described in paragraphs (1) through (5) of section 561(a), shall be deemed to be a master netting agreement only with respect to those agreements or transactions that are described in any one or more of paragraphs (1) through (5) of section 561(a);

"(38B) 'master netting agreement participant' means an entity that, at any time before the date of the filing of the petition, is a party to an outstanding master netting agreement with the debtor;".

(d) SWAP AGREEMENTS, SECURITIES CONTRACTS, COMMODITY CONTRACTS, FORWARD CONTRACTS, REPURCHASE AGREEMENTS, AND MASTER NETTING AGREEMENTS UNDER THE AUTOMATIC-STAY—

(1) IN GENERAL—Section 362(b) of title 11, United States Code, as amended by sections 224, 303, 311, 401, and 718, is amended—

(A) in paragraph (6), by inserting ", pledged to, under the control of," after "held by";

(B) in paragraph (7), by inserting ", pledged to, under the control of," after "held by";

(C) by striking paragraph (17) and inserting the following:

"(17) under subsection (a), of the setoff by a swap participant or financial participant of a mutual debt and claim under or in connection with one or more swap agreements that constitutes the setoff of a claim against the debtor for any payment or other transfer of property due from the debtor under or in connection with any swap agreement against any payment due to the debtor from the swap participant or financial participant under or in connection with any swap agreement or against cash, securities, or other property held by, pledged to, under the control of, or due from such swap participant or financial participant to margin, guarantee, secure, or settle any swap agreement;"; and

(D) by inserting after paragraph (26) the following:

"(27) under subsection (a), of the setoff by a master netting agreement participant of a mutual debt and claim under or in connection with one or more master netting agreements or any contract or agreement subject to such agreements that constitutes the setoff of a claim against the debtor for any payment or other transfer of property due from the debtor under or in connection with such agreements or any contract or agreement subject to such agreements against any payment due to the debtor from such master netting agreement participant under or in connection with such agreements or any contract or agreement subject to such agreements or against cash, securities, or other property held by, pledged to, under the control of, or due from such master netting agreement participant to margin, guarantee, secure, or settle such agreements or any contract or agreement subject to such agreements, to the extent that such participant is eligible to exercise such offset rights under paragraph (6), (7), or (17) for each individual contract covered by the master netting agreement in issue; and".

(2) LIMITATION—Section 362 of title 11, United States Code, as amended by sections 106, 305, 311, and 441, is amended by adding at the end the following:

"(o) The exercise of rights not subject to the stay arising under subsection (a) pursuant to paragraph (6), (7), (17), or (27) of subsection (b) shall not be stayed by any order of a court or administrative agency in any proceeding under this title.".

(e) LIMITATION OF AVOIDANCE POWERS UNDER MASTER NETTING AGREE-MENT—Section 546 of title 11, United States Code, is amended—

(1) in subsection (g) (as added by section 103 of Public Law 101-311)—

(A) by striking "under a swap agreement";

(B) by striking "in connection with a swap agreement" and inserting "under or in connection with any swap agreement"; and

(C) by inserting "or financial participant" after "swap participant"; and

(2) by adding at the end the following:

"(j) Notwithstanding sections 544, 545, 547, 548(a)(1)(B), and 548(b) the trustee may not avoid a transfer made by or to a master netting agreement participant under or in connection with any master netting agreement or any individual contract covered thereby that is made before the commencement of the case, except under section 548(a)(1)(A) and except to the extent that the trustee could otherwise avoid such a transfer made under an individual contract covered by such master netting agreement.".

(f) FRAUDULENT TRANSFERS OF MASTER NETTING AGREEMENTS—Section 548(d)(2) of title 11, United States Code, is amended—

(1) in subparagraph (C), by striking "and" at the end;

(2) in subparagraph (D), by striking the period and inserting "; and"; and

(3) by adding at the end the following new subparagraph:

"(E) a master netting agreement participant that receives a transfer in connection with a master netting agreement or any individual contract covered thereby takes for value to the extent of such transfer, except that, with respect to a transfer under any individual contract covered thereby, to the extent that such master netting agreement participant otherwise did not take (or is otherwise not deemed to have taken) such transfer for value.".

(g) TERMINATION OR ACCELERATION OF SECURITIES CONTRACTS—Section 555 of title 11, United States Code, is amended—

(1) by amending the section heading to read as follows:

"§ 555. Contractual right to liquidate, terminate, or accelerate a securities contract';

and

(2) in the first sentence, by striking "liquidation" and inserting "liquidation, termination, or acceleration".

(h) TERMINATION OR ACCELERATION OF COMMODITIES OR FORWARD CONTRACTS—Section 556 of title 11, United States Code, is amended—

(1) by amending the section heading to read as follows:

"§ 556. Contractual right to liquidate, terminate, or accelerate a commodities contract or forward contract';

(2) in the first sentence, by striking "liquidation" and inserting "liquidation, termination, or acceleration"; and

(3) in the second sentence, by striking "As used" and all that follows through "right," and inserting "As used in this section, the term 'contractual right' includes a right set forth in a rule or bylaw of a derivatives clearing organization (as defined in the Commodity Exchange Act), a multilateral clearing organization (as defined in the Federal Deposit Insurance Corporation Improvement Act of 1991), a national securities exchange, a national securities association, a securities clearing agency, a contract market designated under the Commodity Exchange Act, a derivatives transaction execution facility registered under the Commodity Exchange Act, or a board of trade (as defined in the Commodity Exchange Act) or in a resolution of the governing board thereof and a right,".

(i) TERMINATION OR ACCELERATION OF REPURCHASE AGREEMENTS— Section 559 of title 11, United States Code, is amended—

(1) by amending the section heading to read as follows:

"§ 559. Contractual right to liquidate, terminate, or accelerate a repurchase agreement";

(2) in the first sentence, by striking "liquidation" and inserting "liquidation, termination, or acceleration"; and

(3) in the third sentence, by striking "As used" and all that follows through "right," and inserting "As used in this section, the term 'contractual right' includes a right set forth in a rule or bylaw of a derivatives clearing organization (as defined in the Commodity Exchange Act), a multilateral clearing organization (as defined in the Federal Deposit Insurance Corporation Improvement Act of 1991), a national securities exchange, a national securities association, a securities clearing agency, a contract market designated under the Commodity Exchange Act, a derivatives transaction execution facility registered under the Commodity Exchange Act, or a board of trade (as defined in the Commodity Exchange Act) or in a resolution of the governing board thereof and a right,".

(j) LIQUIDATION, TERMINATION, OR ACCELERATION OF SWAP AGREEMENTS—Section 560 of title 11, United States Code, is amended—

(1) by amending the section heading to read as follows:

"§ 560. Contractual right to liquidate, terminate, or accelerate a swap agreement";

(2) in the first sentence, by striking "termination of a swap agreement" and inserting "liquidation, termination, or acceleration of one or more swap agreements";

(3) by striking "in connection with any swap agreement" and inserting "in connection with the termination, liquidation, or acceleration of one or more swap agreements"; and

(4) in the second sentence, by striking "As used" and all that follows through "right," and inserting "As used in this section, the term 'contractual right' includes a right set forth in a rule or bylaw of a derivatives clearing organization (as defined in the Commodity Exchange Act), a multilateral clearing organization (as defined in the Federal Deposit Insurance Corporation Improvement Act of 1991), a national securities exchange, a national securities association, a securities clearing agency, a contract market designated under the Commodity Exchange Act, a derivatives transaction execution facility registered under the Commodity Exchange Act, or a board of trade (as defined in the Commodity Exchange Act) or in a resolution of the governing board thereof and a right,".

(k) LIQUIDATION, TERMINATION, ACCELERATION, OR OFFSET UNDER A MASTER NETTING AGREEMENT AND ACROSS CONTRACTS—

(1) IN GENERAL—Title 11, United States Code, is amended by inserting after section 560 the following:

"§ 561. Contractual right to terminate, liquidate, accelerate, or offset under a master netting agreement and across contracts; proceedings under chapter 15

"(a) Subject to subsection (b), the exercise of any contractual right, because of a condition of the kind specified in section 365(e)(1), to cause the termination, liquidation, or acceleration of or to offset or net termination values, payment amounts, or other transfer obligations arising under or in connection with one or more (or the termination, liquidation, or acceleration of one or more)—

"(1) securities contracts, as defined in section 741(7);

"(2) commodity contracts, as defined in section 761(4);

"(3) forward contracts;

"(4) repurchase agreements;

"(5) swap agreements; or

"(6) master netting agreements,

shall not be stayed, avoided, or otherwise limited by operation of any provision of this title or by any order of a court or administrative agency in any proceeding under this title.

"(b)(1) A party may exercise a contractual right described in subsection (a) to terminate, liquidate, or accelerate only to the extent that such party could exercise such a right under section 555, 556, 559, or 560 for each individual contract covered by the master netting agreement in issue.

"(2) If a debtor is a commodity broker subject to subchapter IV of chapter 7—

"(A) a party may not net or offset an obligation to the debtor arising under, or in connection with, a commodity contract traded on or subject to the rules of a contract market designated under the Commodity Exchange Act or a derivatives transaction execution facility registered under the Commodity Exchange Act against any claim arising under, or in connection with, other instruments, contracts, or agreements listed in subsection (a) except to the extent that the party has positive net equity in the commodity accounts at the debtor, as calculated under such subchapter; and

"(B) another commodity broker may not net or offset an obligation to the debtor arising under, or in connection with, a commodity contract entered into or held on behalf of a customer of the debtor and traded on or subject to the rules of a contract market designated under the Commodity Exchange Act or a derivatives transaction execution facility registered under the Commodity Exchange Act against any claim arising under, or in connection with, other instruments, contracts, or agreements listed in subsection (a).

"(3) No provision of subparagraph (A) or (B) of paragraph (2) shall prohibit the offset of claims and obligations that arise under—

"(A) a cross-margining agreement or similar arrangement that has been approved by the Commodity Futures Trading Commission or submitted to the Commodity Futures Trading Commission under paragraph (1) or (2) of section 5c(c) of the Commodity Exchange Act and has not been abrogated or rendered ineffective by the Commodity Futures Trading Commission; or

"(B) any other netting agreement between a clearing organization (as defined in section 761) and another entity that has been approved by the Commodity Futures Trading Commission.

"(c) As used in this section, the term 'contractual right' includes a right set forth in a rule or bylaw of a derivatives clearing organization (as defined in the Commodity Exchange Act), a multilateral clearing organization (as defined in the Federal Deposit Insurance Corporation Improvement Act of 1991), a national securities exchange, a national securities association, a securities clearing agency, a contract market designated under the Commodity Exchange Act, a derivatives transaction execution facility registered under the Commodity Exchange Act, or a board of trade (as defined in the Commodity Exchange Act) or in a resolution of the governing board thereof, and a right, whether or not evidenced in writing, arising under common law, under law merchant, or by reason of normal business practice.

"(d) Any provisions of this title relating to securities contracts, commodity contracts, forward contracts, repurchase agreements, swap agreements, or master netting agreements shall apply in a case under chapter 15, so that enforcement of contractual provisions of such contracts and agreements in accordance with their terms will not be stayed or otherwise limited by operation of any provision of this title or by order of a court in any case under this title, and to limit avoidance powers to the same extent as in a proceeding under chapter 7 or 11 of this title (such enforcement not to be limited based on the presence or absence of assets of the debtor in the United States).".

(2) CONFORMING AMENDMENT—The table of sections for chapter 5 of title 11, United States Code, is amended by inserting after the item relating to section 560 the following:

"561. Contractual right to terminate, liquidate, accelerate, or offset under a master netting agreement and across contracts; proceedings under chapter 15.".

(l) COMMODITY BROKER LIQUIDATIONS—Title 11, United States Code, is amended by inserting after section 766 the following:

"§ 767. Commodity broker liquidation and forward contract merchants, commodity brokers, stockbrokers, financial institutions, financial participants, securities clearing agencies, swap participants, repo participants, and master netting agreement participants

"Notwithstanding any other provision of this title, the exercise of rights by a forward contract merchant, commodity broker, stockbroker, financial institution, financial participant, securities clearing agency, swap participant, repo participant, or master netting agreement participant under this title shall not affect the priority of any unsecured claim it may have after the exercise of such rights.".

(m) STOCKBROKER LIQUIDATIONS—Title 11, United States Code, is amended by inserting after section 752 the following:

"§ 753. Stockbroker liquidation and forward contract merchants, commodity brokers, stockbrokers, financial institutions, financial participants, securities clearing agencies, swap participants, repo participants, and master netting agreement participants

"Notwithstanding any other provision of this title, the exercise of rights by a forward contract merchant, commodity broker, stockbroker, financial institution, financial participant, securities clearing agency, swap participant, repo participant, or master netting agreement participant under this title shall not affect the priority of any unsecured claim it may have after the exercise of such rights.".

(n) SETOFF—Section 553 of title 11, United States Code, is amended—

(1) in subsection (a)(2)(B)(ii), by inserting before the semicolon the following: "(except for a setoff of a kind described in section 362(b)(6), 362(b)(7), 362(b)(17), 362(b)(27), 555, 556, 559, 560, or 561)";

(2) in subsection (a)(3)(C), by inserting before the period the following: "(except for a setoff of a kind described in section 362(b)(6), 362(b)(7), 362(b)(17), 362(b)(27), 555, 556, 559, 560, or 561)"; and

(3) in subsection (b)(1), by striking "362(b)(14)," and inserting "362(b)(17), 362(b)(27), 555, 556, 559, 560, 561,".

(o) SECURITIES CONTRACTS, COMMODITY CONTRACTS, AND FORWARD CONTRACTS—Title 11, United States Code, is amended—

(1) in section 362(b)(6), by striking "financial institutions," each place such term appears and inserting "financial institution, financial participant,";

(2) in sections 362(b)(7) and 546(f), by inserting "or financial participant" after "repo participant" each place such term appears;

(3) in section 546(e), by inserting "financial participant," after "financial institution,";

(4) in section 548(d)(2)(B), by inserting "financial participant," after "financial institution,";

(5) in section 548(d)(2)(C), by inserting "or financial participant" after "repo participant";

(6) in section 548(d)(2)(D), by inserting "or financial participant" after "swap participant";

(7) in section 555—

(A) by inserting "financial participant," after "financial institution,"; and

(B) by striking the second sentence and inserting the following: "As used in this section, the term 'contractual right' includes a right set forth in a rule or bylaw of a derivatives clearing organization (as defined in the Commodity Exchange Act), a multilateral clearing organization (as defined in the Federal Deposit Insurance Corporation Improvement Act of 1991), a national securities exchange, a national securities association, a securities clearing agency, a contract market designated under the Commodity Exchange Act, a derivatives transaction execution facility registered under the Commodity Exchange Act, or a board of trade (as defined in the Commodity Exchange Act), or in a resolution of the governing board thereof, and a right, whether or not in writing, arising under common law, under law merchant, or by reason of normal business practice.";

(8) in section 556, by inserting ", financial participant," after "commodity broker";

(9) in section 559, by inserting "or financial participant" after "repo participant" each place such term appears; and

(10) in section 560, by inserting "or financial participant" after "swap participant".

(p) CONFORMING AMENDMENTS—Title 11, United States Code, is amended—

(1) in the table of sections for chapter 5—

(A) by amending the items relating to sections 555 and 556 to read as follows:

"555. Contractual right to liquidate, terminate, or accelerate a securities contract.

"556. Contractual right to liquidate, terminate, or accelerate a commodities contract or forward contract.";

and

(B) by amending the items relating to sections 559 and 560 to read as follows:

"559. Contractual right to liquidate, terminate, or accelerate a repurchase agreement.

"560. Contractual right to liquidate, terminate, or accelerate a swap agreement.";

and

(2) in the table of sections for chapter 7—

(A) by inserting after the item relating to section 766 the following:

"767. Commodity broker liquidation and forward contract merchants, commodity brokers, stockbrokers, financial institutions, financial participants, securities clearing agencies, swap participants, repo participants, and master netting agreement participants.";

and

(B) by inserting after the item relating to section 752 the following:

"753. Stockbroker liquidation and forward contract merchants, commodity brokers, stockbrokers, financial institutions, financial participants, securities clearing agencies, swap participants, repo participants, and master netting agreement participants.".

Sec. 908 RECORDKEEPING REQUIREMENTS.

(a) FDIC-INSURED DEPOSITORY INSTITUTIONS—Section 11(e)(8) of the Federal Deposit Insurance Act (12 U.S.C. 1821(e)(8)) is amended by adding at the end the following new subparagraph:

"(H) RECORDKEEPING REQUIREMENTS—The Corporation, in consultation with the appropriate Federal banking agencies, may prescribe regulations requiring more detailed recordkeeping by any insured depository institution with respect to qualified financial contracts (including market valuations) only if such insured depository institution is in a troubled condition (as such term is defined by the Corporation pursuant to section 32).".

(b) INSURED CREDIT UNIONS—Section 207(c)(8) of the Federal Credit Union Act (12 U.S.C. 1787(c)(8)) is amended by adding at the end the following new subparagraph:

"(H) RECORDKEEPING REQUIREMENTS—The Board, in consultation with the appropriate Federal banking agencies, may prescribe regulations requiring more detailed recordkeeping by any insured credit union with respect to qualified financial contracts (including market valuations) only if such insured credit union is in a troubled condition (as such term is defined by the Board pursuant to section 212).".

Sec. 909 EXEMPTIONS FROM CONTEMPORANEOUS EXECUTION REQUIREMENT.

Section 13(e)(2) of the Federal Deposit Insurance Act (12 U.S.C. 1823(e)(2)) is amended to read as follows:

"(2) EXEMPTIONS FROM CONTEMPORANEOUS EXECUTION REQUIREMENT—An agreement to provide for the lawful collateralization of—

"(A) deposits of, or other credit extension by, a Federal, State, or local governmental entity, or of any depositor referred to in section 11(a)(2), including an agreement to provide collateral in lieu of a surety bond;

"(B) bankruptcy estate funds pursuant to section 345(b)(2) of title 11, United States Code;

"(C) extensions of credit, including any overdraft, from a Federal reserve bank or Federal home loan bank; or

"(D) one or more qualified financial contracts, as defined in section 11(e)(8)(D),

shall not be deemed invalid pursuant to paragraph (1)(B) solely because such agreement was not executed contemporaneously with the acquisition of the collateral or because of pledges, delivery, or substitution of the collateral made in accordance with such agreement.".

Sec. 910 DAMAGE MEASURE.

(a) IN GENERAL—Title 11, United States Code, is amended—

(1) by inserting after section 561, as added by section 907, the following:

"§ 562. Timing of damage measurement in connection with swap agreements, securities contracts, forward contracts, commodity contracts, repurchase agreements, and master netting agreements

"(a) If the trustee rejects a swap agreement, securities contract (as defined in section 741), forward contract, commodity contract (as defined in section 761), repurchase agreement, or master netting agreement pursuant to section 365(a), or if a forward contract merchant, stockbroker, financial institution, securities clearing agency, repo participant, financial participant, master netting agreement participant, or swap participant liquidates, terminates, or accelerates such contract or agreement, damages shall be measured as of the earlier of—

"(1) the date of such rejection; or

"(2) the date or dates of such liquidation, termination, or acceleration.

"(b) If there are not any commercially reasonable determinants of value as of any date referred to in paragraph (1) or (2) of subsection (a), damages shall be measured as of the earliest subsequent date or dates on which there are commercially reasonable determinants of value.

"(c) For the purposes of subsection (b), if damages are not measured as of the date or dates of rejection, liquidation, termination, or acceleration, and the forward contract merchant, stockbroker, financial institution, securities clearing agency, repo participant, financial participant, master netting agreement participant, or swap participant or the trustee objects to the timing of the measurement of damages—

"(1) the trustee, in the case of an objection by a forward contract merchant, stockbroker, financial institution, securities clearing agency, repo participant, financial participant, master netting agreement participant, or swap participant; or

"(2) the forward contract merchant, stockbroker, financial institution, securities clearing agency, repo participant, financial participant, master netting agreement participant, or swap participant, in the case of an objection by the trustee,

has the burden of proving that there were no commercially reasonable determinants of value as of such date or dates."; and

(2) in the table of sections for chapter 5, by inserting after the item relating to section 561 (as added by section 907) the following new item:

"562. Timing of damage measure in connection with swap agreements, securities contracts, forward contracts, commodity contracts, repurchase agreements, or master netting agreements.".

(b) CLAIMS ARISING FROM REJECTION—Section 502(g) of title 11, United States Code, is amended—

(1) by inserting "(1)" after "(g)"; and

(2) by adding at the end the following:

"(2) A claim for damages calculated in accordance with section 562 shall be allowed under subsection (a), (b), or (c), or disallowed under subsection (d) or (e), as if such claim had arisen before the date of the filing of the petition.".

Sec. 911 SIPC STAY.

Section 5(b)(2) of the Securities Investor Protection Act of 1970 (15 U.S.C. 78eee(b)(2)) is amended by adding at the end the following new subparagraph:

"(C) EXCEPTION FROM STAY—

"(i) Notwithstanding section 362 of title 11, United States Code, neither the filing of an application under subsection (a)(3) nor any order or decree obtained by SIPC from the court shall operate as a stay of any contractual rights of a creditor to liquidate, terminate, or accelerate a securities contract, commodity contract, forward contract, repurchase agreement, swap agreement, or master netting agreement, as those terms are defined in sections 101, 741, and 761 of title 11, United States Code, to offset or net termination values, payment amounts, or other transfer obligations arising under or in connection with one or more of such contracts or agreements, or to foreclose on any cash collateral pledged by the debtor, whether or not with respect to one or more of such contracts or agreements.

"(ii) Notwithstanding clause (i), such application, order, or decree may operate as a stay of the foreclosure on, or disposition of, securities collateral pledged by the debtor, whether or not with respect to one or more of such contracts or agreements, securities sold by the debtor under a repurchase agreement, or securities lent under a securities lending agreement.

"(iii) As used in this subparagraph, the term 'contractual right' includes a right set forth in a rule or bylaw of a national securities exchange, a national securities association, or a securities clearing agency, a right set forth in a bylaw of a clearing organization or contract market or in a resolution of the governing board thereof, and a right, whether or not in writing, arising under common law, under law merchant, or by reason of normal business practice.".

TITLE X

PROTECTION OF FAMILY FARMERS AND FAMILY FISHERMEN

Sec. 1001 PERMANENT REENACTMENT OF CHAPTER 12.

(a) REENACTMENT—

(1) IN GENERAL—Chapter 12 of title 11, United States Code, as reenacted by section 149 of division C of the Omnibus Consolidated and Emergency Supplemental Appropriations Act, 1999 (Public Law 105-277), and as in effect on June 30, 2005, is hereby reenacted.

(2) EFFECTIVE DATE OF REENACTMENT—Paragraph (1) shall take effect on July 1, 2005.

(b) AMENDMENTS—Chapter 12 of title 11, United States Code, as reenacted by subsection (a), is amended by this Act.

(c) CONFORMING AMENDMENT—Section 302 of the Bankruptcy Judges, United States Trustees, and Family Farmer Bankruptcy Act of 1986 (28 U.S.C. 581 note) is amended by striking subsection (f).

Sec. 1002 DEBT LIMIT INCREASE.

Section 104(b) of title 11, United States Code, as amended by section 226, is amended by inserting "101(18)," after "101(3)," each place it appears.

Sec. 1003 CERTAIN CLAIMS OWED TO GOVERNMENTAL UNITS.

(a) CONTENTS OF PLAN—Section 1222(a)(2) of title 11, United States Code, as amended by section 213, is amended to read as follows:

"(2) provide for the full payment, in deferred cash payments, of all claims entitled to priority under section 507, unless—

"(A) the claim is a claim owed to a governmental unit that arises as a result of the sale, transfer, exchange, or other disposition of any farm asset used in the debtor's farming operation, in which case the claim shall be treated as an unsecured claim that is not entitled to priority under section 507, but the debt shall be treated in such manner only if the debtor receives a discharge; or

"(B) the holder of a particular claim agrees to a different treatment of that claim;".

(b) SPECIAL NOTICE PROVISIONS—Section 1231(b) of title 11, United States Code, as so designated by section 719, is amended by striking "a State or local governmental unit" and inserting "any governmental unit".

(c) Effective Date; Application of Amendments—This section and the amendments made by this section shall take effect on the date of the enactment of this Act and shall not apply with respect to cases commenced under title 11 of the United States Code before such date.

Sec. 1004 Definition of Family Farmer.

Section 101(18) of title 11, United States Code, is amended—

(1) in subparagraph (A)—

(A) by striking "$1,500,000" and inserting "$3,237,000"; and

(B) by striking "80" and inserting "50"; and

(2) in subparagraph (B)(ii)—

(A) by striking "$1,500,000" and inserting "$3,237,000"; and

(B) by striking "80" and inserting "50".

Sec. 1005 Elimination of Requirement That Family Farmer and Spouse Receive Over 50 Percent of Income From Farming Operation in Year Prior to Bankruptcy.

Section 101(18)(A) of title 11, United States Code, is amended by striking "for the taxable year preceding the taxable year" and inserting the following:

"for—

"(i) the taxable year preceding; or

"(ii) each of the 2d and 3d taxable years preceding;

the taxable year".

Sec. 1006 Prohibition of Retroactive Assessment of Disposable Income.

(a) Confirmation of Plan—Section 1225(b)(1) of title 11, United States Code, is amended—

(1) in subparagraph (A) by striking "or" at the end;

(2) in subparagraph (B) by striking the period at the end and inserting "; or"; and

(3) by adding at the end the following:

"(C) the value of the property to be distributed under the plan in the 3-year period, or such longer period as the court may approve under section 1222(c), beginning on the date that the first distribution is due under the plan is not less than the debtor's projected disposable income for such period.".

(b) Modification of Plan—Section 1229 of title 11, United States Code, is amended by adding at the end the following:

"(d) A plan may not be modified under this section—

"(1) to increase the amount of any payment due before the plan as modified becomes the plan;

"(2) by anyone except the debtor, based on an increase in the debtor's disposable income, to increase the amount of payments to unsecured creditors required for a particular month so that the aggregate of such payments exceeds the debtor's disposable income for such month; or

"(3) in the last year of the plan by anyone except the debtor, to require payments that would leave the debtor with insufficient funds to carry on the farming operation after the plan is completed.".

Sec. 1007 FAMILY FISHERMEN.

(a) DEFINITIONS—Section 101 of title 11, United States Code, is amended—

(1) by inserting after paragraph (7) the following:

"(7A) 'commercial fishing operation' means—

"(A) the catching or harvesting of fish, shrimp, lobsters, urchins, seaweed, shellfish, or other aquatic species or products of such species; or

"(B) for purposes of section 109 and chapter 12, aquaculture activities consisting of raising for market any species or product described in subparagraph (A);

"(7B) 'commercial fishing vessel' means a vessel used by a family fisherman to carry out a commercial fishing operation;"; and

(2) by inserting after paragraph (19) the following:

"(19A) 'family fisherman' means—

"(A) an individual or individual and spouse engaged in a commercial fishing operation—

"(i) whose aggregate debts do not exceed $1,500,000 and not less than 80 percent of whose aggregate noncontingent, liquidated debts (excluding a debt for the principal residence of such individual or such individual and spouse, unless such debt arises out of a commercial fishing operation), on the date the case is filed, arise out of a commercial fishing operation owned or operated by such individual or such individual and spouse; and

"(ii) who receive from such commercial fishing operation more than 50 percent of such individual's or such individual's and spouse's gross income for the taxable year preceding the taxable year in which the case concerning such individual or such individual and spouse was filed; or

"(B) a corporation or partnership—

"(i) in which more than 50 percent of the outstanding stock or equity is held by—

"(I) 1 family that conducts the commercial fishing operation; or

"(II) 1 family and the relatives of the members of such family, and such family or such relatives conduct the commercial fishing operation; and

"(ii)(I) more than 80 percent of the value of its assets consists of assets related to the commercial fishing operation;

"(II) its aggregate debts do not exceed $1,500,000 and not less than 80 percent of its aggregate noncontingent, liquidated debts (excluding a debt for 1 dwelling which is owned by such corporation or partnership and which a shareholder or partner maintains as a principal residence, unless such debt arises out of a commercial fishing operation), on the date the case is filed, arise out of a commercial fishing operation owned or operated by such corporation or such partnership; and

"(III) if such corporation issues stock, such stock is not publicly traded;

"(19B) 'family fisherman with regular annual income' means a family fisherman whose annual income is sufficiently stable and regular to enable such family fisherman to make payments under a plan under chapter 12 of this title;".

(b) WHO MAY BE A DEBTOR—Section 109(f) of title 11, United States Code, is amended by inserting "or family fisherman" after "family farmer".

(c) CHAPTER 12—Chapter 12 of title 11, United States Code, is amended—

(1) in the chapter heading, by inserting "OR FISHERMAN" after "FAMILY FARMER";

(2) in section 1203, by inserting "or commercial fishing operation" after "farm"; and

(3) in section 1206, by striking "if the property is farmland or farm equipment" and inserting "if the property is farmland, farm equipment, or property used to carry out a commercial fishing operation (including a commercial fishing vessel)".

(d) CLERICAL AMENDMENT—In the table of chapters for title 11, United States Code, the item relating to chapter 12, is amended to read as follows:

"12. Adjustments of Debts of a Family Farmer or Family Fisherman with Regular Annual Income . . . . **1201".**

(e) APPLICABILITY—Nothing in this section shall change, affect, or amend the Fishery Conservation and Management Act of 1976 (16 U.S.C. 1801 et seq.).

TITLE XI

HEALTH CARE AND EMPLOYEE BENEFITS

Sec. 1101 DEFINITIONS.

(a) HEALTH CARE BUSINESS DEFINED—Section 101 of title 11, United States Code, as amended by section 306, is amended—

    (1) by redesignating paragraph (27A) as paragraph (27B); and

    (2) by inserting after paragraph (27) the following:

"(27A) 'health care business'—

    "(A) means any public or private entity (without regard to whether that entity is organized for profit or not for profit) that is primarily engaged in offering to the general public facilities and services for—

        "(i) the diagnosis or treatment of injury, deformity, or disease; and

        "(ii) surgical, drug treatment, psychiatric, or obstetric care; and

    "(B) includes—

        "(i) any—

            "(I) general or specialized hospital;

            "(II) ancillary ambulatory, emergency, or surgical treatment facility;

            "(III) hospice;

            "(IV) home health agency; and

            "(V) other health care institution that is similar to an entity referred to in subclause (I), (II), (III), or (IV); and

        "(ii) any long-term care facility, including any—

            "(I) skilled nursing facility;

            "(II) intermediate care facility;

            "(III) assisted living facility;

            "(IV) home for the aged;

            "(V) domiciliary care facility; and

            "(VI) health care institution that is related to a facility referred to in subclause (I), (II), (III), (IV), or (V), if that institution is primarily engaged in offering room, board, laundry, or personal assistance with activities of daily living and incidentals to activities of daily living;".

(b) PATIENT AND PATIENT RECORDS DEFINED—Section 101 of title 11, United States Code, is amended by inserting after paragraph (40) the following:

"(40A) 'patient' means any individual who obtains or receives services from a health care business;

"(40B) 'patient records' means any written document relating to a patient or a record recorded in a magnetic, optical, or other form of electronic medium;".

(c) RULE OF CONSTRUCTION—The amendments made by subsection (a) of this section shall not affect the interpretation of section 109(b) of title 11, United States Code.

Sec. 1102 DISPOSAL OF PATIENT RECORDS.

(a) IN GENERAL—Subchapter III of chapter 3 of title 11, United States Code, is amended by adding at the end the following:

"§ 351. Disposal of patient records

"If a health care business commences a case under chapter 7, 9, or 11, and the trustee does not have a sufficient amount of funds to pay for the storage of patient records in the manner required under applicable Federal or State law, the following requirements shall apply:

"(1) The trustee shall—

"(A) promptly publish notice, in 1 or more appropriate newspapers, that if patient records are not claimed by the patient or an insurance provider (if applicable law permits the insurance provider to make that claim) by the date that is 365 days after the date of that notification, the trustee will destroy the patient records; and

"(B) during the first 180 days of the 365-day period described in subparagraph (A), promptly attempt to notify directly each patient that is the subject of the patient records and appropriate insurance carrier concerning the patient records by mailing to the most recent known address of that patient, or a family member or contact person for that patient, and to the appropriate insurance carrier an appropriate notice regarding the claiming or disposing of patient records.

"(2) If, after providing the notification under paragraph (1), patient records are not claimed during the 365-day period described under that paragraph, the trustee shall mail, by certified mail, at the end of such 365-day period a written request to each appropriate Federal agency to request permission from that agency to deposit the patient records with that agency, except that no Federal agency is required to accept patient records under this paragraph.

"(3) If, following the 365-day period described in paragraph (2) and after providing the notification under paragraph (1), patient records are not claimed by a patient or insurance provider, or request is not granted by a Federal agency to deposit such records with that agency, the trustee shall destroy those records by—

"(A) if the records are written, shredding or burning the records; or

"(B) if the records are magnetic, optical, or other electronic records, by otherwise destroying those records so that those records cannot be retrieved.".

(b) CLERICAL AMENDMENT—The table of sections for subchapter III of chapter 3 of title 11, United States Code, is amended by adding at the end the following:

"351. Disposal of patient records.".

Sec. 1103 ADMINISTRATIVE EXPENSE CLAIM FOR COSTS OF CLOSING A HEALTH CARE BUSINESS AND OTHER ADMINISTRATIVE EXPENSES.

Section 503(b) of title 11, United States Code, as amended by section 445, is amended by adding at the end the following:

"(8) the actual, necessary costs and expenses of closing a health care business incurred by a trustee or by a Federal agency (as defined in section 551(1) of title 5) or a department or agency of a State or political subdivision thereof, including any cost or expense incurred—

"(A) in disposing of patient records in accordance with section 351; or

"(B) in connection with transferring patients from the health care business that is in the process of being closed to another health care business; and".

Sec. 1104 APPOINTMENT OF OMBUDSMAN TO ACT AS PATIENT ADVOCATE.

(a) OMBUDSMAN TO ACT AS PATIENT ADVOCATE—

(1) APPOINTMENT OF OMBUDSMAN—Title 11, United States Code, as amended by section 232, is amended by inserting after section 332 the following:

"§ 333. Appointment of patient care ombudsman

"(a)(1) If the debtor in a case under chapter 7, 9, or 11 is a health care business, the court shall order, not later than 30 days after the commencement of the case, the appointment of an ombudsman to monitor the quality of patient care and to represent the interests of the patients of the health care business unless the court finds that the appointment of such ombudsman is not necessary for the protection of patients under the specific facts of the case.

"(2)(A) If the court orders the appointment of an ombudsman under paragraph (1), the United States trustee shall appoint 1 disinterested person (other than the United States trustee) to serve as such ombudsman.

"(B) If the debtor is a health care business that provides long-term care, then the United States trustee may appoint the State Long-Term Care Ombudsman appointed under the Older Americans Act of 1965 for the State in which the case is pending to serve as the ombudsman required by paragraph (1).

"(C) If the United States trustee does not appoint a State Long-Term Care Ombudsman under subparagraph (B), the court shall notify the State Long-Term Care Ombudsman appointed under the Older Americans Act of 1965 for the State in which the case is pending, of the name and address of the person who is appointed under subparagraph (A).

"(b) An ombudsman appointed under subsection (a) shall—

"(1) monitor the quality of patient care provided to patients of the debtor, to the extent necessary under the circumstances, including interviewing patients and physicians;

"(2) not later than 60 days after the date of appointment, and not less frequently than at 60-day intervals thereafter, report to the court after notice to the parties in interest, at a hearing or in writing, regarding the quality of patient care provided to patients of the debtor; and

"(3) if such ombudsman determines that the quality of patient care provided to patients of the debtor is declining significantly or is otherwise being materially compromised, file with the court a motion or a written report, with notice to the parties in interest immediately upon making such determination.

"(c)(1) An ombudsman appointed under subsection (a) shall maintain any information obtained by such ombudsman under this section that relates to patients (including information relating to patient records) as confidential information. Such ombudsman may not review confidential patient records unless the court approves such review in advance and imposes restrictions on such ombudsman to protect the confidentiality of such records.

"(2) An ombudsman appointed under subsection (a)(2)(B) shall have access to patient records consistent with authority of such ombudsman under the Older Americans Act of 1965 and under non-Federal laws governing the State Long-Term Care Ombudsman program.".

(2) CLERICAL AMENDMENT—The table of sections for subchapter II of chapter 3 of title 11, United States Code, as amended by section 232, is amended by adding at the end the following:

"333. Appointment of ombudsman.".

(b) COMPENSATION OF OMBUDSMAN—Section 330(a)(1) of title 11, United States Code, is amended—

(1) in the matter preceding subparagraph (A), by inserting "an ombudsman appointed under section 333, or" before "a professional person"; and

(2) in subparagraph (A), by inserting "ombudsman," before "professional person".

Sec. 1105 DEBTOR IN POSSESSION; DUTY OF TRUSTEE TO TRANSFER PATIENTS.

(a) IN GENERAL—Section 704(a) of title 11, United States Code, as amended by sections 102, 219, and 446, is amended by adding at the end the following:

"(12) use all reasonable and best efforts to transfer patients from a health care business that is in the process of being closed to an appropriate health care business that—

"(A) is in the vicinity of the health care business that is closing;

"(B) provides the patient with services that are substantially similar to those provided by the health care business that is in the process of being closed; and

"(C) maintains a reasonable quality of care.".

(b) CONFORMING AMENDMENT—Section 1106(a)(1) of title 11, United States Code, as amended by section 446, is amended by striking "and (11)" and inserting "(11), and (12)".

Sec. 1106 EXCLUSION FROM PROGRAM PARTICIPATION NOT SUBJECT TO AUTOMATIC STAY.

Section 362(b) of title 11, United States Code, is amended by inserting after paragraph (27), as amended by sections 224, 303, 311, 401, 718, and 907, the following:

"(28) under subsection (a), of the exclusion by the Secretary of Health and Human Services of the debtor from participation in the medicare program or any other Federal health care program (as defined in section 1128B(f) of the Social Security Act pursuant to title XI or XVIII of such Act).".

TITLE XII

TECHNICAL AMENDMENTS

Sec. 1201 DEFINITIONS.

Section 101 of title 11, United States Code, as amended by this Act, is further amended—

(1) by striking "In this title—" and inserting "In this title the following definitions shall apply:";

(2) in each paragraph (other than paragraph (54A)), by inserting "The term" after the paragraph designation;

(3) in paragraph (35)(B), by striking "paragraphs (21B) and (33)(A)" and inserting "paragraphs (23) and (35)";

(4) in each of paragraphs (35A), (38), and (54A), by striking "; and" at the end and inserting a period;

(5) in paragraph (51B)—

(A) by inserting "who is not a family farmer" after "debtor" the first place it appears; and

(B) by striking "thereto having aggregate" and all that follows through the end of the paragraph and inserting a semicolon;

(6) by striking paragraph (54) and inserting the following:

"(54) The term 'transfer' means—

"(A) the creation of a lien;

"(B) the retention of title as a security interest;

"(C) the foreclosure of a debtor's equity of redemption; or

"(D) each mode, direct or indirect, absolute or conditional, voluntary or involuntary, of disposing of or parting with—

"(i) property; or

"(ii) an interest in property;";

(7) in paragraph (54A)—

(A) by striking "the term" and inserting "The term"; and

(B) by indenting the left margin of paragraph (54A) 2 ems to the right; and

(8) in each of paragraphs (1) through (35), in each of paragraphs (36), (37), (38A), (38B) and (39A), and in each of paragraphs (40) through (55), by striking the semicolon at the end and inserting a period.

Sec. 1202 ADJUSTMENT OF DOLLAR AMOUNTS.

Section 104(b) of title 11, United States Code, as amended by this Act, is further amended—

(1) by inserting "101(19A)," after "101(18)," each place it appears;

(2) by inserting "522(f)(3) and 522(f)(4)," after "522(d)," each place it appears;

(3) by inserting "541(b), 547(c)(9)," after "523(a)(2)(C)," each place it appears;

(4) in paragraph (1), by striking "and 1325(b)(3)" and inserting "1322(d), 1325(b), and 1326(b)(3) of this title and section 1409(b) of title 28"; and

(5) in paragraph (2), by striking "and 1325(b)(3) of this title" and inserting "1322(d), 1325(b), and 1326(b)(3) of this title and section 1409(b) of title 28".

Sec. 1203 EXTENSION OF TIME.

Section 108(c)(2) of title 11, United States Code, is amended by striking "922" and all that follows through "or", and inserting "922, 1201, or".

Sec. 1204 TECHNICAL AMENDMENTS.

Title 11, United States Code, is amended—

(1) in section 109(b)(2), by striking "subsection (c) or (d) of"; and

(2) in section 552(b)(1), by striking "product" each place it appears and inserting "products".

Sec. 1205 PENALTY FOR PERSONS WHO NEGLIGENTLY OR FRAUDULENTLY PREPARE BANKRUPTCY PETITIONS.

Section 110(j)(4) of title 11, United States Code, as so redesignated by section 221, is amended by striking "attorney's" and inserting "attorneys' ".

Sec. 1206 LIMITATION ON COMPENSATION OF PROFESSIONAL PERSONS.

Section 328(a) of title 11, United States Code, is amended by inserting "on a fixed or percentage fee basis," after "hourly basis,".

Sec. 1207 EFFECT OF CONVERSION.

Section 348(f)(2) of title 11, United States Code, is amended by inserting "of the estate" after "property" the first place it appears.

Sec. 1208 ALLOWANCE OF ADMINISTRATIVE EXPENSES.

Section 503(b)(4) of title 11, United States Code, is amended by inserting "subparagraph (A), (B), (C), (D), or (E) of" before "paragraph (3)".

Sec. 1209 Exceptions to Discharge.

Section 523 of title 11, United States Code, as amended by sections 215 and 314, is amended—

(1) by transferring paragraph (15), as added by section 304(e) of Public Law 103-394 (108 Stat. 4133), so as to insert such paragraph after subsection (a)(14A);

(2) in subsection (a)(9), by striking "motor vehicle" and inserting "motor vehicle, vessel, or aircraft"; and

(3) in subsection (e), by striking "a insured" and inserting "an insured".

Sec. 1210 Effect of Discharge.

Section 524(a)(3) of title 11, United States Code, is amended by striking "section 523" and all that follows through "or that" and inserting "section 523, 1228(a)(1), or 1328(a)(1), or that".

Sec. 1211 Protection Against Discriminatory Treatment.

Section 525(c) of title 11, United States Code, is amended—

(1) in paragraph (1), by inserting "student" before "grant" the second place it appears; and

(2) in paragraph (2), by striking "the program operated under part B, D, or E of" and inserting "any program operated under".

Sec. 1212 Property of the Estate.

Section 541(b)(4)(B)(ii) of title 11, United States Code, is amended by inserting "365 or" before "542".

Sec. 1213 Preferences.

(a) In General—Section 547 of title 11, United States Code, as amended by section 201, is amended—

(1) in subsection (b), by striking "subsection (c)" and inserting "subsections (c) and (i)"; and

(2) by adding at the end the following:

"(i) If the trustee avoids under subsection (b) a transfer made between 90 days and 1 year before the date of the filing of the petition, by the debtor to an entity that is not an insider for the benefit of a creditor that is an insider, such transfer shall be considered to be avoided under this section only with respect to the creditor that is an insider.".

(b) Applicability—The amendments made by this section shall apply to any case that is pending or commenced on or after the date of enactment of this Act.

Sec. 1214 POSTPETITION TRANSACTIONS.

Section 549(c) of title 11, United States Code, is amended—

(1) by inserting "an interest in" after "transfer of" each place it appears;

(2) by striking "such property" and inserting "such real property"; and

(3) by striking "the interest" and inserting "such interest".

Sec. 1215 DISPOSITION OF PROPERTY OF THE ESTATE.

Section 726(b) of title 11, United States Code, is amended by striking "1009,".

Sec. 1216 GENERAL PROVISIONS.

Section 901(a) of title 11, United States Code, is amended by inserting "1123(d)," after "1123(b),".

Sec. 1217 ABANDONMENT OF RAILROAD LINE.

Section 1170(e)(1) of title 11, United States Code, is amended by striking "section 11347" and inserting "section 11326(a)".

Sec. 1218 CONTENTS OF PLAN.

Section 1172(c)(1) of title 11, United States Code, is amended by striking "section 11347" and inserting "section 11326(a)".

Sec. 1219 BANKRUPTCY CASES AND PROCEEDINGS.

Section 1334(d) of title 28, United States Code, is amended—

(1) by striking "made under this subsection" and inserting "made under subsection (c)"; and

(2) by striking "This subsection" and inserting "Subsection (c) and this subsection".

Sec. 1220 KNOWING DISREGARD OF BANKRUPTCY LAW OR RULE.

Section 156(a) of title 18, United States Code, is amended—

(1) in the first undesignated paragraph—

(A) by inserting "(1) the term" before "bankruptcy"; and

(B) by striking the period at the end and inserting "; and"; and

(2) in the second undesignated paragraph—

(A) by inserting "(2) the term" before "document"; and

(B) by striking "this title" and inserting "title 11".

Sec. 1221 Transfers Made by Nonprofit Charitable Corporations.

(a) Sale of Property of Estate—Section 363(d) of title 11, United States Code, is amended by striking "only" and all that follows through the end of the subsection and inserting "only—

"(1) in accordance with applicable nonbankruptcy law that governs the transfer of property by a corporation or trust that is not a moneyed, business, or commercial corporation or trust; and

"(2) to the extent not inconsistent with any relief granted under subsection (c), (d), (e), or (f) of section 362.".

(b) Confirmation of Plan of Reorganization—Section 1129(a) of title 11, United States Code, as amended by sections 213 and 321, is amended by adding at the end the following:

"(16) All transfers of property of the plan shall be made in accordance with any applicable provisions of nonbankruptcy law that govern the transfer of property by a corporation or trust that is not a moneyed, business, or commercial corporation or trust.".

(c) Transfer of Property—Section 541 of title 11, United States Code, as amended by section 225, is amended by adding at the end the following:

"(f) Notwithstanding any other provision of this title, property that is held by a debtor that is a corporation described in section 501(c)(3) of the Internal Revenue Code of 1986 and exempt from tax under section 501(a) of such Code may be transferred to an entity that is not such a corporation, but only under the same conditions as would apply if the debtor had not filed a case under this title.".

(d) Applicability—The amendments made by this section shall apply to a case pending under title 11, United States Code, on the date of enactment of this Act, or filed under that title on or after that date of enactment, except that the court shall not confirm a plan under chapter 11 of title 11, United States Code, without considering whether this section would substantially affect the rights of a party in interest who first acquired rights with respect to the debtor after the date of the filing of the petition. The parties who may appear and be heard in a proceeding under this section include the attorney general of the State in which the debtor is incorporated, was formed, or does business.

(e) Rule of Construction—Nothing in this section shall be construed to require the court in which a case under chapter 11 of title 11, United States Code, is pending to remand or refer any proceeding, issue, or controversy to any other court or to require the approval of any other court for the transfer of property.

Sec. 1222 Protection of Valid Purchase Money Security Interests.

Section 547(c)(3)(B) of title 11, United States Code, is amended by striking "20" and inserting "30".

Sec. 1223 BANKRUPTCY JUDGESHIPS.

(a) SHORT TITLE—This section may be cited as the "Bankruptcy Judgeship Act of 2005".

(b) TEMPORARY JUDGESHIPS—

(1) APPOINTMENTS—The following bankruptcy judges shall be appointed in the manner prescribed in section 152(a)(1) of title 28, United States Code, for the appointment of bankruptcy judges provided for in section 152(a)(2) of such title:

(A) One additional bankruptcy judge for the eastern district of California.

(B) Three additional bankruptcy judges for the central district of California.

(C) Four additional bankruptcy judges for the district of Delaware.

(D) Two additional bankruptcy judges for the southern district of Florida.

(E) One additional bankruptcy judge for the southern district of Georgia.

(F) Three additional bankruptcy judges for the district of Maryland.

(G) One additional bankruptcy judge for the eastern district of Michigan.

(H) One additional bankruptcy judge for the southern district of Mississippi.

(I) One additional bankruptcy judge for the district of New Jersey.

(J) One additional bankruptcy judge for the eastern district of New York.

(K) One additional bankruptcy judge for the northern district of New York.

(L) One additional bankruptcy judge for the southern district of New York.

(M) One additional bankruptcy judge for the eastern district of North Carolina.

(N) One additional bankruptcy judge for the eastern district of Pennsylvania.

(O) One additional bankruptcy judge for the middle district of Pennsylvania.

(P) One additional bankruptcy judge for the district of Puerto Rico.

(Q) One additional bankruptcy judge for the western district of Tennessee.

(R) One additional bankruptcy judge for the eastern district of Virginia.

(S) One additional bankruptcy judge for the district of South Carolina.

(T) One additional bankruptcy judge for the district of Nevada.

(2) VACANCIES—

(A) DISTRICTS WITH SINGLE APPOINTMENTS—Except as provided in subparagraphs (B), (C), (D), and (E), the first vacancy occurring in the office of bankruptcy judge in each of the judicial districts set forth in paragraph (1)—

(i) occurring 5 years or more after the appointment date of the bankruptcy judge appointed under paragraph (1) to such office; and

(ii) resulting from the death, retirement, resignation, or removal of a bankruptcy judge;

shall not be filled.

(B) CENTRAL DISTRICT OF CALIFORNIA—The 1st, 2d, and 3d vacancies in the office of bankruptcy judge in the central district of California—

(i) occurring 5 years or more after the respective 1st, 2d, and 3d appointment dates of the bankruptcy judges appointed under paragraph (1)(B); and

(ii) resulting from the death, retirement, resignation, or removal of a bankruptcy judge;

shall not be filled.

(C) DISTRICT OF DELAWARE—The 1st, 2d, 3d, and 4th vacancies in the office of bankruptcy judge in the district of Delaware—

(i) occurring 5 years or more after the respective 1st, 2d, 3d, and 4th appointment dates of the bankruptcy judges appointed under paragraph (1)(F); and

(ii) resulting from the death, retirement, resignation, or removal of a bankruptcy judge;

shall not be filled.

(D) SOUTHERN DISTRICT OF FLORIDA—The 1st and 2d vacancies in the office of bankruptcy judge in the southern district of Florida—

(i) occurring 5 years or more after the respective 1st and 2d appointment dates of the bankruptcy judges appointed under paragraph (1)(D); and

(ii) resulting from the death, retirement, resignation, or removal of a bankruptcy judge;

shall not be filled.

(E) DISTRICT OF MARYLAND—The 1st, 2d, and 3d vacancies in the office of bankruptcy judge in the district of Maryland—

(i) occurring 5 years or more after the respective 1st, 2d, and 3d appointment dates of the bankruptcy judges appointed under paragraph (1)(F); and

(ii) resulting from the death, retirement, resignation, or removal of a bankruptcy judge;

shall not be filled.

(c) EXTENSIONS—

(1) IN GENERAL—The temporary office of bankruptcy judges authorized for the northern district of Alabama, the district of Delaware, the district of Puerto Rico, and the eastern district of Tennessee under paragraphs (1), (3), (7), and (9) of section 3(a) of the Bankruptcy Judgeship Act of 1992 (28 U.S.C. 152 note) are extended until the first vacancy occurring in the office of a bankruptcy judge in the applicable district resulting from the death, retirement, resignation, or removal of a bankruptcy judge and occurring 5 years after the date of the enactment of this Act.

(2) APPLICABILITY OF OTHER PROVISIONS—All other provisions of section 3 of the Bankruptcy Judgeship Act of 1992 (28 U.S.C. 152 note) remain applicable to the temporary office of bankruptcy judges referred to in this subsection.

(d) TECHNICAL AMENDMENTS—Section 152(a) of title 28, United States Code, is amended—

(1) in paragraph (1), by striking the first sentence and inserting the following: "Each bankruptcy judge to be appointed for a judicial district, as provided in paragraph (2), shall be appointed by the court of appeals of the United States for the circuit in which such district is located."; and

(2) in paragraph (2)—

(A) in the item relating to the middle district of Georgia, by striking "2" and inserting "3"; and

(B) in the collective item relating to the middle and southern districts of Georgia, by striking "Middle and Southern . . . . .1".

(e) EFFECTIVE DATE—The amendments made by this section shall take effect on the date of the enactment of this Act.

Sec. 1224 COMPENSATING TRUSTEES.

Section 1326 of title 11, United States Code, is amended—

(1) in subsection (b)—

(A) in paragraph (1), by striking "and";

(B) in paragraph (2), by striking the period at the end and inserting "; and"; and

(C) by adding at the end the following:

"(3) if a chapter 7 trustee has been allowed compensation due to the conversion or dismissal of the debtor's prior case pursuant to section 707(b), and some portion of that compensation remains unpaid in a case converted to this chapter or in the case dismissed under section 707(b) and refiled under this chapter, the amount of any such unpaid compensation, which shall be paid monthly—

"(A) by prorating such amount over the remaining duration of the plan; and

"(B) by monthly payments not to exceed the greater of—

"(i) $25; or

"(ii) the amount payable to unsecured nonpriority creditors, as provided by the plan, multiplied by 5 percent, and the result divided by the number of months in the plan."; and

(2) by adding at the end the following:

"(d) Notwithstanding any other provision of this title—

"(1) compensation referred to in subsection (b)(3) is payable and may be collected by the trustee under that paragraph, even if such amount has been discharged in a prior case under this title; and

"(2) such compensation is payable in a case under this chapter only to the extent permitted by subsection (b)(3).".

Sec. 1225 AMENDMENT TO SECTION 362 OF TITLE 11, UNITED STATES CODE.

Section 362(b)(18) of title 11, United States Code, is amended to read as follows:

"(18) under subsection (a) of the creation or perfection of a statutory lien for an ad valorem property tax, or a special tax or special assessment on real property whether or not ad valorem, imposed by a governmental unit, if such tax or assessment comes due after the date of the filing of the petition;".

Sec. 1226 JUDICIAL EDUCATION.

The Director of the Federal Judicial Center, in consultation with the Director of the Executive Office for United States Trustees, shall develop materials and conduct such training as may be useful to courts in implementing this Act and the amendments made by this Act, including the requirements relating to the means test under section 707(b), and reaffirmation agreements under section 524, of title 11 of the United States Code, as amended by this Act.

Sec. 1227 RECLAMATION.

(a) RIGHTS AND POWERS OF THE TRUSTEE—Section 546(c) of title 11, United States Code, is amended to read as follows:

"(c)(1) Except as provided in subsection (d) of this section and in section 507(c), and subject to the prior rights of a holder of a security interest in such goods or the proceeds thereof, the rights and powers of the trustee under sections 544(a), 545, 547, and 549 are subject to the right of a seller of goods that has sold goods to the debtor, in the ordinary course of such seller's business, to reclaim such goods if the debtor has received such goods while insolvent, within 45 days before the date of the commencement of a case under this title, but such seller may not reclaim such goods unless such seller demands in writing reclamation of such goods—

"(A) not later than 45 days after the date of receipt of such goods by the debtor; or

"(B) not later than 20 days after the date of commencement of the case, if the 45-day period expires after the commencement of the case.

"(2) If a seller of goods fails to provide notice in the manner described in paragraph (1), the seller still may assert the rights contained in section 503(b)(9).".

(b) ADMINISTRATIVE EXPENSES—Section 503(b) of title 11, United States Code, as amended by sections 445 and 1103, is amended by adding at the end the following:

"(9) the value of any goods received by the debtor within 20 days before the date of commencement of a case under this title in which the goods have been sold to the debtor in the ordinary course of such debtor's business.".

Sec. 1228 PROVIDING REQUESTED TAX DOCUMENTS TO THE COURT.

(a) CHAPTER 7 CASES—The court shall not grant a discharge in the case of an individual who is a debtor in a case under chapter 7 of title 11, United States Code, unless requested tax documents have been provided to the court.

(b) CHAPTER 11 AND CHAPTER 13 CASES—The court shall not confirm a plan of reorganization in the case of an individual under chapter 11 or 13 of title 11, United States Code, unless requested tax documents have been filed with the court.

(c) DOCUMENT RETENTION—The court shall destroy documents submitted in support of a bankruptcy claim not sooner than 3 years after the date of the conclusion of a case filed by an individual under chapter 7, 11, or 13 of title 11, United States Code. In the event of a pending audit or enforcement action, the court may extend the time for destruction of such requested tax documents.

Sec. 1229 ENCOURAGING CREDITWORTHINESS.

(a) SENSE OF THE CONGRESS—It is the sense of the Congress that—

(1) certain lenders may sometimes offer credit to consumers indiscriminately, without taking steps to ensure that consumers are capable of repaying the resulting debt, and in a manner which may encourage certain consumers to accumulate additional debt; and

(2) resulting consumer debt may increasingly be a major contributing factor to consumer insolvency.

(b) STUDY REQUIRED—The Board of Governors of the Federal Reserve System (hereafter in this section referred to as the "Board") shall conduct a study of—

(1) consumer credit industry practices of soliciting and extending credit—

(A) indiscriminately;

(B) without taking steps to ensure that consumers are capable of repaying the resulting debt; and

(C) in a manner that encourages consumers to accumulate additional debt; and

(2) the effects of such practices on consumer debt and insolvency.

(c) REPORT AND REGULATIONS—Not later than 12 months after the date of enactment of this Act, the Board—

(1) shall make public a report on its findings with respect to the indiscriminate solicitation and extension of credit by the credit industry;

(2) may issue regulations that would require additional disclosures to consumers; and

(3) may take any other actions, consistent with its existing statutory authority, that the Board finds necessary to ensure responsible industry-wide practices and to prevent resulting consumer debt and insolvency.

Sec. 1230 PROPERTY NO LONGER SUBJECT TO REDEMPTION.

Section 541(b) of title 11, United States Code, as amended by sections 225 and 323, is amended by adding after paragraph (7), as added by section 323, the following:

"(8) subject to subchapter III of chapter 5, any interest of the debtor in property where the debtor pledged or sold tangible personal property (other than securities or written or printed evidences of indebtedness or title) as collateral for a loan or advance of money given by a person licensed under law to make such loans or advances, where—

"(A) the tangible personal property is in the possession of the pledgee or transferee;

"(B) the debtor has no obligation to repay the money, redeem the collateral, or buy back the property at a stipulated price; and

"(C) neither the debtor nor the trustee have exercised any right to redeem provided under the contract or State law, in a timely manner as provided under State law and section 108(b); or".

Sec. 1231 TRUSTEES.

(a) SUSPENSION AND TERMINATION OF PANEL TRUSTEES AND STANDING TRUSTEES—Section 586(d) of title 28, United States Code, is amended—

(1) by inserting "(1)" after "(d)"; and

(2) by adding at the end the following:

"(2) A trustee whose appointment under subsection (a)(1) or under subsection (b) is terminated or who ceases to be assigned to cases filed under title 11, United States Code, may obtain judicial review of the final agency decision by commencing an action in the district court of the United States for the district for which the panel to which the trustee is appointed under subsection (a)(1), or in the district court of the United States for the district in which the trustee is appointed under subsection (b) resides, after first exhausting all available administrative remedies, which if the trustee so elects, shall also include an administrative hearing on the record. Unless the trustee elects to have an administrative hearing on the record, the trustee shall be deemed to have exhausted all administrative remedies for purposes of this paragraph if the agency fails to make a final agency decision within 90 days after the trustee requests administrative remedies. The Attorney General shall prescribe procedures to implement this paragraph. The decision of the agency shall be affirmed by the district court unless it is unreasonable and without cause based on the administrative record before the agency.".

(b) EXPENSES OF STANDING TRUSTEES—Section 586(e) of title 28, United States Code, is amended by adding at the end the following:

"(3) After first exhausting all available administrative remedies, an individual appointed under subsection (b) may obtain judicial review of final agency action to deny a claim of actual, necessary expenses under this subsection by commencing an action in the district court of the United States for the district where the individual resides. The decision of the agency shall be affirmed by the district court unless it is unreasonable and without cause based upon the administrative record before the agency.

"(4) The Attorney General shall prescribe procedures to implement this subsection.".

Sec. 1232 BANKRUPTCY FORMS.

Section 2075 of title 28, United States Code, is amended by adding at the end the following:

"The bankruptcy rules promulgated under this section shall prescribe a form for the statement required under section 707(b)(2)(C) of title 11 and may provide general rules on the content of such statement.".

Sec. 1233 DIRECT APPEALS OF BANKRUPTCY MATTERS TO COURTS OF APPEALS.

(a) APPEALS—Section 158 of title 28, United States Code, is amended—

(1) in subsection (c)(1), by striking "Subject to subsection (b)," and inserting "Subject to subsections (b) and (d)(2),"; and

(2) in subsection (d)—

(A) by inserting "(1)" after "(d)"; and

(B) by adding at the end the following:

"(2)(A) The appropriate court of appeals shall have jurisdiction of appeals described in the first sentence of subsection (a) if the bankruptcy court, the district court, or the bankruptcy appellate panel involved, acting on its own motion or on the request of a party to the judgment, order, or decree described in such first sentence, or all the appellants and appellees (if any) acting jointly, certify that—

"(i) the judgment, order, or decree involves a question of law as to which there is no controlling decision of the court of appeals for the circuit or of the Supreme Court of the United States, or involves a matter of public importance;

"(ii) the judgment, order, or decree involves a question of law requiring resolution of conflicting decisions; or

"(iii) an immediate appeal from the judgment, order, or decree may materially advance the progress of the case or proceeding in which the appeal is taken;

and if the court of appeals authorizes the direct appeal of the judgment, order, or decree.

"(B) If the bankruptcy court, the district court, or the bankruptcy appellate panel—

"(i) on its own motion or on the request of a party, determines that a circumstance specified in clause (i), (ii), or (iii) of subparagraph (A) exists; or

"(ii) receives a request made by a majority of the appellants and a majority of appellees (if any) to make the certification described in subparagraph (A);

then the bankruptcy court, the district court, or the bankruptcy appellate panel shall make the certification described in subparagraph (A).

"(C) The parties may supplement the certification with a short statement of the basis for the certification.

"(D) An appeal under this paragraph does not stay any proceeding of the bankruptcy court, the district court, or the bankruptcy appellate panel from which the appeal is taken, unless the respective bankruptcy court, district court, or bankruptcy appellate panel, or the court of appeals in which the appeal in pending, issues a stay of such proceeding pending the appeal.

"(E) Any request under subparagraph (B) for certification shall be made not later than 60 days after the entry of the judgment, order, or decree.".

(b) PROCEDURAL RULES—

(1) TEMPORARY APPLICATION—A provision of this subsection shall apply to appeals under section 158(d)(2) of title 28, United States Code, until a rule of practice and procedure relating to such provision and such appeals is promulgated or amended under chapter 131 of such title.

(2) CERTIFICATION—A district court, a bankruptcy court, or a bankruptcy appellate panel may make a certification under section 158(d)(2) of title 28, United States Code, only with respect to matters pending in the respective bankruptcy court, district court, or bankruptcy appellate panel.

(3) PROCEDURE—Subject to any other provision of this subsection, an appeal authorized by the court of appeals under section 158(d)(2)(A) of title 28, United States Code, shall be taken in the manner prescribed in subdivisions (a)(1), (b), (c), and (d) of rule 5 of the Federal Rules of Appellate Procedure. For purposes of subdivision (a)(1) of rule 5—

(A) a reference in such subdivision to a district court shall be deemed to include a reference to a bankruptcy court and a bankruptcy appellate panel, as appropriate; and

(B) a reference in such subdivision to the parties requesting permission to appeal to be served with the petition shall be deemed to include a reference to the parties to the judgment, order, or decree from which the appeal is taken.

(4) FILING OF PETITION WITH ATTACHMENT—A petition requesting permission to appeal, that is based on a certification made under subparagraph (A) or (B) of section 158(d)(2) shall—

(A) be filed with the circuit clerk not later than 10 days after the certification is entered on the docket of the bankruptcy court, the district court, or the bankruptcy appellate panel from which the appeal is taken; and

(B) have attached a copy of such certification.

(5) REFERENCES IN RULE 5—For purposes of rule 5 of the Federal Rules of Appellate Procedure—

(A) a reference in such rule to a district court shall be deemed to include a reference to a bankruptcy court and to a bankruptcy appellate panel; and

(B) a reference in such rule to a district clerk shall be deemed to include a reference to a clerk of a bankruptcy court and to a clerk of a bankruptcy appellate panel.

(6) APPLICATION OF RULES—The Federal Rules of Appellate Procedure shall apply in the courts of appeals with respect to appeals authorized under section 158(d)(2)(A), to the extent relevant and as if such appeals were taken from final judgments, orders, or decrees of the district courts or bankruptcy appellate panels exercising appellate jurisdiction under subsection (a) or (b) of section 158 of title 28, United States Code.

Sec. 1234 INVOLUNTARY CASES.

(a) AMENDMENTS—Section 303 of title 11, United States Code, is amended—

(1) in subsection (b)(1), by—

(A) inserting "as to liability or amount" after "bona fide dispute"; and

(B) striking "if such claims" and inserting "if such noncontingent, undisputed claims"; and

(2) in subsection (h)(1), by inserting "as to liability or amount" before the semicolon at the end.

(b) EFFECTIVE DATE; APPLICATION OF AMENDMENTS—This section and the amendments made by this section shall take effect on the date of the enactment of this Act and shall apply with respect to cases commenced under title 11 of the United States Code before, on, and after such date.

Sec. 1235 FEDERAL ELECTION LAW FINES AND PENALTIES AS NONDISCHARGEABLE DEBT.

Section 523(a) of title 11, United States Code, as amended by section 314, is amended by inserting after paragraph (14A) the following:

"(14B) incurred to pay fines or penalties imposed under Federal election law;".

TITLE XIII

CONSUMER CREDIT DISCLOSURE

Sec. 1301 ENHANCED DISCLOSURES UNDER AN OPEN END CREDIT PLAN.

(a) MINIMUM PAYMENT DISCLOSURES—Section 127(b) of the Truth in Lending Act (15 U.S.C. 1637(b)) is amended by adding at the end the following:

"(11)(A) In the case of an open end credit plan that requires a minimum monthly payment of not more than 4 percent of the balance on which finance charges are accruing, the following statement, located on the front of the billing statement, disclosed clearly and conspicuously: 'Minimum Payment Warning: Making only the minimum payment will increase the interest you pay and the time it takes to repay your balance. For example, making only the typical 2% minimum monthly payment on a balance of $1,000 at an interest rate of 17% would take 88 months to repay the balance in full. For an estimate of the time it would take to repay your balance, making only minimum payments, call this toll-free number: __.' (the blank space to be filled in by the creditor).

"(B) In the case of an open end credit plan that requires a minimum monthly payment of more than 4 percent of the balance on which finance charges are accruing, the following statement, in a prominent location on the front of the billing statement, disclosed clearly and conspicuously: 'Minimum Payment Warning: Making only the required minimum payment will increase the interest you pay and the time it takes to repay your balance. Making a typical 5% minimum monthly payment on a balance of $300 at an interest rate of 17% would take 24 months to repay the balance in full. For an estimate of the time it would take to repay your balance, making only minimum monthly payments, call this toll-free number: __.' (the blank space to be filled in by the creditor).

"(C) Notwithstanding subparagraphs (A) and (B), in the case of a creditor with respect to which compliance with this title is enforced by the Federal Trade Commission, the following statement, in a prominent location on the front of the billing statement, disclosed clearly and conspicuously: 'Minimum Payment Warning: Making only the required minimum payment will increase the interest you pay and the time it takes to repay your balance. For example, making only the typical 5% minimum monthly payment on a balance of $300 at an interest rate of 17% would take 24 months to repay the balance in full. For an estimate of the time it would take to repay your balance, making only minimum monthly payments, call the Federal Trade Commission at this toll-free number: __.' (the blank space to be filled in by the creditor). A creditor who is subject to this subparagraph shall not be subject to subparagraph (A) or (B).

"(D) Notwithstanding subparagraph (A), (B), or (C), in complying with any such subparagraph, a creditor may substitute an example based on an interest rate that is greater than 17 percent. Any creditor that is subject to subparagraph (B) may elect to provide the disclosure required under subparagraph (A) in lieu of the disclosure required under subparagraph (B).

"(E) The Board shall, by rule, periodically recalculate, as necessary, the interest rate and repayment period under subparagraphs (A), (B), and (C).

"(F)(i) The toll-free telephone number disclosed by a creditor or the Federal Trade Commission under subparagraph (A), (B), or (G), as appropriate, may be a toll-free telephone number established and maintained by the creditor or the Federal Trade Commission, as appropriate, or may be a toll-free telephone number established and maintained by a third party for use by the creditor or multiple creditors or the Federal Trade Commission, as appropriate. The toll-free telephone number may connect consumers to an automated device through which consumers may obtain information described in subparagraph (A), (B), or (C), by inputting information using a touch-tone telephone or similar device, if consumers whose telephones are not equipped to use such automated device are provided the opportunity to be connected to an individual from whom the information described in subparagraph (A), (B), or (C), as applicable, may be obtained. A person that receives a request for information described in subparagraph (A), (B), or (C) from an obligor through the toll-free telephone number disclosed under subparagraph (A), (B), or (C), as applicable, shall disclose in response to such request only the information set forth in the table promulgated by the Board under subparagraph (H)(i).

"(ii)(I) The Board shall establish and maintain for a period not to exceed 24 months following the effective date of the Bankruptcy Abuse Prevention and Consumer Protection Act of 2005, a toll-free telephone number, or provide a toll-free telephone number established and maintained by a third party, for use by creditors that are depository institutions (as defined in section 3 of the Federal Deposit Insurance Act), including a Federal credit union or State credit union (as defined in section 101 of the Federal Credit Union Act), with total assets not exceeding $250,000,000. The toll-free telephone number may connect consumers to an automated device through which consumers may obtain information described in subparagraph (A) or (B), as applicable, by inputting information using a touch-tone telephone or similar device, if consumers whose telephones are not equipped to use such automated device are provided the opportunity to be connected to an individual from whom the information described in subparagraph (A) or (B), as applicable, may be obtained. A person that receives a request for information described in subparagraph (A) or (B) from an obligor through the toll-free telephone number disclosed under subparagraph (A) or (B), as applicable, shall disclose in response to such request only the information set forth in the table promulgated by the Board under subparagraph (H)(i). The dollar amount contained in this subclause shall be adjusted according to an indexing mechanism established by the Board.

"(II) Not later than 6 months prior to the expiration of the 24-month period referenced in subclause (I), the Board shall submit to the Committee on Banking, Housing, and Urban Affairs of the Senate and the Committee on Financial Services of the House of Representatives a report on the program described in subclause (I).

"(G) The Federal Trade Commission shall establish and maintain a toll-free number for the purpose of providing to consumers the information required to be disclosed under subparagraph (C).

"(H) The Board shall—

"(i) establish a detailed table illustrating the approximate number of months that it would take to repay an outstanding balance if a consumer pays only the required minimum monthly payments and if no other advances are made, which table shall clearly present standardized information to be used to disclose the information required to be disclosed under subparagraph (A), (B), or (C), as applicable;

"(ii) establish the table required under clause (i) by assuming—

"(I) a significant number of different annual percentage rates;

"(II) a significant number of different account balances;

"(III) a significant number of different minimum payment amounts; and

"(IV) that only minimum monthly payments are made and no additional extensions of credit are obtained; and

"(iii) promulgate regulations that provide instructional guidance regarding the manner in which the information contained in the table established under clause (i) should be used in responding to the request of an obligor for any information required to be disclosed under subparagraph (A), (B), or (C).

"(I) The disclosure requirements of this paragraph do not apply to any charge card account, the primary purpose of which is to require payment of charges in full each month.

"(J) A creditor that maintains a toll-free telephone number for the purpose of providing customers with the actual number of months that it will take to repay the customer's outstanding balance is not subject to the requirements of subparagraph (A) or (B).

"(K) A creditor that maintains a toll-free telephone number for the purpose of providing customers with the actual number of months that it will take to repay an outstanding balance shall include the following statement on each billing statement: 'Making only the minimum payment will increase the interest you pay and the time it takes to repay your balance. For more information, call this toll-free number: ___.' (the blank space to be filled in by the creditor).".

(b) REGULATORY IMPLEMENTATION—

(1) IN GENERAL—The Board of Governors of the Federal Reserve System (hereafter in this title referred to as the "Board") shall promulgate regulations implementing the requirements of section 127(b)(11) of the Truth in Lending Act, as added by subsection (a) of this section.

(2) EFFECTIVE DATE—Section 127(b)(11) of the Truth in Lending Act, as added by subsection (a) of this section, and the regulations issued under paragraph (1) of this subsection shall not take effect until the later of—

(A) 18 months after the date of enactment of this Act; or

(B) 12 months after the publication of such final regulations by the Board.

(c) STUDY OF FINANCIAL DISCLOSURES—

(1) IN GENERAL—The Board may conduct a study to determine the types of information available to potential borrowers from consumer credit lending institutions regarding factors qualifying potential borrowers for credit, repayment requirements, and the consequences of default.

(2) FACTORS FOR CONSIDERATION—In conducting a study under paragraph (1), the Board should, in consultation with the other Federal banking agencies (as defined in section 3 of the Federal Deposit Insurance Act), the National Credit Union Administration, and the Federal Trade Commission, consider the extent to which—

(A) consumers, in establishing new credit arrangements, are aware of their existing payment obligations, the need to consider those obligations in deciding to take on new credit, and how taking on excessive credit can result in financial difficulty;

(B) minimum periodic payment features offered in connection with open end credit plans impact consumer default rates;

(C) consumers make only the required minimum payment under open end credit plans;

(D) consumers are aware that making only required minimum payments will increase the cost and repayment period of an open end credit obligation; and

(E) the availability of low minimum payment options is a cause of consumers experiencing financial difficulty.

(3) REPORT TO CONGRESS—Findings of the Board in connection with any study conducted under this subsection shall be submitted to Congress. Such report shall also include recommendations for legislative initiatives, if any, of the Board, based on its findings.

Sec. 1302 ENHANCED DISCLOSURE FOR CREDIT EXTENSIONS SECURED BY A DWELLING.

(a) OPEN END CREDIT EXTENSIONS—

(1) CREDIT APPLICATIONS—Section 127A(a)(13) of the Truth in Lending Act (15 U.S.C. 1637a(a)(13)) is amended—

(A) by striking "CONSULTATION OF TAX ADVISER—A statement that the" and inserting the following: "TAX DEDUCTIBILITY—A statement that—

"(A) the"; and

(B) by striking the period at the end and inserting the following: "; and

"(B) in any case in which the extension of credit exceeds the fair market value (as defined under the Internal Revenue Code of 1986) of the dwelling, the interest on the portion of the credit extension that is greater than the fair market value of the dwelling is not tax deductible for Federal income tax purposes.".

(2) CREDIT ADVERTISEMENTS—Section 147(b) of the Truth in Lending Act (15 U.S.C. 1665b(b)) is amended—

(A) by striking "If any" and inserting the following:

"(1) IN GENERAL—If any"; and

(B) by adding at the end the following:

"(2) CREDIT IN EXCESS OF FAIR MARKET VALUE—Each advertisement described in subsection (a) that relates to an extension of credit that may exceed the fair market value of the dwelling, and which advertisement is disseminated in paper form to the public or through the Internet, as opposed to by radio or television, shall include a clear and conspicuous statement that—

"(A) the interest on the portion of the credit extension that is greater than the fair market value of the dwelling is not tax deductible for Federal income tax purposes; and

"(B) the consumer should consult a tax adviser for further information regarding the deductibility of interest and charges.".

(b) NON-OPEN END CREDIT EXTENSIONS—

(1) CREDIT APPLICATIONS—Section 128 of the Truth in Lending Act (15 U.S.C. 1638) is amended—

(A) in subsection (a), by adding at the end the following:

"(15) In the case of a consumer credit transaction that is secured by the principal dwelling of the consumer, in which the extension of credit may exceed the fair market value of the dwelling, a clear and conspicuous statement that—

"(A) the interest on the portion of the credit extension that is greater than the fair market value of the dwelling is not tax deductible for Federal income tax purposes; and

"(B) the consumer should consult a tax adviser for further information regarding the deductibility of interest and charges."; and

(B) in subsection (b), by adding at the end the following:

"(3) In the case of a credit transaction described in paragraph (15) of subsection (a), disclosures required by that paragraph shall be made to the consumer at the time of application for such extension of credit.".

(2) CREDIT ADVERTISEMENTS—Section 144 of the Truth in Lending Act (15 U.S.C. 1664) is amended by adding at the end the following:

"(e) Each advertisement to which this section applies that relates to a consumer credit transaction that is secured by the principal dwelling of a consumer in which the extension of credit may exceed the fair market value of the dwelling, and which advertisement is disseminated in paper form to the public or through the Internet, as opposed to by radio or television, shall clearly and conspicuously state that—

"(1) the interest on the portion of the credit extension that is greater than the fair market value of the dwelling is not tax deductible for Federal income tax purposes; and

"(2) the consumer should consult a tax adviser for further information regarding the deductibility of interest and charges.".

(c) REGULATORY IMPLEMENTATION—

(1) IN GENERAL—The Board shall promulgate regulations implementing the amendments made by this section.

(2) EFFECTIVE DATE—Regulations issued under paragraph (1) shall not take effect until the later of—

(A) 12 months after the date of enactment of this Act; or

(B) 12 months after the date of publication of such final regulations by the Board.

Sec. 1303 DISCLOSURES RELATED TO "INTRODUCTORY RATES".

(a) INTRODUCTORY RATE DISCLOSURES—Section 127(c) of the Truth in Lending Act (15 U.S.C. 1637(c)) is amended by adding at the end the following:

"(6) ADDITIONAL NOTICE CONCERNING 'INTRODUCTORY RATES'—

"(A) IN GENERAL—Except as provided in subparagraph (B), an application or solicitation to open a credit card account and all promotional materials accompanying such application or solicitation for which a disclosure is required under paragraph (1), and that offers a temporary annual percentage rate of interest, shall—

"(i) use the term "introductory" in immediate proximity to each listing of the temporary annual percentage rate applicable to such account, which term shall appear clearly and conspicuously;

"(ii) if the annual percentage rate of interest that will apply after the end of the temporary rate period will be a fixed rate, state in a clear and conspicuous manner in a prominent location closely proximate to the first listing of the temporary annual percentage rate (other than a listing of the temporary annual percentage rate in the tabular format described in section 122(c)), the time period in which the introductory period will end and the annual percentage rate that will apply after the end of the introductory period; and

"(iii) if the annual percentage rate that will apply after the end of the temporary rate period will vary in accordance with an index, state in a clear and conspicuous manner in a prominent location closely proximate to the first listing of the temporary annual percentage rate (other than a listing in the tabular format prescribed by section 122(c)), the time period in which the introductory period will end and the rate that will apply after that, based on an annual percentage rate that was in effect within 60 days before the date of mailing the application or solicitation.

"(B) EXCEPTION—Clauses (ii) and (iii) of subparagraph (A) do not apply with respect to any listing of a temporary annual percentage rate on an envelope or other enclosure in which an application or solicitation to open a credit card account is mailed.

"(C) CONDITIONS FOR INTRODUCTORY RATES—An application or solicitation to open a credit card account for which a disclosure is required under paragraph (1), and that offers a temporary annual percentage rate of interest shall, if that rate of interest is revocable under any circumstance or upon any event, clearly and conspicuously disclose, in a prominent manner on or with such application or solicitation—

"(i) a general description of the circumstances that may result in the revocation of the temporary annual percentage rate; and

"(ii) if the annual percentage rate that will apply upon the revocation of the temporary annual percentage rate—

"(I) will be a fixed rate, the annual percentage rate that will apply upon the revocation of the temporary annual percentage rate; or

"(II) will vary in accordance with an index, the rate that will apply after the temporary rate, based on an annual percentage rate that was in effect within 60 days before the date of mailing the application or solicitation.

"(D) DEFINITIONS—In this paragraph—

"(i) the terms 'temporary annual percentage rate of interest' and 'temporary annual percentage rate' mean any rate of interest applicable to a credit card account for an introductory period of less than 1 year, if that rate is less than an annual percentage rate that was in effect within 60 days before the date of mailing the application or solicitation; and "(ii) the term 'introductory period' means the maximum time period for which the temporary annual percentage rate may be applicable.

"(E) RELATION TO OTHER DISCLOSURE REQUIREMENTS—Nothing in this paragraph may be construed to supersede subsection (a) of section 122, or any disclosure required by paragraph (1) or any other provision of this subsection.".

(b) REGULATORY IMPLEMENTATION—

(1) IN GENERAL—The Board shall promulgate regulations implementing the requirements of section 127(c)(6) of the Truth in Lending Act, as added by this section.

(2) EFFECTIVE DATE—Section 127(c)(6) of the Truth in Lending Act, as added by this section, and regulations issued under paragraph (1) of this subsection shall not take effect until the later of—

(A) 12 months after the date of enactment of this Act; or

(B) 12 months after the date of publication of such final regulations by the Board.

Sec. 1304 INTERNET-BASED CREDIT CARD SOLICITATIONS.

(a) INTERNET-BASED SOLICITATIONS—Section 127(c) of the Truth in Lending Act (15 U.S.C. 1637(c)) is amended by adding at the end the following:

"(7) INTERNET-BASED SOLICITATIONS—

"(A) IN GENERAL—In any solicitation to open a credit card account for any person under an open end consumer credit plan using the Internet or other interactive computer service, the person making the solicitation shall clearly and conspicuously disclose—

"(i) the information described in subparagraphs (A) and (B) of paragraph (1); and

"(ii) the information described in paragraph (6).

"(B) FORM OF DISCLOSURE—The disclosures required by subparagraph (A) shall be—

"(i) readily accessible to consumers in close proximity to the solicitation to open a credit card account; and

"(ii) updated regularly to reflect the current policies, terms, and fee amounts applicable to the credit card account.

"(C) DEFINITIONS—For purposes of this paragraph—

"(i) the term 'Internet' means the international computer network of both Federal and non-Federal interoperable packet switched data networks; and

"(ii) the term 'interactive computer service' means any information service, system, or access software provider that provides or enables computer access by multiple users to a computer server, including specifically a service or system that provides access to the Internet and such systems operated or services offered by libraries or educational institutions.".

(b) REGULATORY IMPLEMENTATION—

(1) IN GENERAL—The Board shall promulgate regulations implementing the requirements of section 127(c)(7) of the Truth in Lending Act, as added by this section.

(2) EFFECTIVE DATE—The amendment made by subsection (a) and the regulations issued under paragraph (1) of this subsection shall not take effect until the later of—

(A) 12 months after the date of enactment of this Act; or

(B) 12 months after the date of publication of such final regulations by the Board.

Sec. 1305 DISCLOSURES RELATED TO LATE PAYMENT DEADLINES AND PENALTIES.

(a) DISCLOSURES RELATED TO LATE PAYMENT DEADLINES AND PENALTIES—Section 127(b) of the Truth in Lending Act (15 U.S.C. 1637(b)) is amended by adding at the end the following:

"(12) If a late payment fee is to be imposed due to the failure of the obligor to make payment on or before a required payment due date, the following shall be stated clearly and conspicuously on the billing statement:

"(A) The date on which that payment is due or, if different, the earliest date on which a late payment fee may be charged.

"(B) The amount of the late payment fee to be imposed if payment is made after such date.".

(b) REGULATORY IMPLEMENTATION—

(1) IN GENERAL—The Board shall promulgate regulations implementing the requirements of section 127(b)(12) of the Truth in Lending Act, as added by this section.

(2) EFFECTIVE DATE—The amendment made by subsection (a) and regulations issued under paragraph (1) of this subsection shall not take effect until the later of—

(A) 12 months after the date of enactment of this Act; or

(B) 12 months after the date of publication of such final regulations by the Board.

Sec. 1306 PROHIBITION ON CERTAIN ACTIONS FOR FAILURE TO INCUR FINANCE CHARGES.

(a) PROHIBITION ON CERTAIN ACTIONS FOR FAILURE TO INCUR FINANCE CHARGES—Section 127 of the Truth in Lending Act (15 U.S.C. 1637) is amended by adding at the end the following:

"(h) PROHIBITION ON CERTAIN ACTIONS FOR FAILURE TO INCUR FINANCE CHARGES—A creditor of an account under an open end consumer credit plan may not terminate an account prior to its expiration date solely because the consumer has not incurred finance charges on the account. Nothing in this subsection shall prohibit a creditor from terminating an account for inactivity in 3 or more consecutive months.".

(b) REGULATORY IMPLEMENTATION—

(1) IN GENERAL—The Board shall promulgate regulations implementing the requirements of section 127(h) of the Truth in Lending Act, as added by this section.

(2) EFFECTIVE DATE—The amendment made by subsection (a) and regulations issued under paragraph (1) of this subsection shall not take effect until the later of—

(A) 12 months after the date of enactment of this Act; or

(B) 12 months after the date of publication of such final regulations by the Board.

Sec. 1307 DUAL USE DEBIT CARD.

(a) REPORT—The Board may conduct a study of, and present to Congress a report containing its analysis of, consumer protections under existing law to limit the liability of consumers for unauthorized use of a debit card or similar access device. Such report, if submitted, shall include recommendations for legislative initiatives, if any, of the Board, based on its findings.

(b) CONSIDERATIONS—In preparing a report under subsection (a), the Board may include—

(1) the extent to which section 909 of the Electronic Fund Transfer Act (15 U.S.C. 1693g), as in effect at the time of the report, and the implementing regulations promulgated by the Board to carry out that section provide adequate unauthorized use liability protection for consumers;

(2) the extent to which any voluntary industry rules have enhanced or may enhance the level of protection afforded consumers in connection with such unauthorized use liability; and

(3) whether amendments to the Electronic Fund Transfer Act (15 U.S.C. 1693 et seq.), or revisions to regulations promulgated by the Board to carry out that Act, are necessary to further address adequate protection for consumers concerning unauthorized use liability.

Sec. 1308 STUDY OF BANKRUPTCY IMPACT OF CREDIT EXTENDED TO DEPENDENT STUDENTS.

(a) STUDY—

(1) IN GENERAL—The Board shall conduct a study regarding the impact that the extension of credit described in paragraph (2) has on the rate of cases filed under title 11 of the United States Code.

(2) EXTENSION OF CREDIT—The extension of credit described in this paragraph is the extension of credit to individuals who are—

(A) claimed as dependents for purposes of the Internal Revenue Code of 1986; and

(B) enrolled within 1 year of successfully completing all required secondary education requirements and on a full-time basis, in postsecondary educational institutions.

(b) REPORT—Not later than 1 year after the date of enactment of this Act, the Board shall submit to the Senate and the House of Representatives a report summarizing the results of the study conducted under subsection (a).

Sec. 1309 CLARIFICATION OF CLEAR AND CONSPICUOUS.

(a) REGULATIONS—Not later than 6 months after the date of enactment of this Act, the Board, in consultation with the other Federal banking agencies (as defined in section 3 of the Federal Deposit Insurance Act), the National Credit Union Administration Board, and the Federal Trade Commission, shall promulgate regulations to provide guidance regarding the meaning of the term "clear and conspicuous", as used in subparagraphs (A), (B), and (C) of section 127(b)(11) and clauses (ii) and (iii) of section 127(c)(6)(A) of the Truth in Lending Act.

(b) EXAMPLES—Regulations promulgated under subsection (a) shall include examples of clear and conspicuous model disclosures for the purposes of disclosures required by the provisions of the Truth in Lending Act referred to in subsection (a).

(c) STANDARDS—In promulgating regulations under this section, the Board shall ensure that the clear and conspicuous standard required for disclosures made under the provisions of the Truth in Lending Act referred to in subsection (a) can be implemented in a manner which results in disclosures which are reasonably understandable and designed to call attention to the nature and significance of the information in the notice.

TITLE XIV

PREVENTING CORPORATE BANKRUPTCY ABUSE

Sec. 1401 EMPLOYEE WAGE AND BENEFIT PRIORITIES.

Section 507(a) of title 11, United States Code, as amended by section 212, is amended—

(1) in paragraph (4) by striking "90" and inserting "180", and

(2) in paragraphs (4) and (5) by striking "$4,000" and inserting "$10,000".

Sec. 1402 FRAUDULENT TRANSFERS AND OBLIGATIONS.

Section 548 of title 11, United States Code, is amended—

(1) in subsections (a) and (b) by striking "one year" and inserting "2 years",

(2) in subsection (a)—

(A) by inserting "(including any transfer to or for the benefit of an insider under an employment contract)" after "transfer" the 1st place it appears, and

(B) by inserting "(including any obligation to or for the benefit of an insider under an employment contract)" after "obligation" the 1st place it appears, and

(3) in subsection (a)(1)(B)(ii)—

(A) in subclause (II) by striking "or" at the end,

(B) in subclause (III) by striking the period at the end and inserting "; or", and

(C) by adding at the end the following:

"(IV) made such transfer to or for the benefit of an insider, or incurred such obligation to or for the benefit of an insider, under an employment contract and not in the ordinary course of business.".

(4) by adding at the end the following:

"(e)(1) In addition to any transfer that the trustee may otherwise avoid, the trustee may avoid any transfer of an interest of the debtor in property that was made on or within 10 years before the date of the filing of the petition, if—

"(A) such transfer was made to a self-settled trust or similar device;

"(B) such transfer was by the debtor;

269

"(C) the debtor is a beneficiary of such trust or similar device; and

"(D) the debtor made such transfer with actual intent to hinder, delay, or defraud any entity to which the debtor was or became, on or after the date that such transfer was made, indebted.

"(2) For the purposes of this subsection, a transfer includes a transfer made in anticipation of any money judgment, settlement, civil penalty, equitable order, or criminal fine incurred by, or which the debtor believed would be incurred by—

"(A) any violation of the securities laws (as defined in section 3(a)(47) of the Securities Exchange Act of 1934 (15 U.S.C. 78c(a)(47))), any State securities laws, or any regulation or order issued under Federal securities laws or State securities laws; or

"(B) fraud, deceit, or manipulation in a fiduciary capacity or in connection with the purchase or sale of any security registered under section 12 or 15(d) of the Securities Exchange Act of 1934 (15 U.S.C. 78l and 78o(d)) or under section 6 of the Securities Act of 1933 (15 U.S.C. 77f).".

Sec. 1403 PAYMENT OF INSURANCE BENEFITS TO RETIRED EMPLOYEES.

Section 1114 of title 11, United States Code, is amended—

(1) by redesignating subsection (l) as subsection (m), and

(2) by inserting after subsection (k) the following:

"(l) If the debtor, during the 180-day period ending on the date of the filing of the petition—

"(1) modified retiree benefits; and

"(2) was insolvent on the date such benefits were modified;

the court, on motion of a party in interest, and after notice and a hearing, shall issue an order reinstating as of the date the modification was made, such benefits as in effect immediately before such date unless the court finds that the balance of the equities clearly favors such modification.".

Sec. 1404 DEBTS NONDISCHARGEABLE IF INCURRED IN VIOLATION OF SECURITIES FRAUD LAWS.

(a) PREPETITION AND POSTPETITION EFFECT—Section 523(a)(19)(B) of title 11, United States Code, is amended by inserting ", before, on, or after the date on which the petition was filed," after "results".

(b) EFFECTIVE DATE UPON ENACTMENT OF SARBANES-OXLEY ACT—The amendment made by subsection (a) is effective beginning July 30, 2002.

Sec. 1405 APPOINTMENT OF TRUSTEE IN CASES OF SUSPECTED FRAUD.

Section 1104 of title 11, United States Code, is amended by adding at the end the following:

"(e) The United States trustee shall move for the appointment of a trustee under subsection (a) if there are reasonable grounds to suspect that current members of the governing body of the debtor, the debtor's chief executive or chief financial officer, or members of the governing body who selected the debtor's chief executive or chief financial officer, participated in actual fraud, dishonesty, or criminal conduct in the management of the debtor or the debtor's public financial reporting.".

Sec. 1406 EFFECTIVE DATE; APPLICATION OF AMENDMENTS.

(a) EFFECTIVE DATE—Except as provided in subsection (b), this title and the amendments made by this title shall take effect on the date of the enactment of this Act.

(b) APPLICATION OF AMENDMENTS—

(1) IN GENERAL—Except as provided in paragraph (2), the amendments made by this title shall apply only with respect to cases commenced under title 11 of the United States Code on or after the date of the enactment of this Act.

(2) AVOIDANCE PERIOD—The amendment made by section 1402(1) shall apply only with respect to cases commenced under title 11 of the United States Code more than 1 year after the date of the enactment of this Act.

TITLE XV

GENERAL EFFECTIVE DATE; APPLICATION OF AMENDMENTS

Sec. 1501 EFFECTIVE DATE; APPLICATION OF AMENDMENTS.

(a) EFFECTIVE DATE—Except as otherwise provided in this Act, this Act and the amendments made by this Act shall take effect 180 days after the date of enactment of this Act.

(b) APPLICATION OF AMENDMENTS—

(1) IN GENERAL—Except as otherwise provided in this Act and paragraph (2), the amendments made by this Act shall not apply with respect to cases commenced under title 11, United States Code, before the effective date of this Act.

(2) CERTAIN LIMITATIONS APPLICABLE TO DEBTORS—The amendments made by sections 308, 322, and 330 shall apply with respect to cases commenced under title 11, United States Code, on or after the date of the enactment of this Act.

Sec. 1502 TECHNICAL CORRECTIONS.

(a) CONFORMING AMENDMENTS TO TITLE 11 OF THE UNITED STATES CODE—Title 11 of the United States Code, as amended by the preceding provisions of this Act, is amended—

(1) in section 507—

(A) in subsection (a)—

(i) in paragraph (5)(B)(ii) by striking "paragraph (3)" and inserting "paragraph (4)"; and

(ii) in paragraph (8)(D) by striking "paragraph (3)" and inserting "paragraph (4)";

(B) in subsection (b) by striking "subsection (a)(1)" and inserting "subsection (a)(2)"; and

(C) in subsection (d) by striking "subsection (a)(3)" and inserting "subsection (a)(1)";

(2) in section 523(a)(1)(A) by striking "507(a)(2)" and inserting "507(a)(3)";

(3) in section 752(a) by striking "507(a)(1)" and inserting "507(a)(2)";

(4) in section 766—

(A) in subsection (h) by striking "507(a)(1)" and inserting "507(a)(2)"; and

(B) in subsection (i) by striking "507(a)(1)" each place it appears and inserting "507(a)(2)";

(5) in section 901(a) by striking "507(a)(1)" and inserting "507(a)(2)";

(6) in section 943(b)(5) by striking "507(a)(1)" and inserting "507(a)(2)";

(7) in section 1123(a)(1) by striking "507(a)(1), 507(a)(2)" and inserting "507(a)(2), 507(a)(3)";

(8) in section 1129(a)(9)—

(A) in subparagraph (A) by striking "507(a)(1) or 507(a)(2)" and inserting "507(a)(2) or 507(a)(3)"; and

(B) in subparagraph (B) by striking "507(a)(3)" and inserting "507(a)(1)";

(9) in section 1226(b)(1) by striking "507(a)(1)" and inserting "507(a)(2)"; and

(10) in section 1326(b)(1) by striking "507(a)(1)" and inserting "507(a)(2)".

(b) RELATED CONFORMING AMENDMENT—Section 6(e) of the Securities Investor Protection Act of 1970 (15 U.S.C. 78fff(e)) is amended by striking "507(a)(1)" and inserting "507(a)(2)".